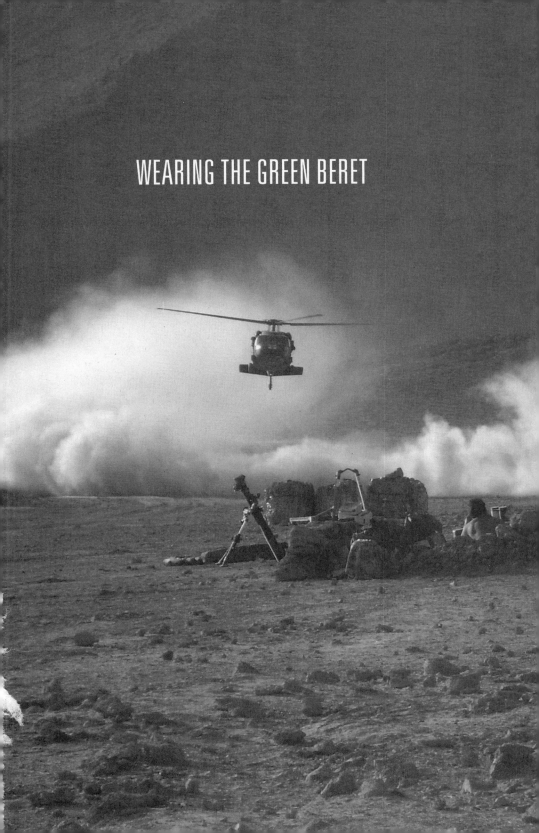

WEARING THE GREEN BERET

Overleaf: A Danish Blackhawk comes in to take out some of the MOG's wounded.

A CANADIAN WITH THE ROYAL MARINE COMMANDOS

WEARING THE GREEN BERET

JAKE OLAFSEN

McClelland & Stewart

Library and Archives Canada Cataloguing in Publication

Olafsen, Jake
Wearing the green beret : a Canadian with the Royal Marine Commandos / Jake Olafsen.

Also issued in electronic format.
ISBN 978-0-7710-6852-2

1. Olafsen, Jake. 2. Afghan War, 2001– – Personal narratives, Canadian.
3. Great Britain. Royal Marines – Biography. 4. Soldiers – Canada – Biography.
I. Title.

DS371.413.O43 2011   958.104'7092   C2010-904128-3

We acknowledge the financial support of the Government of Canada through the Book Publishing Industry Development Program and that of the Government of Ontario through the Ontario Media Development Corporation's Ontario Book Initiative. We further acknowledge the support of the Canada Council for the Arts and the Ontario Arts Council for our publishing program.

Published simultaneously in the United States of America by McClelland & Stewart Ltd., P.O. Box 1030, Plattsburgh, New York 12901

Library of Congress Control Number: 2010937149

All photos courtesy of the author.

Typeset in Dante by M&S, Toronto
Printed and bound in Canada

ANCIENT FOREST
FRIENDLY

This book is printed on acid-free paper that is 100% recycled, ancient-forest friendly (100% post-consumer waste).

McClelland & Stewart Ltd.
75 Sherbourne Street
Toronto, Ontario
M5A 2P9
www.mcclelland.com

1   2   3   4   5   15   14   13   12   11

CONTENTS

PART 3 – THE LONG WAY HOME

PROLOGUE

Something big was in the pipeline and the whole company knew it. After all, it's not every day we put our heavy artillery out in front of our positions. The big guns are normally miles to the rear, not five hundred metres from the enemy. If you start sticking 105 mm howitzers outside someone's house and firing over open sights, you mean business. We were definitely about to kill some Taliban.

I was a member of Zulu Company from 45 Commando Royal Marines (RM), and we had been operating in the area for a couple of months. We spent most of our time formed up in the desert as Mobile Operations Group (MOG) South and had been cruising around attacking various Taliban targets up and down the Helmand River. Because we moved around constantly, every day was different, with no shortage of action. Our job was to attack Taliban, and there were Taliban everywhere. The area was definitely what the RM called "target rich."

The routine was that after a spell in the desert and an operation or two we would return to the District Centre in the town of Garmsir. The DC was a compound that British forces had recently wrestled from the Taliban and our company was now using as a base. We were preparing to launch another big attack from the DC on another big Taliban-held compound. But the only information we had so far was what we'd heard through the grapevine and from people talking shit.

But as with all things in the Royal Marines, once the ball gets rolling, it rolls fast, and it doesn't stop until something spectacular happens. On March 6, the ball got rolling. It would be one hell of a show, and I had front-row tickets. Zulu Company was called into orders. I love going into orders before a decent operation. First, I finally learn what role I will be playing (and then try to estimate the odds of getting shot), and second, this is when adrenalin starts pumping. I find it very exciting to learn that the next day I will be storming into a compound with confirmed enemy in it or that soon I will be machine gunning people as they try to kill me and my friends. It sure beats paperwork.

In orders, we all sit around a large 3D map laid out on the floor and made from string, grass and other bits of trash. We sit in our troops (units the same size as what the army calls platoons) and the company commander spills the beans. This time we were going to attack a series of Taliban-held compounds called Sheppys, Strongbow, and Vodka, named after various drinks that were popular with the lads. Sheppys has a special place in many Royal Marines' hearts: It's the name of a powerful cider made at a small farm a few miles from the RM base in Taunton (incidentally, the county town of Somerset, England) and anyone who has served with 40 Commando has at least one Sheppys tee-shirt and numerous Sheppys hangovers under his belt.

These enemy positions were very close to one of our own checkpoints and we exchanged fire with them from these spots on a daily basis. They sniped at us constantly and loved to let rip with RPGs (rocket-propelled grenades) before scurrying for cover. The time had come to spank these guys with a big stick and let them know who was boss. And a big stick it was going to be. The whole company (about 100 guys), was going into the attack and we had numerous Brigade-level assets attached to us. We had a section of engineers, a battery of artillery, and lots of aircraft to support us. We would have a B1 heavy bomber, F-18s, A-10s, an AC130 Spectre gunship, as many Apache attack helicopters as we wanted, and a Nimrod surveillance plane to watch and record the action. We also had a Marine-manned mortar line in the DC for extra measure. I would be going in with a general-purpose medium machine gun (GPMG), plenty of link, and a pouch filled with grenades. My friend Jay was another machine gunner in the troop and we would be sticking together. Our two guns together packed a tremendous amount of power, and it was going to be our job to stop any baddies trying to get in among our guys from the north side as they worked to clear the compounds.

These Taliban compounds were separated from our area by a fifty-foot-wide canal. Its water was too deep and fast to wade across, and the nearest bridge was nearly two miles to the north. The bridge was in our hands, but it was far too likely an approach route. This canal posed a problem for us, but it also provided some serious advantages. To get us across the canal the engineers would have to quickly assemble, at night and possibly while under fire, one of their infantry assault bridge kits. We would have to get an entire company of marines across this narrow, lightweight bridge, stir up a serious shit storm, then try to get back the same way. The possible problems with this plan were obvious. If that bridge took too much fire or was destroyed, there could be a lot of casualties. Marines excel at working around water (we are, after all, the U.K.'s amphibious assault nucleus), but nobody floats very well when he is wearing a load of weapons, belts of ammunition, and body armour. The advantages, however, outweighed the risk. The enemy knew we were planning on shooting them up because of our newest gun emplacements, but they wouldn't expect us to storm across the canal. The Taliban felt secure in their belief that the canal was an obstacle that wouldn't be crossed in force. They figured their western flank was protected, so they had few defences set up on that side. Unfortunately for them, they underestimated the Royal Marines. Surprise would be on our side.

Once orders were finished, it was time to prepare for the task at hand. We weren't heading off until the next night so we had plenty of time to catch up on sleep, get a few meals down our necks, and sort out our weapons. To give the guys a chance to rest nobody went out on patrol that night. Some of the lads wrote letters home but most just sat around and smoked like chimneys, engrossed in their own thoughts. We had gone on the attack a number of times already, but the anticipation is always intense. Your brain can play all sorts of funny tricks while your body is waiting for action. I try not to think of home too much at these times – better to focus on the job ahead and think about how I can do it better than I did it last time.

We spent the next day tinkering with our kit. Most of what we take with us is carried in a vest that zips up the front and is covered in pouches and pockets. No matter how many times you adjust it and pack it all away, you can always pack it better. Ammo can always be stored in a more efficient way for better access, a tighter fit, or just plain more of it. Aside from all the ammunition, you have to figure out the best way to wear or carry your body armour, water, snacks, first-aid kit, self-administered morphine injections, radio, compass, map, batteries, knife, and grenades. You might remove small things from your pouches to reduce weight, only to later decide you actually want to keep them, so you pack it all over again. We call it kit tinkering, and soldiers love it. It passes the time, and well-packed kit helps to keep you fighting in comfort and without pause. We test-fired our guns off a compound roof out into the river and made sure we had fresh batteries on the radios and in our NVGs. I went around the DC to see mates in other troops and wished everyone luck. As the hours ticked by, the excitement began to mount. The Taliban sent a few rockets our way just to remind us that they were still there and waiting for us. Little did they know we were on our way.

Darkness fell and we all started to get our kit on and get organized into the order of march. We wouldn't step off (start walking) until complete darkness – we had lots of night vision kit, including individual infrared night vision goggles and thermal imagery rifle sights, so we figured we might as well use it. The attack was scheduled to start with a rain of bombs at 2100, so at 2030 we left the DC in a long snake of one hundred soldiers and began to thread our way southeast. We silently made our way through the deserted streets of Garmsir and by one of our checkpoints as we passed into the fields and ditches beyond the town. With the checkpoint behind us, we had just crossed into no man's land. Everything to our east, south, and west was enemy territory. Target recognition was not a problem in these circumstances. There were no civilians here, only them and us.

We were treading lightly and slowly, trying not to bring any attention to ourselves. The snake silently wove its way among the ditches in the fields and covered over a kilometre before we halted. We dropped to sit on the ground with a long dirt bank between us and the target area. We were happy to lean back and get the weight off our shoulders for a moment. I was carrying one hundred pounds of machine gun and ammunition. We were only about one hundred metres from our crossing point, and so far the enemy was unaware of our approach. Everything was going according to plan. Things began to happen very quickly at this point. The engineers were constructing the bridge. It comes in ten-foot sections and there is a float on one end. As you connect each section, you push the bridge farther and farther across the gap. For this job the engineers had four or five sections to sort out. When it reaches the other side, one or two brave engineers have to run across and secure it to the far bank. At that point, there are just two of them over there, and a shitload of bad guys. Not a comfortable position.

While this was happening we had teams setting up security just south of the near end of our bridge. They were getting in place with Javelin missiles, which lock in on heat sources (vehicles or people); .50-calibre heavy machine guns; and our brand-new Heckler & Koch GMGS – machine guns that launch grenades. It was a ton of firepower, to help ensure no baddies could sneak up from the south. Our guys were isolating the battlefield.

Over the radio the company got the message to try and keep down: a 2,000-pound bomb was heading for our main target, Vodka. Thirty seconds until impact is the usual message, but with all the delays of relaying messages it is usually almost instantly. Nothing quite breaks up a quiet night like 2,000 pounds of high explosive. A fraction of a second before it hits, you can hear it approaching like a freight train – and then *BOOM!* It is awesome to be huddled down as close as you can get to something like that. I recommend it.

After that first bomb hit, we let all hell loose on Vodka. Heavy bombers way overhead slammed down bombs, and then the artillery started to unload on the target. Mortars jumped in the game too, and soon it was one long continuous roar of explosions. I can't imagine being on the receiving end of something like that. The sheer number and violence of the explosions was awesome. There were secondary explosions starting to go off in Vodka as we struck Taliban ammunition and weapons caches, and still the barrage seemed to grow in intensity.

I was sitting facing away from Vodka, my back to the dirt pile, helping to keep an eye on our exposed western flank. I pulled out a tin of chewing tobacco and had a dip. The Brits don't do chewing tobacco, and neither do I normally, but things are different on operations. "Anybody want a dip?" I asked the guys up and down the line, offering the tin to anyone within reach. "Fuck that shit," most of them said. There was only one taker, a real athletic guy born in England and raised in Spain. It was funny because he could speak English better than you or me but couldn't write it worth a shit. All of his schooling had been in Spanish. "Give me some of that crap," he said. So there we sat, each with a gob full of spit, me just taking it all in, and him turning green.

The bombs continued to fall on our target. The wind was blowing from Vodka towards us. The smell of cordite and scorched earth was very strong and we were being covered in a blanket of dust and soot. In fact, the dust and smoke in the air was becoming so thick that it was starting to cause a bit of concern. The level of visibility was rapidly dropping, and it is difficult enough to see in the dark without trying to do it in a dust and smoke storm. Word came back down the line. "Prepare to move." We had been there about ten minutes.

As the whole company of us struggled up off of the ground with all of our kit, our heads came up above the dirt pile and we got a view of what was happening to Vodka. The heavy bombing from above had stopped by now because we were heading straight into the blast zone, but the mortars and artillery kept pounding. Explosions and rumbles continued to fill the air, and when the volume dropped it was just enough to let us hear the whine and moan of the incoming artillery shells. In the time it took us to get up and step off, the dust and smoke had grown so heavy that it was hard to see even a few metres in front of us. I was worried I'd lose sight of the guy in front of me. This was no time to wander off on your own. We tightened up the single file line as we moved and guys joked back and forth to each other about the dust. There was no need to be quiet now.

But as we got closer and closer to the bridge leading to Vodka, things began to get more serious. I felt like I was walking in a World War I battlefield, about to go "over the top." With the massive bombardment still going on, all the shit in the air, the bulk of the company behind me in line, and the expectation that in a moment I would have to run into a hail of gunfire across that little bridge, I was in a strange place in my head. I wouldn't say I was frightened, but I was definitely concerned. We moved up to the edge of the canal and stopped again, waiting for our turn to make for the bridge. The company had to make its way over the canal in single file; one or two guys at a time. The engineers were crouched down at the bank to direct movement over the bridge. I only knew we were near the canal because an engineer told us we were, the visibility was that bad.

The artillery barrage continued and I could hear jet engines scream-ing overhead. The first guys in my troop were on the other side of the bridge already so it was time for us to go. My buddies across the bridge would be very grateful for the 2 GPMGS Jay and I were carrying, so we had to get a move on. An engineer grabbed me by the shoulder and gave the two of us the green light to move. Apparently the bridge was only a few metres away, but I still couldn't see shit. We shuffled forward and the air began to fill with new noises. Small sharp snaps began to sur-round us. Nothing too intense compared to what we had experienced on previous operations, but there was no doubt that the enemy were now shooting at us. *Cheers for that*, I thought to myself. I would have preferred they had waited until I was over the bridge.

I was close to the bridge now and could see about halfway across its span. Two more engineers were crouched at my end to tell us when to go. The bridge was easily overloaded and they didn't want too many people on the flimsy bridge at once. It was also a good idea to leave big gaps between people so a single burst of automatic fire or an RPG couldn't take out a lot of soldiers at once. As I stepped onto the bridge the enemy fire seemed to grow in intensity. Maybe I was imagining it, but it sure felt like they were cranking it up just for me. It was my turn to run across the bridge and into the dust and smoke on the other shore. Beyond the bridge, in the unknown, the artillery and mortars were still landing on the target, creating flashes in the haze. The earth was vibrating under the barrage. Jay tapped me on the shoulder with a big grin on his face. "Living the dream!" he said. I couldn't help but smile. "Ain't that the truth!" I replied. No matter what was happening we would always say that we were living the dream or that "civvies would pay thousands for this."

But was I really living the dream? Is this what I had imagined when I first thought of signing up with the Royal Marines? *A small-town boy, from the West Coast of Canada, caught up in this shit.* This was one of those moments when I found myself asking the same old thing. *How in the hell did I end up here?*

PART 1
BUILDING A BOOTNECK

CHAPTER 1

EARLY DAYS

I was born in a small town on Vancouver Island off the coast of British Columbia in 1979 and my first home was a cabin surrounded by forests and wildlife. I lived in that little cabin with my mom, my dad, and my brother, who was three years older than me. My dad was building a nice family home on the property and the cabin was just a temporary measure as the house came together. My parents spent a few years in it, I think, but I barely did one. So, living miles away from the nearest town, I grew up playing with slingshots and wooden swords my dad made out of plywood. We had a few pigs and some chickens, and sometimes I couldn't go out to play because of bears or wolves in the yard. I thought it was a fantastic place to live. I was never bored, and my mother made sure that I was on the soccer and T-ball teams or involved with kids' clubs to keep me busy. When I wasn't up to that stuff I was back in the bush, throwing rocks at the snake nest or setting the tent up in the yard to sleep out at night. I loved it.

When I was about six my parents got divorced. My mom and my brother and I moved about fifty miles away to Comox and I had a whole new batch of friends. I was a little farther from the bush than I would have liked, but there were still some parks where I could crawl around in the trees and play soldier with my new mates. My dad had moved up to a more secluded town with plenty of bush around, so when I was visiting him I still managed to get my fill. I got to go fishing and camping, and learned to shoot in the local gravel pits at a young age.

High school came very quickly, and I excelled in every subject. Book work came easily to me and every few months my dreams of what I wanted to do when I grew up changed. Just before graduation we started having interviews and meetings with school and career counsellors about what options we had for the future. I had always thought of a career in the military, and was almost decided that that was what I was going to do. This counsellor who had been assigned to me actually spent most of his time trying to talk me out of it. The counsellor told me it was a horrible career choice, that the military as a whole was a huge waste of taxpayers' money and that no self-respecting person would serve in the forces. My dad attended one of these meetings and I think he told this guy to piss off and mind his own business and then dragged me out of that office. Thinking back, it frustrates me to think that a professional providing career advice to kids would be so biased and unobjective. A career in the forces is a great option for many young people, and I hope that guy changed his tune over the years.

I couldn't quite make up my mind about what I wanted to do and ended up going to college for a year in my town, taking some general courses that I could use towards university if I decided to go down that road. But I was always a bit hesitant about committing to four years of classrooms so I never did apply to go to university. A year later I moved to Vancouver and enrolled in technical school for two years to study finance. As interesting as the program was, I never fully enjoyed my time there. I was just too much of a small-town boy and I couldn't figure out how everyone got along without the camping and fishing.

. I was still kicking around the idea of joining the military and all I had in mind was some good old-fashioned infantry action. I loved being in the outdoors and hiking and shooting so it seemed like it might be a good fit. I started the recruiting process with the Canadian Forces. I wasn't sure I wanted to commit to something full-time so I started my career with the Reserve Force, joining an army reserve unit in Vancouver. This way there was no real contractual commitment and I could leave if it wasn't my cup of tea. I joined the Seaforth Highlanders of Canada and started heading down to the armoury once a week. I was very proud to be in the Canadian Forces uniform, and wearing the Canadian maple leaf flash on my shoulder was an amazing feeling. In the summer of 2003, I headed off to train full time with the army. I was happy: Wearing a uniform every day, doing drill, marching, learning all about machine guns and grenades. I found that I was actually pretty good at soldiering and placed second in each of my courses. It was a fantastic experience and when I moved back to Vancouver Island a few months later I transferred to another unit, the Canadian Scottish Regiment, to carry on. In the C-Scots I made some good friends and attended everything there was to attend. I was there for every weekend exercise and every Thursday night I turned up full of enthusiasm. I was dismayed to find that some of the other reservists weren't as dedicated and wouldn't turn up for exercises if the weather forecast wasn't good. But I put in everything I had. I signed up for every possible course and was looking forward to going away again in the coming summer to complete my training.

In the meantime I found a new girl in my home town. Her name was Jennifer, and she was lovely. We worked together, in a big parts warehouse, so I had plenty of opportunity to flirt with her. Before I knew it we were going out together, and everything seemed to be going really well for me. The army thing was progressing nicely, I had a decent job, and there was a great girl on my arm. Life was good. As the summer rolled nearer I started to make plans at work for my absence when I would be off training. I was getting excited and couldn't stop talking about it, but a few weeks before I should have headed off to Alberta for the course, I got a phone call to tell me that there weren't enough places and I would have to wait another year. Bombshell. I was pissed off. It got worse when I saw who was actually getting to go on course. I was livid. People who didn't show up when it rained were on course. People who did poorly on previous courses were on this one. A light went on. Hard work and dedication, it seemed to me, didn't mean shit here. That sounds a little harsh now, but at the time, when I was angry and stinging from a decision that made no sense to me, that is what I thought. I knew then that if I wanted to do any real soldiering, I would have to look elsewhere. Cue my friend John.

John is a great guy and an even better soldier. I met him in basic training with the Reserves and we got along splendidly from the first day. He was serving with the Royal Westminster Regiment on the mainland. He is a sucker for physical punishment and loves the outdoors just as much as I do, if not more. We had already been on a few good hiking trips together, pushing deep into Strathcona Provincial Park and on to Della Falls. One day, not long after I got the bad news about the course, he mentioned something called the Royal Marine Corps. I had heard of them before as I was a bit of a history buff but it had not occurred to me that I could join them. I really knew very little about the Royal Marines. Well, John decided it was a good idea to put in an application, so the next day at work, out of curiosity, I went onto their website and did a little research. It turned out that the Royal Marine Commandos were a hard-core bunch of guys. They form the

Royal Navy's "go anywhere" amphibious force and are a key component in the United Kingdom's global Rapid Reaction Force. Training looked intense and there was a lot of travelling so I was intrigued. I did a bit more reading, and then click, click, click, I'd requested an information package too. I never told Jennifer, because I wasn't taking the idea entirely seriously. But the Corps was taking it *very* seriously. They were heavily committed in the Iraqi invasion and Afghanistan and needed manpower. I was just what they were looking for. When I had applied to join the Canadian Forces, the process had been long and tedious. Delays were common and expected. In contrast, three days after I applied online to the Royal Marines I received a huge application and information package in my mailbox. Three days to hear from England, three weeks to hear when I tried to apply in Canada. These guys meant business, and it was a breath of fresh air.

John and I filled in our applications and sent them back to England, not knowing what would happen next. But the more we talked about it and the more we looked into the Corps, the more we knew we had to give it a shot. It would mean abandoning everything I had going for me in Canada. It would mean leaving a good job that I enjoyed, it would mean leaving my girl, and it would mean leaving my favourite place on earth, Vancouver Island. My family would be left behind, I'd take a huge pay cut from my job in the warehouse, and any thoughts I had of starting a family would be put on hold. My freedom to do what I wanted when I wanted would be gone. I was twenty-four years old and figured that was pretty much the cut-off age for me to make a choice. The Corps will let you join up until age thirty, but I figured that if I spent, say, five years with them starting now, I'd be enlisted while I was in my physical prime and before I had any children. It was a classic now-or-never decision, and I chose now. I knew that the Royal Marines always saw action. The Canadian army at this time was only just start-ing to get committed in Afghanistan, and nobody then could have foreseen how involved they would ultimately get. I figured joining the Corps was a sure bet to get some trigger time, and I was not wrong.

As spring turned into summer, John and I quietly kept up the application process. Soon we had to pick a date to head over to England for our interviews and an intense selection process to see if we were suitable to attempt Royal Marine training. This would involve four days of fitness assessments, team work, and tests. It would be anything but easy, going by what we were reading. We figured we would need a few months to get in shape, so we picked December 7, 2004, as the day we would show up at the Commando Training Centre, Royal Marines, in Lympstone, Devon. It was about this time I broke the news to everybody. Jennifer was surprisingly supportive but I think she might have reacted a little differently if she had really known what we were getting ourselves into. I had no idea either how difficult the separation would eventually become. But for now all was well.

For the next few months John and I gradually ramped up our exercise program and little by little prepared ourselves. I was nervous and wasn't sure how fit we would really need to be to get in. We booked our flights to London but about two weeks before we were scheduled to fly, John called me up and gave me some terrible news. "Things are not good," John said. "I injured my knee. I can't make it." And that was that. I was on my own.

CHAPTER 2

THE BEGINNING

Early on in the application process I had to choose a recruiting office in England. Not knowing my way around the U.K. at the time, I picked a location on the southern coast, thinking that it would be better weather when I headed over in December. I chose Brighton out of all the possibilities, and it turned out to be a pretty good choice. It was not a bad place at all, and it was there that I made my first stop in the U.K. When I arrived there was a lot of paperwork to do and physical tests to go through. The docs had to verify that my ears and eyes worked and that my heart was strong. I was staying in a hostel a few blocks away from the recruiting office and going for runs most days to keep up my fitness. Once the application and interviews were complete I had a few days to kill before I headed west down the coast to a little village called Lympstone. This was the home of CTC and where I would get my first taste of what commando training entailed. I had a lot of work ahead of me just to see if I had what it took to actually be accepted into the Corps as a recruit.

I took a train to Exeter, a city just up the River Exe from Lympstone, and got myself a room at a B&B. I went down to a pub and had a few beers to calm my nerves. I was more nervous than I had ever been before, and I hadn't even set eyes on the training centre yet. The beers did me a world of good and I sauntered off to bed ready for whatever the morning should bring.

The next day I experienced a feeling that only a Royal Marine will understand. CTC has its own train station reserved for people that have business at the training centre, and as the train begins to slow for the stop it passes by the whole commando assault course. There, laid out in front of you, is an area where blood, sweat, and tears are a daily reality, and it is rare that you won't see some recruits getting thrashed all over that course with full kit and rifles on. You can see recruits running and climbing over obstacles, carrying each other and crawling on the ground with instructors screaming in their ears. The recruits were filthy, soaking wet and looked worse than miserable. I felt sick to my stomach as the train came to a stop. Good old nervousness had been joined by an entirely new feeling. That new feeling was fear, and it is something every Royal Marine recruit feels that first day. In fact, it is something that sticks with us forever. I have taken that train ride a hundred times now in my life, and every single time I get the same sick feeling as I pass by that scene.

There were about fifty of us on that train, all feeling the same. As we got off together we looked each other up and down, each trying to gauge if he was in the company of supermen or just normal guys like himself. We were all dressed in slacks and wearing ties, just as we'd been instructed. There was a Royal Marine waiting at the gate to let us in and as we passed by he ticked our names off a list. Once we were inside, the gate slammed shut and we were officially there. He led us up a path and wound us through the camp until we found where we would be staying. Groups of recruits were marching and jogging all over the place. Some looked smart in drill uniforms; others looked exhausted, their fatigues covered in mud, sweat, and spit. It all looked pretty hard-core to me. Everything appeared highly organized and professional and I was amazed at the number of recruits on camp. Everywhere you looked you'd see another group of thirty or forty and the groups were all rushing off in different directions. It was a big change from what I had seen as a recruit with the Canadian Reserves at a small armoury in Vancouver.

The next few days went very quickly. We got assigned some accommodation (barracks) and were issued old uniforms before our assessments began. Before we knew it we were running around in the gym and doing push-ups by the dozen, sit-ups and sprints and all that good stuff. We went on runs that were a few miles long and spent some time crawling around in the mud on the bottom field (that's what the assault course area is called). We had a lot of lectures on what the Royal Marines were all about and what opportunities there were for us. But mostly it seemed to be a physical assessment, and we had some team games to do in the gym, all of which involved a lot of sweat. They had to make sure we weren't afraid of heights so they had us running along planks way up in the air. They were long and tiring days and I have to admit I was very happy when it was all over.

Before we left we all assembled to find out who had passed and who hadn't. I made it through and was given a little "well done" cer-tificate and a large information package on what exercise I should be doing before I showed up for training. Some of the guys were going to start training within a few weeks, but I would be waiting for a while. They do extensive security and background checks on all potential recruits, but they didn't start that process for me until after I passed the selection. The security screening takes more time when it is an international effort, and they weren't going to waste any effort before I had at least proven I was a candidate. But this delay suited me fine. From what I had seen, I could handle putting everything on hold for a few months.

I left CTC in good spirits, pleased with what I had accomplished, and took a train straight to the airport as I was out of money and couldn't afford a hotel. I had about fifteen hours to kill before my flight but had planned ahead. I pulled a light sleeping bag out of my backpack and found a nice quiet spot behind some seats in a corner of the terminal. I got in that bag, went straight to sleep, and slept like a log for about eight hours. When I woke up there were people everywhere and a man was nudging a large floor-polishing machine at my toes.

At home I dropped back into the familiar routine. I worked hard and played hard, and spent a great deal of time thinking about my future. After a few weeks the Royal Marines gave me a call, and told me that all of the security checks were complete and everything was good to go. All I had to do was pick a date that I wanted to head over there, sign a contract, and get on with it. I told the guy I would call him back the next day with an answer and hung up the phone.

I was faced with the biggest decision of my life. Here it was. *Now or never.* Well, I had always figured it was better to do something than do nothing, so I grabbed the phone and called the guy right back. I picked a date from his possible list, and that was that. On July 25, 2005, my life would change dramatically. I still had four months before I had to show up in England so I just carried on as usual, never really letting it all sink in. But what could I really let sink in? To be honest, I had no idea what I had just committed to.

Four months later I sat in that recruiting office again in Brighton with a contract laid out on the table before me. I asked a lot of questions about the fine print, and made doubly sure that I didn't actually have to do the entire contract's term. A complete term is for twenty-two years. That is how long it takes to qualify for a full pension.

No, he assured me, I could give twelve months' notice to leave any time after three years had been served. Well, that I figured I could do. I signed my name, slid the papers across the desk, and was handed a train ticket to Lympstone. Next stop, the Commando Training Centre, Royal Marines.

I headed a day early into Exeter so that I wouldn't have to travel very far in the morning before reporting for duty on July 25. I stayed in the same B&B I had stayed in seven months before, and went to the same pub and had a few of the same beers to calm the same nerves as I had done last time. I was even more nervous this time around, as now there was no escape. I only had a couple of beers as I really didn't want to take on the next day with a hangover, so I went up to bed quite early, but as you can imagine I lay there wide awake all night. I got up early with no sleep and put on the same pair of slacks and same tie as the last time. I got on the train and again it was full of about fifty young guys with short haircuts, slacks, and ties. We all looked each other over again and you could tell everyone felt the same nerves. As the train approached the stop at CTC, that sick feeling crept back into my guts, and seeing recruits crawling in the mud and in anguish made me feel worse. The train stopped and we all got out. The routine from before was repeated: Everybody through the gate as a Marine ticks off your name, and then SLAM!, the gate shuts. This was it. I had arrived.

We got formed up into some sort of body of men and marched our way across the camp to a building where all of the recruits spend the first two weeks of their lives at CTC. We halted outside the building and the first member of our training team came out and made an appearance. I know him now as a regular guy in the Corps, but that first day I thought he was some sort of super soldier. We all did. Royal Marine. Crisp drill uniform. Mirror-like boots. And most importantly, his green beret. He looked the part, and all of us wanted to be like him. I suppose that was the point. For the next eight months, everything that I did for every second of every day would all be aimed at achieving one thing and one thing only. I wanted a green beret of my own. A green beret that very few people attempt to get, and even fewer will ever possess. I was here, and there was work to do.

CHAPTER 3

A NEW WORLD ORDER

It was July 25, 2005, and I knew only shitty things were coming my way for a very long time, but I did my best to take it with a grin. I'd realize later that the first day was actually fairly chilled out in comparison to some of my time at CTC, but that didn't make it any easier. The Drill Leader got us standing at attention in three ranks. He went through his nominal list to see who had bothered to show up and if anybody had dared to be late on Day 1. A few of the guys on the list were absent. They simply never showed up. We got marched to our first accommodation, called the foundation block, and found ourselves in a large rectangular room with sixty beds and lockers, lined up against the wall, all the way around the room. The middle of the room was empty, except for a few tables and some lockers with glass fronts on them. These lockers were there as examples, and our lockers were to look exactly like these ones. They were immaculate, with everything pressed perfectly and folded to the regulation dimensions. This didn't look like it was going to be a whole lot of fun.

We got assigned our beds and dumped our civilian duffel bags on the floor by our lockers. There were a lot of ironing boards around and everyone had a million questions, but there was no time to chat to the other guys, who were looking around with the same blank face that I had. We were off for a haircut and a busy day. Buzz, buzz – off came the hair. Straight into a lecture hall, where we all stood up and made our oath of allegiance to the Queen. After that we legally had to do as we were told. Too bad.

The whole week proved to be very tiring and very busy. We never got to bed before 1:00 a.m. and were up at five each morning. This was a schedule that would certainly take a little getting used to, as sadly there were no midday naps scheduled. The week was packed with events such as physical fitness assessments, dental checkups, immunization shots galore, and plenty of kit issues. The training team came around and showed us how to put all of our backpacks and webbing together and how to pack some basic kit for the field. A lot of time was devoted to learning how to iron our rig properly, and we had to iron everything. Sheets, socks, hats, everything. We got issued with dark blue berets and spent a lot of time trying to form them so we didn't look like complete idiots. Folding our kit properly took a lot of time and patience. Long johns were particularly tricky to get into the regulation dimensions. By the third day people were beginning to get very tired. Four hours of sleep a night is hardly sufficient for most people, and we were no exception. Our days were mentally as well as physically exhausting. We were constantly in and out of the gym for physical assessments, and swim tests were conducted to see if we were fish or bricks.

To fill the day it certainly helped that all of our laundry had to be done by hand, and this included our sheets. There were plenty of washers and dryers on camp but until we had proven we could do it the hard way we weren't allowed to entertain the thought of doing it the easy way. Everyone jockeyed for position at the limited number of sinks each night, and battled for a space to hang his stuff in the drying room. Early in the morning you had to gather up your dry laundry and iron it, fold it, and stow it away in your locker for morning inspection. It was a hell of a week. More dental checkups, ID issues, Corps history lectures, career advisor interviews, banking lectures, math and English tests, cleaning, cleaning, and more cleaning, drill, marching, group photos, blood tests, more PT, and yet more kit issues. It just went on and on and on.

And just when you thought you had everything squared away and were about to drop your tired ass in bed, the training team would pop a surprise locker inspection. Everybody had to spring up and be dressed in two minutes with their lockers open, standing to attention beside their beds. Then the fun would start. One of the instructors would inspect a locker, looking for the most minor infraction. A speck of dust, an imperfectly folded shirt, whatever. It didn't really matter if there was anything there or not. The training team had gone through this when they were recruits, and they would be damned if they weren't going to pass on the tradition. So they would find something, and then they would trash your locker. Everything would come flying out into a heap or be sent skidding across the room. Boots scuffed, ironed and folded rig tied into knots. Clothes rubbed into the floor. It was all funny as hell until they got to your locker. *Bam!* There goes your locker too. Funny until you realize it will take you four hours or so to put it all back together, and it had all better be back in there for the morning inspection. No sleep again. The scene in that room was really something else. Four Royal Marines wandering around having a grand time, and fifty recruits looking miserable with their hard work all mixed up all over the room. Inevitably some guy who couldn't stop laughing would be sentenced to hop on one leg in the middle of the room the whole time. Or a mattress would go out the window. Or some guy would be on the table in the push-up position in the middle of the room singing his national anthem. We had South Africans, Scots, and Welshmen. It was always something different. It was always funny as hell. The Corps has a great sense of humour, and this was our first taste of it. The scene was often the same again first thing in the morning.

I noticed early on a guy whose bed was right across from mine, and he always seemed to do everything with ease. His locker always hit a very high standard even though he often disappeared for hours each evening and was in bed before everyone else. He took everything in stride and never seemed flustered or worked up at all. He had something up his sleeve, and I wanted some of it. I wandered over one day and started chatting to him. Sure enough, he had plenty of tricks up his sleeve. Turns out Steve had been through all of this before. Two years previously he had gotten all the way to the last week of training before being kicked out for basically being a shit disturber. He had an ND (negligent discharge) with his rifle on the final exercise and that had been the last straw. Now, amazingly, he had volunteered to go through all of this shit a second time. If anybody wanted a green beret, it was Steve. It was great to have him on board. He knew all the tricks to make life easy as a recruit. He knew where the bar (Jollies) was and where we could use washers and dryers without getting caught. He also knew where to find the late-night greasy spoon on camp so we could get some extra food. It was always open until two or three in the morning. After Steve and I became friends things got a lot easier.

The training team made everything as humorous as possible, in a sick kind of bootneck way. That's the slang term for a Royal Marine. We are called bootnecks. On one occasion as they were showing us how to wash and take care of yourself properly in the field, one of the corporals got naked and started to wash. He explained how important it was to clean your balls and penis, and while doing this he pulled back his foreskin and removed a dime-size piece of cheese he had stuck there for just this occasion. "Ya gotta keep it clean or this shit builds up – dick cheese!" he exclaimed. Classic bootneck humour.

As usual, the following morning our lockers were systematically destroyed by the training team. Steve had a good angle on this, from experience. When they went to trash his locker, he would ask very politely if he could trash his own locker. Slightly amused, they would let him, and he would very tactfully tear everything out and throw it on the floor so that much of it was still folded nicely. Yep, I had a lot to learn from this guy.

The next day we had to clear out of the foundation block and move into the residence where we would stay for the duration of training. I figured it would be nice to get into a smaller room – out of fifty guys in one room, the chances were pretty damn good that a few would snore like Satan. Our new rooms were six-man rooms and in a nice new clean building. This was good in one sense, but it also meant that we would be expected to keep everything that much more immaculate. We moved over to our new block and set up our lockers just like we had in foundation. Things were beginning to look up a little bit for us, until we were introduced to the troop sergeant. Up until this point we had pretty much been in the clutches of our Drill Leader, but once foundation ended, the troop was properly formed.

The original fifty guys formed up in three ranks and then stood to attention when he came down out of the office. Our new sergeant was a fairly big guy with broad shoulders and an experienced face that looked aged beyond its years. He had dark hair and thick eyebrows and looked like he could kick my ass. As he approached the troop he walked slowly and deliberately with absolutely no doubt in his mind of who was in charge. He had one hell of a scowl on his face and he just stood there looking at us for a few minutes in complete silence, daring anyone to look him in the eye. He left without saying a word and called for one of the corporals to follow him in. The message relayed to us by the corporal when he returned was that we looked like such a bag of shit, the sergeant refused to even address us. He would deal with us later when he had calmed down a bit.

With time, we would learn what this guy was all about, and so will you. For now, let's just say that he was not very nice and that I lost a lot of sleep in my life spending it jumping when that prick said jump.

Training is broken down into separate weeks, each one being a hurdle in its own way. Some focus on lectures and written tests on camp, some are spent in the field, and others are spent preparing for and tackling the final Commando tests. These four tests are the culmination of eight months of physical training, and every recruit fears them from day one. The tests are done on four consecutive days and are designed to see if you have the endurance, determination, and physical fitness to carry on, no matter what.

Every two weeks there is a new injection of fifty to sixty recruits to start at Week 1. Every two weeks there is also a group of about twenty recruits known as the King's Squad who put on a big display of arms drill for friends and family, and get marched off to their duties within the Corps. Excluding our scheduled holidays at Christmas, Easter, and in the summer, thirty-two weeks of pain separate the two groups. Each week or two throughout training you have certain tests and if you are successful you advance to the next week with your troop. If you are unsuccessful you will be back-trooped, which means you move back down the list of troops an appropriate number of weeks, to do some part of training again and tackle the tests at a later date. You will never rejoin your original troop, and back-troopers are abundant. A recruit who is deep into training enjoys great prestige at being an original in his troop. Out of twenty guys passing out from CTC every two weeks, perhaps ten will be originals.

There are also many ways to get kicked right out of training as opposed to merely being back-trooped. If you have already been back-trooped many times, you can easily just be binned. If you have a generally shitty attitude, can't learn fast enough, don't pull your own weight, simply don't like being cold and wet or develop an allergy, you can be sent packing. Many other recruits get back-trooped or sent home for good because of injuries. When you start to carry a lot of weight as fast as you can over rough terrain, knees, ankles, and backs buckle and break under the strain. Some bodies can handle it, and others can't.

The training team is made up of eight key members, and they are responsible for getting a particular troop through training from start to finish. There are other specialist instructors the recruits will learn from along the way, but these are the core eight. First there is the troop commander, usually a captain. Then there is the troop 2ic (second in command). This is a sergeant, and he is the brawn behind the leadership in the troop. There will be four corporals who are the troop section commanders and they will teach you how to live in the field, give you lectures, teach you to shoot, stalk, and generally be an effective soldier in the field. The troop is broken down into sections and each corporal is responsible for a section. Recruits are rarely moved between sections. You will have a PTI (Physical Training Instructor) who kicks the shit out of you in the gym and all over the bottom field. He will also take you through your commando tests. And last but not least, you have a DL (Drill Leader), who is there to teach you how to dress, act, salute, talk, eat, wash, and march. He is usually one mean son of a bitch with a hell of a sense of humour. When you are standing to attention on the parade square for inspection, you can bet on him cracking some witty jokes and getting some poor bugger to break out laughing. Inevitably this ends in a lot of sweat and tears for whoever couldn't hold in the laughter. The immaculate Royal Marine we met the very first day was our troop's Drill Leader.

CHAPTER 4

NODS

Week 3 of training started out quickly, and we were introduced to our rifles. Most British forces use the SA-80. It is a short, heavy weapon in a bullpup design (the action and the magazine are located behind the trigger and alongside the shooter's face). When originally issued it was a temperamental bit of kit. Magazines would fall off or a bit of dirt would cause stoppages. But Heckler & Koch, the German firearm makers, got their hands on it and made some changes and the latest model has proven to be very reliable. The more I used it the more I liked it. The first day they just showed us how to make sure it wasn't loaded and how to take it apart. Basic stuff again, but all interesting when learning a new weapon system.

We began to have a shitload of drill thrown at us, and for the most part I didn't like it. It basically involves putting on an immaculate semi-dress uniform and learning how to stand perfectly still. Rain or shine, you go out and learn how to stand still for a few hours. Sometimes you get to march around, but inevitably you spend most of the time like a statue while the DL walks up and down the ranks inspecting you and ensuring you had put in the time and effort to have a perfect uniform. Lots of fun.

The lectures continued as usual, one or two a day. In the warm classrooms the guys would naturally start to fall asleep, because we were still going to bed late and getting up very early. All around heads would be bobbing and chins bouncing off chests as guys nodded off to sleep. Royal Marine recruits are known as "nods" for this very reason. They spend eight months of their lives nodding away in this fashion.

The physical training was really ramping up as well. Being a good nod means being very fit and anyone who couldn't keep up would find themselves out of the troop in a blink of an eye. We had many CV (cardio-vascular) circuits in the gymnasium, and we swam a lot – not so much doing laps as doing push-ups on the edge of the pool. Push-ups, push-ups, and more push-ups. Sometimes it seemed there was rarely a moment in the day when we didn't find ourselves in the push-up position. Every time someone was late the whole troop would get down in the push-up position and wait for the person like that. If we were getting a talking to, we would normally be down in the push-up position. It was very tiring but certainly helped to build upper body strength, which it turns out makes life as a soldier much easier.

Some nights the sergeant would make an appearance, and it could be at any hour. He would have everyone up and outside in seconds, standing in three ranks to attention as usual. He would come down out of the office and slowly put on his beret while scowling at us. We were learning that this was a bad sign. No beret meant no pain. A beret slowly donned meant something bad was coming our way. He rarely yelled at us, but to be fair there was no need to yell at all. He would tell us how angry he was and then he would put us in various stress positions while he talked at length. He really loved to have us squat down with our thighs parallel to the ground and hold our arms straight out in front of us. It's easy for a few seconds, but after five minutes things get a little painful. He would walk up and down the ranks telling us how dirty the accommodation was (it wasn't dirty at all) or how we had been late again (when they gave us thirty seconds to get changed) or had committed some other trivial infraction.

After he had us doing this shit for half an hour in the middle of the night he would take us down to the field and have us crawl around in the grass and the mud before being released. This was to ensure we would not get any sleep that night. After all, your clothes had to be clean and immaculate in your locker for the morning inspection, and that included the ones you had been crawling around in at 2:00 a.m. We were still limited to hand washing our clothing and hanging it to dry, so it was obviously impossible to have it ready in three hours, but that wasn't the point. This just gave the training team an excuse to trash our lockers and make us crawl in the mud a bit more. It all became very frustrating and you can see why a lot of people were choosing to quit.

Outside the team office they had a picture of the troop that was taken in the first few days, and when a person left, his face and body were carefully blacked out with a marker, never to be a part of the troop again. It was a little creepy, but also a little satisfying to look at that picture with the black blobs slowly multiplying and spreading out all around your own face. As long as the blob didn't cover you up, you were still okay.

We began to do a lot of rifle drills during this third long week and were learning about how to shoot properly, trajectories, theories of flight, and all sorts of good stuff. We would go down to these little brick buildings and have our weapon lessons in them. They were open on one side and really just a concrete floor, a roof, and some benches. We stripped and reassembled our rifles over and over again, and we were getting faster and faster each time. As we would be putting our rifles together the instructor would wander around asking questions about the effective range of the weapon, or what the name of some small part was. If you didn't answer fast enough or simply didn't know, there was always some sort of punishment waiting for you. A common one was called the fruit bat. The rafters supporting the roofs of these little brick buildings are thin steel horizontal beams that are stood on edge. You would have to jump up and hang from the rafters for a given amount of time, usually a few minutes. The edge of the rafters really cut into your fingers and it hurt like hell with all the weight you were carrying. There you would hang, just like a fruit bat. Genius!

Some of the lads one night got really drunk and started puking all over. A few of these guys started storming around camp pissed up and acting like they owned the place. They were picking fights with anyone who came near and smashing glasses. This was not the sort of thing a Week-3 nod should be getting up to if he knows what is good for him. Naturally our sergeant was contacted and came down on the guys like a hurricane. Three of them were thrown in the cells that night and the rest of us were up all night cleaning the accommodation. We had the next day off (Sunday) for once, and Steve and I made a plan to get up early and get the hell off camp as quick as we could to avoid the shit storm. We were allowed to leave camp at 0700 and at 0659 we stood at the gate ready to go. We got off camp and started to walk to the bus stop, and a minute or so later heard over the camp's loudspeakers that our entire troop was to muster outside the guardroom immediately. "Whaddaya think?" Steve asked me. "Fuck that!" I said. "Let's haul ass!" Steve and I ran away, heading for the next bus stop. We went into town for the whole day and didn't sign in again until 1959, one minute before curfew. We had dodged a bullet. All the other guys had had to get up and in a long line sweep the streets in the camp all day. Strangely, nothing was ever said to us by the stripey (the sergeant) about our absence. It was eerie. And to this day I have no explanation for his oversight. The troop was prohibited from drinking alcohol, and we settled into bed nice and early in anticipation of a terrible Monday morning. There was no way the sergeant was going to accept a little bit of sweeping as payment for the troop disgracing itself on his watch.

We received a dressing down from the company commander for our antics over the weekend, and while this was happening we could see the sergeant standing off to the flank with his blood boiling. After the Major left he explained a few things to us. "You fuckers are gonna get it. Here on camp there are little officers and welfare people to keep tabs on things, but out in the field it's only me. The gloves are off!" Nobody was looking forward to going in the field now. Not ever. But in two weeks that is exactly where we would find ourselves.

CHAPTER 5

TO THE FIELD

Week 5 started out like every other at CTC. We had a full kit and locker inspection that resulted in lockers being trashed all over the place. Beds were overturned and uniforms were tied in knots. The sergeant was on his hands and knees in the bathroom to make sure they were clean enough behind the toilets. It was something right out of a Hollywood movie. Imagine it, a sergeant in the Royal Marines on the floor with a recruit lying beside him, peering up under and behind a toilet to try and see exactly what speck of dirt was about to get the troop in the shit. It was bloody ridiculous. Not that we would ever say anything like that to him. To him it was all, "Yes, sergeant. I see it, sergeant. We'll clean that right away, sergeant. Won't happen again, sergeant. Downstairs, sergeant? You want to have a word with the troop, sergeant? In drill rig in two minutes, sergeant? Right away, sergeant!" That is how it went, and a few moments later we would all be out there in his favourite stress position with him yelling away. "Thighs parallel to the deck, you! Arms out straight, you! Stop shaking! Get a fuckin' grip of yourself! Take control of your body!" And after he had kept us long enough to have his fill, he would release us to get to our first lesson or phys period, for which we would inevitably be late, and for which we would inevitably be punished. And so it went on.

We spent a lot of time in the swimming pool as well. We were all getting ready for our battle swim test, to take place in two weeks, and I wasn't looking forward to it. I wasn't a very good swimmer, never really had been. Failing the swim test meant you got back-trooped; if you failed it three times you were out. I was in the brick section in the pool, which meant I spent most of my time in the shallow end getting lessons on how to breast stroke while the bulk of the troop messed around in the deep end. It would have been embarrassing if it wasn't for the fact that there were about eight of us bricks. But it all turned out well, as this is where I got to know a guy from Grimsby who became a very good friend of mine.

Tom was a brick like me, couldn't swim for shit. He was covered in tattoos, scrawny like me too, and a comedian. To this day I have never seen Tom in a shitty mood. Ever. Cold, wet, muddy, tired, shot, blown up, it doesn't matter. He has been there, done that, and he did it all with a grin on his face. I admire him for that. Very few people out there drive over land mines and get shot in the head and laugh it off as a bit of bad luck. Or good luck. Depends how you look at it. Anyway, Tom and I became great friends and our routes through the Corps were to follow parallel paths for several years.

The day after I had met Tom in the shallow end of the pool the troop was back in the gym bright and early in the morning for our normal pre-field deployment thrash session. The training team always wanted us to be physically tired before we headed into the field to teach us that you may not always get to soldier only when you are well rested. Once the PTI had his way with us we were all off to pack up the stores for the exercise. We all carried our ridiculously large and heavy bergens across camp and lined them up on the ground in the cold English rain. They were about eighty pounds and we were happy to set them down. The troop loaded up all the crap we would need onto trucks, and it took a few hours to get it all together. Ammunition, food, and water were the basics. Then came all the luxuries for the training team. Massive tents for them, cot beds, stoves, field toilets, fresh rations, umbrellas, tables, chairs, coffee pots, the lot. But such is the life of a nod; all of the work and none of the pleasures. Once all the stores were loaded we drew our weapons from the armoury and jumped into the back of some big trucks. While we were transported to a training area known as Woodbury Common, most of us tried to catch a bit of sleep, nodding away as the truck bounced and jolted over the potholes. Woodbury Common is a rough area of moorland and woodland terrain, interspersed with thick stands of gorse and prickle bushes. It is a fine place to thrash nods, and much too soon the truck stopped and the tailgate dropped. We looked out at the rain pouring down, shook our heads, and jumped down into the mud. It was something we would end up getting used to. It was only late September and at least the days were still warm. January would be different, but for the moment we tried not to think about that.

First job was offload the stores and set up the training team tent as quickly as you could. The training team didn't like standing around in the rain, and we were all flapping around like headless chickens trying to figure out how to put this tent together in the rain with the training team barking out orders and pointing at various poles and pegs. It was all turning into a fiasco and the whole operation was stopped. The troop was formed up in three ranks and the sergeant came over to have a word to motivate us to work together. A bunch of push-ups, standing to attention with your rifle held out in front of you with straight arms, a bit more mud crawling, and a couple of sprints sorted us right out. We all got around the tent again and finally got it set up. It could sleep about twenty people on cot beds but there would only be five in there, the four section commanders and the sergeant. We quickly got all of their other kit in out of the rain and set up their tables and chairs. The propane was hooked up to the stove and all the pots and pans laid out nice and neat. Once they were satisfied, they kicked us back out into the elements and got ready to get on with the training.

Later that day the training started with field lectures. We all scribbled in our little notebooks about how to properly camouflage ourselves and make best use of cover and about general observation skills. In these early field exercises we followed a basic pattern: a day or two of field lectures, then a few days of putting it all into practice. We went and set up a harbour position in the trees. This is just a fancy word for our little camp, but it was all set up in a specific way. We were laid out in a large triangle with everybody facing outwards. Headquarters was in the middle of the triangle, and the three corners had both day and night sentry positions with machine guns always manned. We were still in the early non-tactical phase of training so there were no enemy about and the routines were fairly relaxed, but we were slowly being introduced to a very strict way of soldier life that is designed to save lives. We had all been paired up with a bivvy partner from within our sections and unfortunately I was not paired up with my first choice. I got Brad. Brad was only seventeen, very unsure of himself and not the sharpest tool in the shed. I had to do pretty much everything when it came to setting up our shelter and managing our time and throughout training I constantly had to remind him to pack this or that away, clean his weapon or change his socks. The worst part was that the pairing was permanent, until you finished training or one of you quit.

With our shelter finally up that first night of the exercise I was tasked to make a sentry list that was to run through the night, two men on and staggered. We would stagger the shifts so that someone fresh was always on, and through your hour shift you would have two different partners, which helped to keep you awake. The night went smoothly for the most part, although as expected some lads fell back asleep a few seconds after you woke them up to come and relieve you, and many had trouble packing away all of their kit in the dark. Every time you got out of your sleeping bag, everything had to be packed away as if you were about to yomp (march with bergen) from that location. This was all done so that if things were real, you would always be ready to move if the enemy attacked you without warning. Everything was done for a reason, and our routines and rules were designed to save lives so that you could carry on in strength and defeat the enemy.

As far as guys falling back asleep and not turning up to relieve you, my partner was the worst of the bunch. I would creep back to our bivvy from the sentry position and give Brad a shake. He would wake up and I would sit there for a second talking to him to make sure he was actually awake and knew what was going on. Then I would crawl back to my post, happy to know that in a few minutes I would get to catch a few hours of wonderful sleep in my warm sleeping bag. I would wait five minutes, then ten, and then finally I would head on back to the bivvy to find Brad fast asleep again. I would shake him and sit there. A moment later I would shake him again, harder and harder until finally he would get very pissed off and start swearing at me for acting like an asshole. I wasn't going to let things go along like this forever. But for now, I was prepared to give him the benefit of the doubt and chalk it up as a whole new experience for him. Once I had seen him physically crawl out of his bag and start packing it away I would head on back to the sentry position and whisper to the other guy about what a shit I had been paired up with. Finally, twenty or twenty-five minutes late, he would crawl up in a bad mood and take over for me, acting like I was the dickhead.

In the field we were always up long before first light, and after we were all washed, and carrying clean rifles, we had to assemble out in an open area in sections to lay out all of our kit for a full kit muster. This was a major pain in the ass and was designed to ensure we could all take care of ourselves and our kit in field conditions and to prove we hadn't lost anything and were carrying everything on the kit list. Nothing more, nothing less. Each recruit would lay out his poncho on the ground and empty the contents of his bergen onto it. Everything had to be laid out in a specific format. Clothing at the top, spare socks, dirty socks, thirty metres of string, boot polish, rations, sleeping bag, shelter, mess tins, cooking blocks, matches, waterproof bags, ammunition, radios, maps, gloves, warm hat, toothbrush, razor, flashlight, glowsticks, spare batteries, lighter, everything. The boot polish tin had to be over 95 per cent full. Water bottles topped up. Magazines stripped down and cleaned for inspection. Weapons cleaning kit laid out. Rifle fully disassembled and ready to be checked for cleanliness and proper oiling. Even our garbage was laid out to prove that we had been eating all of our rations that we were supposed to have eaten by that point in the exercise. Later on we would even have to lay out bags of shit to prove we had left no sign behind for the enemy. We had about ten minutes to lay it all out and go over our weapons one last time. The training team would count down the last few seconds and everybody would scramble around until we were all standing to attention at the foot of our kit with our rifle barrel over our shoulder for easy inspection. This was what we did every single morning in the field in the first half of training, and we did it regardless of the weather. Rain, hail, or shine, it made no difference.

Our section commander would then come up to each person and check over all his stuff. Rifles and individuals were inspected the most closely. He would slowly pick up each piece of rifle and check it for dirt and rust, and then he would check over the person. He wanted to see clean and polished boots, a clean shave, and no cam cream anywhere on your face. Most people would still have a bit on their ear or neck.

If a fault was found in any of your kit you were put on the flank. When you were told you were on the flank you had to run off to the side of the kit musters and stand there, as more and more people ran over to join you. At the end of it all, the majority of the troop was on the flank and in for a little fun. While the other guys who had dodged the flanking bullet packed away their kit and got on a cup of tea, those on the flank got a fifteen-minute thrashing. Usually they would have to run and dive into various bushes, taking cover and crawling around with their rifles. They could be seen running around the country side with their rifles up over their heads, or carrying their friends on their backs as they ran to keep up with the sergeant. It was not designed to be pleasant, and nobody ever came back from a flanking with a smile. Never. We were not yet at the Royal Marines' famed state of mind, "Cheerfulness in the face of adversity." Once the thrash session was done, the punished nods would all rush back and pack away their kit as fast as they could as the training team yelled at them to hurry up. The whole troop would put their bergens in a big pile under a tree and fall into three ranks, ready for a day of training.

This was all usually done by 0700, sometimes earlier. How does your morning routine compare?

Midday on the second day of the exercise we went for a little jog down to a pond called Peter's Pool and jumped in wearing all of our kit. Throughout training we would become very intimate with this pond, but this was our first taste of its cold, filthy water. We were submerged to ensure that we were thoroughly soaked before we moved into our new troop harbour and got settled into our night routine. This night we would be introduced to another advancement on staying alive in adverse conditions, and as usual it would prove to be anything but comfortable. We learned what the wet-and-dry routine was all about. Before you went to sleep you dug around in your bergen and got into a nice dry set of clothes. You would then place all of your soaking wet clothes in a plastic bag and pack it away, ready to move off at a moment's notice. Every time you got up for your shift on sentry you would dig out your wet clothes and put them back on, stowing away the dry ones for later. You always had to make sure you had a dry set of clothes so that if you started to go down with hypothermia you could get warm again. Two sets of wet clothes was useless. It doesn't sound like too big of a deal, but I can assure you it takes a lot of motivation to crawl out of your warm sleeping bag at three in the morning, wipe the frost off of the top of your bergen, and dig out some half-frozen clothes to put on. By January we would literally have to smack our clothes against a tree to break the ice off them before we put them on again. Once your freezing clothes were on, you would crawl out into a frozen bush and lie there for an hour shivering and muttering to yourself about how you would never complain about being hot again. It was at times like these that you'd be really pissed off if your relief on sentry was even a few minutes late.

Once the training team had had its fill of the field we had to pack up their tent and all of their stores. On this first time out, it was still raining as we packed up, and we were still not working fast enough for them. We were all very tired, not just from the last few days but from the last few weeks, and it was starting to show. More crawling and a little mud motivated us again and the job was finally completed. We scrambled up into the back of the trucks and immediately fell asleep as we headed back to CTC. As much as we would have liked to just go have a shower and crawl into bed, when we got back there was a lot of work to do. We all woke with a shudder as the trucks went over the speed bumps on the way into camp, and then, before we knew it, we were all standing out in the rain again. We were covered in bits of bushes and cam cream, half asleep, hungry, covered in mud and shivering. We all got our tasks and set to work trying to clean and return all of the training team's field stores. We marched off to the accommodation and sat outside on our bergens while we cleaned our weapons. We couldn't go inside as we were simply too filthy, and the rifles took priority over a shower.

We got around the rifles for a few hours and once they had been inspected by the sergeant we could march across camp to hand them into the armoury. Then we would march back to our building and strip down outside to keep as much mud and crap out of our rooms as we could. After hitting the showers, getting on a clean uniform and a hot meal down our necks, it was time to start sorting all of our muddy and wet field kit out. It didn't matter what we had been doing the day before, the morning locker and accommodation inspections were a sure thing. We were up until two or three in the morning scrubbing our bergens and washing bits and pieces of field kit, and up again at five or six to make sure it all got out of the drying rooms and neatly into our lockers. Later on in training I would actually think back to these days and wish I was back there getting as much sleep as we were. I simply didn't realize it at the time, but when pushed to its limits, the human body can do just about anything.

CHAPTER 6

SERGEANT PSYCHO

We still had lots of guys leaving the troop for all sorts of reasons and the rapid decline in our numbers was starting to catch the attention of people up top. In only five weeks of training we had lost twenty people, bringing the troop strength down to thirty-four. The black blobs on the troop photo were spreading and oozing over many faces. The training team was very pleased with the results so far. A smaller troop meant less paperwork and better quality training. They had only one concern, and that was to produce quality, not quantity.

We kept on swimming in preparation for the BST (battle swim test) that was looming on the horizon. Some of the other bricks had been upgraded to fish and were now in the deep end with the rest of the troop, but not Tom and me. We were bricks through and through, still splashing around in the shallow end. Any time we did manage to do a length, technique played no part, it was through sheer brute strength and moving massive amounts of water. But Tom was always smiling and cracking jokes about it all. He had such a good attitude and it carried outside the pool as well. He was a musician and could play guitar and harmonica. He once wrote a song about training and life as a nod. He set it to a basic blues riff and it was a big hit. He called it "The Nod Song."

I woke up this morning
At 5 a.m.
Went to scran
Had rounds again
I fucking failed
No change there
That's why I'm stood here with my weapon in the air

One day I found him in the centre of the accommodation, having been press-ganged into entertaining the training team. He had his harmonica in his mouth, was strumming his guitar, and banging mess tins together with his knees. Talented guy.

One afternoon at the end of Week 6 we had a locker inspection that the sergeant had promised was going to be unusually thorough. This was bad news, and as we all stood to attention next to our wide-open lockers we braced ourselves for the inevitable shit storm. Over the next couple of hours every single locker was trashed and mine was no exception. Because the dryers had been taken away from us I had a pair of socks folded and put away that was still slightly damp. I knew that was a big mistake but I had no choice. If the socks weren't there I was fucked, if they were dirty I was fucked, and if they were damp I was fucked. All you can do is try and get fucked with a grin on your face. Cheerfulness in the face of adversity. It was time to try it out.

The contents of our lockers were dumped in a huge pile in the centre of the building and all mixed together. Foot powder was sprayed on our kit and stuff went out the windows into the dirt below.

Guys were doing push-ups and in stress positions all over the place and a few were leopard crawling up and down the stairs, polishing the floors with their stomachs. Most inspections ended in a bad way, but today was special. The sergeant absolutely snapped and we all knew this was way beyond his normal rants. He rarely yelled, but today he was screaming at the top of his lungs to crawl faster and to get out of the way as he trashed another locker. He had foam and spit coming out of his mouth and the veins in his face and forehead were nearly bursting. If it didn't all translate into so much work for us it would have been comical. He started to get us doing quick changes and in a few minutes we were all outside in our best drill rig. We crawled through the grass and dirt and headed straight back in to get into another uniform and do it again. We went through every bit of clothing we had except for one uniform he let us keep clean for dinner that evening. Absolutely everything was filthy and covered in foot powder, grass stains, and mud. It was a nightmare. When we had finished trashing our last set of rig we were formed up in the standard three ranks and stuck in the standard half-squat stress position as he ranted and raved about what a shit troop we were. He promised us that we would keep doing this until someone cried and quit training and sure enough after a few minutes a few of the younger lads started to cry. That really got him going.

I fully expected him to start kicking and hitting us as we squatted there, shaking and grunting as we fought gravity, but he managed to restrain himself at least that much. Not that he didn't want to hit us. He certainly told us he did, and that he wished he had been in charge of us twenty years earlier when he could have kicked the shit out of us with impunity. Finally, after what seemed like an age, he had had enough of us and stormed off, leaving us to begin sorting our shit out. The last thing he had done was warn us that there would be a full kit muster in the morning. He had made his point and the effects were immediate. Several of the guys made a decision to abandon their dreams and quit training then and there.

Still in shock, we slunk back to our rooms and stared around at the leftovers of the tornado that had ripped through the place. It was nearly dinner time now and we were in for a very long night. If we had any chance to try and get it all squared away we had to get started right away. Little by little, hour by hour, the place gradually got back to normal. Everything we owned had to be washed and scrubbed by hand, dried, ironed, and folded perfectly to the regulation dimensions. It was a huge headache and we all knew that no matter how much effort we put in, it would never be enough. But putting in no effort was not an option, so we did what we were being trained to do. Shut up and get on with the job.

It turned out, luckily for us, that the sergeant had been sent home to cool off for the weekend, so we avoided the kit muster the next morning. Instead, we had four periods of drill on a chilly Saturday morning, which, as painful as that was, was a far better option. And Sunday was bliss, with no screaming sergeant to get in the way of a little laundry.

CHAPTER 7

SLEEP?

We were up early Monday morning and cleaned the accommodation with trepidation, knowing what lay in store for us for the week; another field exercise. It was only Week 7 and already we were sick of the whole routine. So far we had done very little real soldiering and wanted to get out there and do more exciting stuff. Where were all the helicopters, parachutes, and live-fire exercises we saw in the recruiting videos and brochures? So far all we had done was iron and clean, or get cold and wet and fucked around.

We loaded up for another field exercise and headed off camp. We were soon in the training area, and sure enough it had started to rain while we were on the move. The team tent went up much smoother this time and the training team was pleased that all of their stuff was still nice and dry. Of course, our bergens and kit were lying out in the rain, but I suppose there was no point in waterproofing everything in our bergens if they weren't going to get wet. We got ourselves coated in cam cream and had a moment to attach bits of grass and brush to our helmets and webbing. Once we were cammed out and had checked each other over, the section commander had a look and pointed out all of our mistakes. Broken ends of twigs were visible and had to be covered with brown cam cream, grass that had been stuffed in upside down had to be re-stuffed right side up, and people who had failed to put cam cream all over their hands had to go back and do a touch-up. This may all seem like minor stuff that nobody would really notice when you were crouched in a bush, but if a well-trained enemy sniper happened to be looking for you, the smallest mistake could cost you big-time, and you might end up with piece of your skull decorating that bush.

We crawled all day long, and by the time night fell we had been out and about in the rain for five or six hours and were thoroughly soaked through. It was chilly sitting there on the hillside and the training team could see that some of us were beginning to shiver quite severely. "Anyone getting a little cold out here?" the team asked the troop. Many of the guys put their hands up. I suspected a trick and kept my eye on my buddy Steve, the veteran. His hand stayed firmly on his knee, and as cold as I was, my hand stayed down too. It was a smart move and the rest of the troop was about to learn another lesson in how the game is played. "All you bitches with your hands in the air, get your kit on and line up on the track. You're about to get warm!" The training team told the rest of us to chill out and get some hot wets (drinks) on. We knew the drill and within seconds our group had little fires going and hot, sweet tea on the brew. This was our reward for not admitting we were cold. The team was teaching us that being uncomfortable does not mean you are cold. Being cold means you are going to die or the mission will be compromised unless you take drastic measures to warm yourself up. Shivering, blowing on your hands, and stamping your feet count as being uncomfortable, not cold. We were in the field and you were supposed to be uncomfortable. That was the point. As for the rest of the troop who had put their hands up, well, they would be warm enough in a few minutes. The team made sure of that.

After the troop's little session the team got their sections and told us to grab our bergens and follow them. We set off on a little yomp, winding in and out around dark stands of trees and across fields of knee-high, wet grass. It wasn't long before even those of us who had sat out the phys session were sweating heavily. With sweat and cam cream running out from under our helmets and into our eyes we stopped just short of a large stand of dense hemlock trees. Our section commander told us that unlike the last field exercise, this time we were going to be a bit more tactical about the whole thing. No lights and no talking above a very quiet whisper were going to be tolerated, and infractions would have repercussions. So knowing what was surely coming our way we set up our shelters and sorted out our kit.

I suspected the team was going to have a go at the troop any second, but I rolled the dice, changed into my dry clothes, and got into my slug (sleeping bag) to sleep for a few hours before my first sentry shift started. Brad followed suit and we just lay there listening to the other members of the troop around us, thrashing about in the trees and bushes. The section commanders were sitting in the edge of the wood line, watching and listening to the troop flap about. They had their night vision goggles on and could clearly see everything that was going on. They were always making mental notes of who was doing what they had been taught and who wasn't. Much to my surprise, though, they didn't do anything right then and just let everyone slowly get set up and settle into the sentry routine. As Brad began to snore quietly beside me I thought of home and blissfully thought of my girlfriend, Jennifer, picturing her naked. Jennifer's breasts definitely made a much softer pillow than the webbing I had stuffed under my head, and I couldn't wait to see her at Christmas. I quickly fell asleep with my mind happily in the gutter, hoping this whole experience was just a bad dream.

After a few hours the sentry duties came down the line as far as me and I crawled out of my warm, dry clothes and slowly got on my wet and cold ones. This was one of those things that never got easier, and for the next few moments I tried leaning very far forward so that my cold shirt didn't touch my chest. I packed up my sleeping bag and roll mat, grabbed my rifle, and crawled up to take my post as a sentry in a freezing puddle.

Ten minutes before Brad was to relieve me I crawled back to wake him up. As usual, he didn't want to get up, so I sat beside him and poked him every few seconds. Pretty soon I was smacking him on the head, then kicking him in the ribs. That did the trick. He was halfway out of his slug and calling me names again as I headed back to the position. With his poor organization and relaxed pace he still showed up twenty minutes late. I told him what was on my mind and got myself into my slug and back to my dirty dreams as fast as I could. I was quickly learning that my sleeping bag was actually one of the nicest places on earth, and I wanted to stay there forever if I could. Before I knew it the shift had come around again and the whole thing was repeated. My clothes were still freezing, it was still raining, and Brad was still a nightmare to handle.

Stand-to came shortly before first light and we packed away all of our kit and faced outwards, ready to fend off any dawn attack. We cracked on with the standard field morning routine and finished it all with a lovely kit muster. As we crouched over our kit and cleaned the last few bits of our rifles, the training team was standing in their massive tent with the end flaps wide open so they could watch us getting everything ready. They were eating bacon and eggs, drinking hot coffee, and having a good laugh. It was very demoralizing and got even worse when the egg toss started. The team started chucking eggs at us from about a hundred feet away. It was a nasty thing to do, as all of our kit was laid out on our ponchos and the targets were huge. A few guys started to move out of the way when an egg was heading for them and the team barked out the rules of the game. "Oi! You there! Don't even think about moving out of the way! Carry on doing what you're doing and *do not* pay attention to what's happening over here. Just ignore the eggs or else!" We had to carry on as if there were no eggs raining down on us. This wasn't quite funny enough for the team so they gave me a slice of cooked ham and told me I had to carry that with me and lay it out for inspection each morning with the rest of my kit. Bootneck humour; you gotta love it.

Our PTI showed up in the field that morning to take us for our first proper field phys session. We went off running in our boots for a few miles across country and made sure we went through every bit of mud we could find. We were just in tee-shirts and the cool light rain felt good. Yes, we were soaked and muddy, but for once we weren't overheating.

More lectures were crammed into the afternoon and we finally got to practise the fire and movement tactic a bit. Individuals or groups would move towards the objective while others covered the target with fire. Then the groups would switch roles and leapfrog each other. We were all shooting off a ton of blanks and shouting our lungs out as we tried to move smoothly towards the objectives as a section. It was very tiring work but much more satisfying than lectures. This was the kind of training we'd been waiting for, and from here on in it would only get better, with slicker weapon drills and more exciting objectives to attack. As a team, we would begin to develop more fluid movements and better communication. We carried on like that for the rest of the afternoon, crawling and running, shouting and shooting. As the day neared last light, we got on our dinner and rolled into the night harbour routine. We had a dry evening and the stars were visible through the treetops. I always took comfort in looking up at the stars in southern England, which is at pretty much the same latitude as my home in Canada, so I'd see the same night sky. For a second or two, as I looked up, I could pretend that I was actually home. But only for a second or two . . .

The next morning it was pissing out as I stood for our inspection, with my piece of ham laid out nice and neat beside my immaculate rifle. More guys than usual got themselves on the flank this morning because they were starting to get tired and a little lethargic. A pattern was already starting to emerge in the troop, and it was usually the same guys who ended up on the flank each morning. Some of them were just generally not very good at doing all they had to do, and others had gotten onto the team's bad list and were being driven out of the troop. Our favourite PTI showed up again after this and took us for another long run through the mud and gorse to keep us getting fit at the prescribed rate. It didn't matter where we were or what we were doing, we could always count on him to come out and show us a good time.

We speed-marched with all of our kit back to camp a few days later, and all of it was filthy as usual and caked in mud. We had a full kit inspection at 0600 the next day and couldn't afford to waste any time. Jollies would have to wait for another day. I got to sleep at 0330 and was up again at 0500 to finish what needed to be done. Everything had to be laid out just as we had done in the field, but it had to meet the standard of perfection, as did our lockers and the accommodation. I was way past being tired by this time, I was on autopilot, none too sure what was going on. I figured I had had about eleven hours of sleep in the last four nights, and considering all the physical punishment we were being subjected to, it felt like even less. The inspection turned out to be very lenient, as the sergeant wasn't around and the section commanders knew we were in a shit state. They still checked over everything and pointed out the problems, but no lockers were trashed and nobody had to crawl around.

The very last thing we had scheduled for Week 7 was the battle swim test, and as tired as we were, there was no avoiding it. We headed off to the pool and there was no time to piss around. Every one of us lined up, fully clothed, put on twenty-two pounds of kit, slung a ten-pound rifle on his back, and waited his turn to climb up to the high diving board. The test was to jump in with all the kit on, swim a length, take the kit off while treading water, pass the kit out of the pool without touching the side of the pool, then tread water for ten minutes. The test was easy for the fish in the troop, but I knew it was going to be hard for the bricks. Treading water was no problem, but swimming with kit was very difficult. So when my turn came I jumped in there and after what seemed like an eternity my head broke the surface and I went off splashing and gasping down the pool. I made it the length and as I was trying to remove my webbing and rifle I was going straight to the bottom. The PTI was yelling at me. "Relax! Take your time! Stop fucking flapping about and chill!" But I thought I was going to drown so I grabbed the edge of the pool, and that was it for me. Fail.

I crawled out of the pool still wearing my kit and the PTI shook his head. "Get a grip on yourself," he told me. "Go to the back of the line. You will pass this, Olafsen." I would try again in about five minutes. I stood there wondering how in the hell I was going to get out of this one, but before I could find a good answer I was climbing the steps and launching myself off the diving board. I decided as I surfaced that I was going to drown or pass, and that seemed to do the trick. I had no intention of drowning that day, so that only left me with one option. And pass I did. Once I managed to get my kit off and hand it up and out of the pool it was all downhill. I lay back and treaded water, staring at the clock, knowing that in only ten more minutes I could lay this week to rest. It was a great motivator, and soon the minutes had wound down and I was out of the pool, getting showered and changed. I was happy that the swim test was over and I had passed, and that now there was cold beer on my horizon.

CHAPTER 8

RESPITE

The troop was looking forward to Weeks 8 and 9. The last week had been particularly tiring, and two weeks on camp would suit us just fine. Not that being on camp was a cake walk or anything, but at least you knew you would usually get more than an hour or two of sleep a night. As with all of our time on camp, we spent most of it in the lecture room studying maps and taking a million pages of notes on a whole range of subjects, from the realities of war to first aid to English and math lessons.

We carried on with our drill lessons, all polished up and learning how to stand still. We spent a lot of time marching around, turning in formation, and just generally trying to look good for the DL. Everything was actually coming together pretty well on the parade square, and we were starting to look like a troop of professional soldiers when we wanted to. Sadly, we also spent a lot of time slow marching, because this is how you march when you carry a casket at a bootneck funeral. Marines were being killed in Iraq at this time, and though the slow march was a skill nobody wanted to use, learning it was unfortunately necessary.

On one particular day there were three troops out there all doing drill at the same time. We were all in different weeks of training, and the DLs were having a laugh among themselves off to one side. We could see they were scheming and were pretty sure that whatever fun they had in mind would be at our expense. They didn't keep us in suspense long. It was nearing the end of the drill session when they called us all into the big hangar and told us the plan. They had decided that the three troops were going to have a dance-off to see which troop would be dismissed from the drill lesson first. Each troop had to pick their best dancer and their worst dancer and also had to form a band that could only make music with what they had with them, which was, of course, nothing but their lungs. Our troop nominated our dancers (I could have easily been picked as the worst dancer but dodged that bullet) and formed up the band, and the other troops did the same.

The lads all started trying their best to make music while the best dancers got out front and showed us their moves. Some guys were breakdancing and standing on their heads while others did the worm all over the dirty floor in their immaculate drill rig. The troops, along with the DLs, were in stitches, and it only got better when the worst dancers stepped out front. Everyone was in hysterics watching these guys twist and contort to their friends' howls, but the DLs just couldn't decide who had been the best or who had been the worst. They decided to solve the problem by having a new contest.

Whichever troop could produce the most disgusting man boobs would walk, and immediately we knew that our troop was going to win. We had a secret weapon for this one. We had a guy who was not exactly an attractive man. He was very hairy, very spotty, and looked like a caveman with an enormous nose. He had long pointy boobs with nipples that looked like they belonged to an orangutan that had just had a dozen young apes sucking on them for the last hour. We let the other troops produce their goods first and we all had a laugh at the tits on some of these guys, but once we unleashed our beast it was all over. Nobody had to declare us the winner, it was obvious. Our DL thanked the other DLS for their time, formed us up into three ranks, and smartly marched us out of the hangar and off the parade square. We were already changed and having a cup of tea by the time the other troops got to leave. A great victory for the troop.

Towards the end of Week 9 we made it up to our local gorse plantation for an afternoon. We did a quick daytime navigation exercise and tore ourselves to bits as we waded through seas of my favourite prickly plant. I remember this day well because for once it didn't rain, and for some reason the team never made us crawl through the gorse, crawl through any mud, or dive into Peter's Pool. I was confused, but rather than ask why they were treating us well, I thought it was best just to keep my mouth shut. As we all sat around eating our crappy rations, the training team, who had made a run to the local fish and chip shop, were stuffing their faces in front of us and loving every second of it. One of the team wandered over and said he would give one of his sausages to anyone who could tell him what the capital city of Mongolia was. Oddly, I had recently been looking into the train route from Beijing to Moscow as a potential trip to make one day, and knew damn well the train passed through the Mongolian capital. "Ulaanbaatar," I said and he walked over and handed me a large, batter-coated, deep-fried sausage. He told me that when he had been a nod his training team had asked him the exact same question and when he had given the right answer he'd been awarded with a battered sausage. I guess the lesson to be learned here is that knowledge can get you meat.

CHAPTER 9

SPOONING

Much sooner than we would have liked, we found ourselves packing for the field again and the weather reports were predicting we would not be getting off easy. We were heading up into Dartmoor for all of Week 10. This was our first trip up onto Dartmoor, and the troop would learn to hate and fear it. It is a huge area of high hills covered in wet knee-deep grass and separated by marshlands. Somehow, on the moor, even the hilltops are soggy. There are no trees and the wind and weather rip across the moor unhindered. It rains heavily and constantly. There is the odd path and dirt track that crosses the area, but in the autumn and winter it is a desolate place. It is a few thousand feet up and famous for its heavy fog, which can roll in with alarming speed. Many nods have gotten lost on Dartmoor, and there is at least one memorial for bootnecks who have died of exposure there.

After an early-morning kit muster we got everything loaded up onto a bus and headed off. We took a bus this time because the trip was three hours long and the troop was travelling light. The instructors would be living out of their bergens like the rest of us. The training team was really starting to hammer the navigation lessons into us and along the way we studied maps, pressing compasses to them and scribbling calculations down in our notebooks. We were all openly praying that the bus would break down and the exercise would be delayed or cancelled, but our luck wasn't that good. The bus kept pressing towards our destination as the sky grew darker and darker with thick, low clouds. We all looked at each other and shook our heads, feeling sick to our stomachs as we thought about what was ahead. As we looked out the windows the view gradually changed from trees and houses to the hills of Dartmoor looming up out of the mist. Rain began streaking down the windows, and the driver cranked his windshield wipers up from low to high. The team told us to start packing our shit away and to wake up those who had managed to drift off. By the time the bus slowed down and stopped in the middle of the moor, it was absolutely pissing down. Nobody was in a very good mood, not even the team. There was no tent or cots or any other little luxuries for the team on this exercise, although they would manage to spend much of their time in a derelict stone house out on the moor.

We all piled off the bus and dug out our overloaded packs. In no time everything was completely soaked, and our bergens were getting heavier by the minute as they tried to absorb all the water in Southwest England. I remember this rain storm clearly because of how high the rain was bouncing off the road. Everything below my knees was hidden in mist and spray and the rain was pouring off my beret and down my face. It was cascading down my neck and shoulders and I was drenched before I had even gotten my bergen heaved up onto my back. Nobody wanted to stay put for long because we would get very cold very fast if we just stood around. The team had the same idea and we headed off into the moor, heads down and miserable. We formed up into a long troop snake and began to wind our way up and around the soggy hill-sides, sloshing through streams and finding bogs all around. We went for about twelve kilometres and yomped down into a small, steep-sided valley with a few trees at one end and a large stone house at the other. Around the house was a network of low stone walls that looked like they had been there for five hundred years. The house looked just as old, and cold and foreboding in the darkening mist. There was no electricity out here. The house was next to a stream, running quickly, swollen with all the rain. It wasn't a very nice-looking place, but it was going to be home for the next four nights or so. Not that the troop would ever be allowed in the house – we would be set up under our little shelters in the walled sections while the team set up inside.

Everyone's priority was to get up a shelter, get some hot food on, and get as dry as possible. The team had nothing planned for us that evening so we were pretty much just left to get on with it. The weather was too foul for the team to come out and mess with us, and as long as we maintained the normal sentry routine we would, in theory, be left alone. Brad and I (though with not much help from Brad) got our shelter up in record time and hunkered down under it to get some hot dinner on the go. The shelter was just a small camou-flage tarp so it went up quickly after a bit of practice. I was starting to get very cold as soon as I wasn't working and just wanted to get into my dry kit and into my warm sleeping bag. With a bit of a struggle and a few swear words I managed to get myself sorted out. There isn't much room under our shelters at the best of times, and with two men trying to get changed under there while keeping all of their kit tucked in out of the rain it is a tight squeeze. But once I slid into my bag I was in a little piece of heaven. We ate our meals while wrapped in our bags, packed our spoons and little pots away in preparation for a crash move, and lay there in the dark, listening to the rain still pelting down above us.

My sentry shift came along as swiftly as ever, and using every ounce of motivation I could muster I crawled out of my slug and fished my cold, wet clothes out of my bergen. It was so tempting to cheat the system. We carried a Gore-Tex jacket and Gore-Tex pants with us everywhere we went, and it would have been so easy to put them on over my dry clothes for the next hour, but our dry kit had to stay dry, no matter what the cost. With this in mind, I slipped on my wet kit with the routine wince, packed away all of my kit into my bergen, and headed out into the storm. We had more sentry positions than normal at this location, so we only had one person on each spot. This was a major drag, as it is much more difficult to keep yourself awake when you have nobody to whisper back and forth with. As I crawled up to the lad I was taking over for, I saw that he had a massive smile on his face. He was going back to his bit of heaven and wasn't trying to hide his happiness. "Enjoy yourself, dickhead," he said to me as he crawled away. "Piss off, cock muncher," was a suitable reply.

I lay down there for a full hour, shivering away and thinking about warm beaches and mugs of steaming coffee. My sentry position was in a depression behind one of the stone walls and it was filling up with water. Nothing beats lying in a pool of freezing water by yourself in the middle of the night. I crawled back when my time was nearly up and started to go through the routine of waking up Brad. The shittier the weather, the longer he took to get out of his slug, and I expected him tonight to take a very long time indeed. I gave him a shake, several kicks, and swatted him on the head a few times to let him know that I meant business, and slowly but surely, with the customary remarks about me being a prick, he crawled out into the cold night. I got back to the sentry spot and waited for Brad. I didn't have to go back to wake him up again, which was a nice change, but he was still nearly ten minutes late. Next time I would just have to wake him up earlier. Three hours later I was back in my wet kit and out in the rain for my next shift.

As the drizzly, grey dawn broke out over Dartmoor the troop stripped down to tee-shirts and headed off for a little morning phys, trying to keep up with the PTI who had been kind enough to head out to us for a little visit. We ran all over that place, up and down hill after hill, stopping now and then to do some sprints or sit-ups in the mud. We carried each other around distant rocks and crawled on command until the PTI had had enough.

We got kitted up and went straight into what we had come here for: navigation practice, and lots of it. We got our bergens on and headed off in sections to take turns leading the group from checkpoint to checkpoint. We were going to be putting on a lot of hard miles throughout the week, and our feet and shoulders were going to pay the price. We kept breaking down into smaller and smaller groups as the day progressed, and eventually were navigating around by ourselves. I preferred this, to be honest. By yourself or in pairs was best because you could move a lot quicker, and I got a little frustrated sometimes standing there with a heavy bergen on while someone with half a brain stared at an upside down map for hours on end.

It got dark and we just kept on walking all over Dartmoor. Sometime around midnight we reached the last checkpoint, which was kindly placed nowhere near the troop harbour. We formed up into a tight unit and were led off into the darkness at a slow run. One last bit of phys to end the day. My feet were in agony now, and looking around at the other guys I knew that I was not alone. We ran on, over the hills for a few miles, slowing down to a walk as we approached the position. We were all dead tired. It had been a very long day and I hoped we would manage to avoid any shenanigans that evening. We set up the sentry rotation and got ourselves firmly embedded in our sleeping bags.

Ten minutes later all hell broke loose. Someone in the troop had decided he was too exhausted to bother getting into his dry clothes and had actually crawled into his sleeping bag soaking wet. The team had obviously been watching for just such a lapse and sprang at the opportunity to fuck with us. With shouts and prods, they made us get back into our wet kit and pack away our shelters, and formed us up in three ranks, at which point they found that one of the guys on sentry had the balls to be wearing a warm hat underneath his helmet. Things were rapidly going from bad to worse. Clearly, the lads were getting complacent again, and it was time to thrash that out of them. We packed our bergens at breakneck speed and crawled down to the stream on our elbows and knees. In the dark, and absolutely freezing now, we all crawled into the stream and got in the push-up position, waiting for our little evening phys session to start. The team was all out there and wanted a bit of the action. We started exercising in unison to their shouts. "Arms bend! Stretch! Bend! Stretch! Bend! Stretch!" – and each time we went down our faces got closer and closer to the water as our hands sunk deeper into the mud. Quickly onto our backs for some underwater sit-ups, then sprint up the hill to try and get some feeling back into our bodies. Back in the stream, push-ups, sit-ups, sprints, push-ups, sit-ups, sprints. God only knows how long this lasted, but the sprints weren't helping much. Lying in that stream was really taking its toll, and my whole body was starting to go numb. I wished I had a little more fat on me for warmth, but with all this phys there wasn't much chance of that happening any time soon.

As the troop froze in the stream that night, you might think this is the part where most of us break mentally, and I assure you some of the lads did, but many of us were actually smiling again. It was so ridiculous to be in that stream, and we were so cold and miserable, the experience had passed to the realm of comical. Grins were passed from man to man as the team shouted and pointed at us, and as the pain of extreme cold crept up my limbs I knew I couldn't be beaten. Not this easily at least. Cheerfulness in the face of adversity. It's not always easy to find, but once you have it, life becomes a heck of a lot easier.

Once the team had had their fun with us we were sent back to sort out our shit with one final warning not to cut any corners. As we were struggling to get command of our fingers and get our shelters up the sergeant came out to address the troop. He told us to ensure our shelters were placed in perfect, parallel rows before we carried on with the sentry routine. And then he left us, scrambling to get up some cover. We were all freezing and nearly falling asleep as we worked. It was very dark and, with the state the troop was in, the likelihood of getting perfectly aligned shelters was slim. We tried our best, but most of the guys were beyond caring. They wanted to be in their slugs and that was it. Sure enough, ten minutes after we all got settled down and were just starting to get warm again, the sergeant was back outside like a thunder clap.

He was swearing and yelling and it was back into our wet kit, tear down the shelters, and get our bergens packed. We got on our webbing and helmets and grabbed our rifles for another quick phys session. He had us doing some sprints and a bit of crawling, as usual. We were all slowing down by this point, and it was apparent the team's goals were being met. They wanted us fatigued for this exercise, and they were delivering in spades. This time, as quickly as it had started, it was all over. "Straight lines!" we were told as the sergeant stormed away, and we did it all over again. Setting up cold and wet, trying to get the shelters in straight lines but failing miserably. We all rolled the dice and got in our bags, knowing the sergeant could come out again any second. But he didn't. It was nearly three in the morning already, we would be up by six, and I had to squeeze in another hour on sentry before then. I grabbed a little bit of sleep that night but kept dreaming about cleaning my rifle. There was just no getting away from it any more.

At 0600 we were all back in the fucking stream and back up that fucking hill. I don't know what was propelling me up that hill that morning. It certainly wasn't me. I was out of energy and too tired to focus on much more than breathing and reminding my heart to keep on beating. I was on autopilot, and not looking forward to trying to focus on a map later that day. After some basic crawling and push-ups and sit-ups in the stream and running around the hills, we switched it up by carrying each other uphill on our backs, and sometimes like a groom carries his bride over the threshold. We crawled and dove and carried and sprinted for ages. It was a serious thrashing we were getting, and I knew damn well we hadn't screwed up badly enough to deserve this. This was nothing personal: just part of the program. The team wanted to know where our limits were, and they sought them out that morning. When we finally stopped, the troop was broken. Some guys were sobbing and snivelling to themselves. I was completely exhausted, walking in a daze. Most of us had puked up our breakfast with the phys, and that was a real shame. We needed all the energy we could get.

We sunk down to sit on our bergens and stared at the ground with bloodshot eyes and looks of disbelief. We had only been out for two nights, and I was already firmly in the hurt locker. It was the same for everybody. There is plenty of room in the hurt locker. And for the next several days we stayed right where we were; in the Dartmoor hurt locker.

Things changed when we were finally yomping off across Dartmoor again with our bergens biting into our shoulders. The bergens weighed a ton now. They had soaked up plenty of water and were just one more thing to piss you off. There was nothing to do but trudge on, and after a few miles we all piled onto a few trucks to take us to another training area for the start of our survival exercise.

I closed my eyes for one long, drawn-out blink of sleep before the trucks stopped with a shudder. The troop jumped down into the mud with its kit and, shouldering our dripping bergens, we prepared to move. Off we went in sections, crossing fences and streams as we got closer and closer to a forest way up on a distant hillside. Eight miles or so later we found ourselves scrambling up a steep, muddy trail, clinging to roots and each other to try to keep gravity at bay. Once we were all at the top it was a quick yomp down an old track and we were at the survival exercise site. We all turned in our bergens, shelters, and sleeping bags and formed up into ranks. The team took our webbing and rifles from us. Then they took away our jackets and made us empty out our pockets. Then they took away our belts, bootlaces, and watches. They made us hand over our lighters and small flashlights we were wearing on a length of string around our necks. We even had to drop our pants to prove we had hidden nothing away. We were being stripped down to the bare minimum.

We all pulled our pants up and then were handed back our knives and small survival kits we had put together a few weeks before. That was all we would have to work with for the next two days. So there we were, standing in nothing but tee-shirts in the autumn wind and rain, freezing our asses off and trying to think of happier times. This situation would have been unpleasant at the best of times, but after the last few days we were already in a world of hurt. We were all weakened by hunger, dehydration, cold, and mental fatigue.

They broke us up into groups of four and gave each group a live chicken, a live rabbit, and a large empty baked-bean can. Then they left us to our own devices. It was nearly 1700 and the light was already starting to fade. We had to work fast if we didn't want this adventure to turn into an absolute fiasco. We killed the animals and skinned them as fast as we could, making a mess of it but managing to get some good meat chunks in the pot. I quickly tried to take control of our broken little group and get something organized. I got two of the guys trying to get up some sort of a shelter with a spot at one end for a fire, and then Brad and I headed off to search for some firewood. The problem was clearly going to be getting our hands on wood that was dry enough to burn. It had been raining steadily for the last couple of thousand years in England, and we were in a particularly wet area.

We scrambled around as fast as we could, grabbing whatever didn't release water when you squeezed it, and got up a pile that would with luck get us through the night. The shelter wasn't too bad, but when you're in a hurry in failing light, it's not easy to make anything completely waterproof. Like I said, we were all pretty much moving like zombies by this point, and even simple tasks were proving very difficult. We got to work on the fire and actually got one going when the rain let up a bit. But we were destined to be screwed. As we all huddled around the pathetic little fire in the dripping shelter, our eyes stinging from the smoke, the heavens opened up on us. It was hopeless. The fire was doused and what we had to work with was just too wet. We weren't going to be able to cook our dinner, we weren't going to get any warmth, and we weren't going to be let off easy. There was nothing we could do but wait until first light when we could get a better handle on the situation. Water was pouring through the roof of the shelter and the boughs we had set down on the ground were already getting swallowed up by the mud. I was freezing. Being cold is one thing on its own and I can deal with that. Being wet is nothing by itself, and hunger on its own is manageable. But if you are dealing with extreme cold, total saturation, and acute hunger at the same time, you will find yourself firmly back in the hurt locker.

As we all got colder and colder there was nothing left to do but huddle together for warmth. In a few minutes four men were lying together in the mud, spooning each other as tightly as they possibly could. We were shivering in unison and weren't getting any warmer. Another group's shelter collapsed, so those four guys went crawling about in the rain and mud to try and find refuge in other people's shelters. Shortly after that, a refugee arrived at our address and squeezed in to join the spoon-fest. We were packed in there like sardines. I wished with every fibre they hadn't taken away my jacket.

It was the middle of November, and the temperature was dropping fast. By now it was about eight o'clock, still early, and we were going to have to lie there, shivering and sinking into the mud, with no chance of sleep, for another ten hours or so. We were squeezed together so tightly that it was impossible to move even an arm or your head. Once you took the chill off the patch of mud beneath you, the last thing you wanted to do was squirm about to warm up more mud. Unbelievably, the rain picked up. It was coming through the roof of our shelter in small rivers. I was lucky enough to have a little stream of ice-cold water start pouring directly into my left ear. I didn't move. I couldn't move. I just lay there and wondered what time it was, when dawn was going to arrive, and how much more of this I could take. My mind began to wander away from my cold and battered body. I closed my eyes, and ignoring the water pouring into my ear, drifted away. I drifted away from Dartmoor, away from the spoon-fest and the mud. I went home to see my sweet Jennifer and I crawled into her warm bed and snuggled up to her body.

CHAPTER 10

FIND A HAPPY PLACE

I was in my happy place, thinking about how wonderful and comfortable my life had been. Jennifer and I got along so well and always made each other laugh and smile. At home we hung out all the time, usually just the two of us. We could have the most wonderful time, just us and a few bottles of wine. We watched a lot of movies, curled up on the couch together, and spent a lot of time in bed. God, how I wished I was in bed with her at that moment. Or maybe in a hot shower with her.

My brother and his wife had a daughter and a son, and I loved my niece and nephew. I used to go over and play with them all the time, and they would come over to their uncle's for sleepovers as often as I would have them. There was no doubt that I was the coolest uncle in the world, and I was wishing I could be home to give them a big bear hug.

A year before I enlisted, I took Jennifer up a mountain on a warm summer evening just as it was getting dark. We had blankets and wine, and as we lay down together we gazed up at the stars. That night as we sat there, wrapped in thick blankets and each other's warmth, we watched a spectacular meteor shower. The shooting stars were filling the sky, and I couldn't have dreamed of a better way to experience such a show. We talked about everything and we talked about nothing. We were comfortable in each other's silence too. Her body pressed tightly to mine said it all.

I was so happy to be there in my mind, and not on Dartmoor with the rain pouring into my left ear.

I dreamed about being at my father's house by the river. For years I had slept with my bedroom window open so that I could hear the river, and now, as I drifted, I was at my father's, lying in a large hammock under some big trees by the patio. Large, lazy clouds were lounging in the sky and the sun fell on me in patches through the branches. I could hear the river, and was at peace as a small breeze rustled the flowering shrubs and leaves all around. The family dog was lying beside the hammock in the cool, green grass with not a care in the world. Everyone was lazy, and it was perfect. I kept my eyes closed and felt the hammock swaying ever so slightly. I let my arm fall from the side of the hammock and my fingertips touched the grass that was just about long enough for a fresh cut. I could smell the grass and the freshness of the air, and I breathed deep. It just didn't get any better than this.

I went back home again and was having dinner with my family at my mom's place. My niece and nephew were there and I was so happy, surrounded by those that I loved the most. We ate and laughed and afterwards I played with the kids, giving them piggyback rides and spinning them to make them dizzy. Their uncle was in top form and the kids were loving every minute of it. They didn't want their uncle to move to England, and he didn't want to go.

I went from there to sitting on a little plane that was going to take me from my home town to Vancouver, where I would take another flight, to London. I sat next to a window, and as the little plane taxied along, I could see my brother and his wife standing at the fence watching me leave. My little niece was holding her mother's hand and my nephew was sitting up on his dad's shoulders. The whole family was waving goodbye to me as the plane gathered speed down the runway and took me away. I waved back but doubted they could see me. My eyes filled with tears as I turned away, and for the first time in many years a tear rolled down my cheek. I wiped it away and blinked a few times, and when my vision cleared, the airplane was gone. Everything was black and I was fucking freezing. I was shivering uncontrollably, lying in the mud in a tee-shirt in November, and I had a stream of water pouring into my ear. Reality was back, and it was kicking my ass.

For hour after hour I took the pain, struggling the whole time to find that magical "cheerfulness in the face of adversity." I thought about all the plans I had for how to improve the shelter and how great it was going to be when the sky finally grew light. But that was still an eternity away, and many more precious calories would be burned up between now and then as I shivered in the mud. We all needed food in a bad way. This wasn't a matter of just wanting some food because you are hungry. This was science, pure and simple. Our bodies needed fuel to burn, or before long we would stop shivering and bad things would follow. My mind raced all that long night and I encouraged it throughout. The more I thought, the less I noticed the cold biting into me. The wet ground was sucking the warmth right out of me, and I tried again and again to go back home, but my mind wouldn't let me go again. It needed me to stay focused on what was happening. It needed me to pay attention to my body, but there was nothing I could do but wait, and wait we did. I waited until I could wait no longer, and then waited some more. Perhaps I fell asleep for a bit, perhaps not. I have no idea. What I do know is that this was the longest night of my life, and when a bit of light finally started to pierce the rain clouds I felt ten years older.

Ever so slowly it began to grow light, and with the dawn we crawled out of our meagre shelter and stood up to survey the scene. The rain had stopped and as the trees dripped on our soggy frames we could see our breath. We blew on our hands and jogged on the spot to try and get a little blood flowing through our frozen limbs. We had no idea when the next downpour would come but suspected it wasn't far off. With this in mind we set to work squaring everything away. We fanned out to collect more branches and boughs for the shelter, and hoped we would be able to stumble across some bits of wood that were even marginally dry. But little did we know that as we struggled with our simple tasks, something genuinely good was being organized for us.

The team had decided it was time to go back to CTC, and when they came up to tell us that the exercise was over we simply didn't believe them. But they were serious, and told us to get our asses down to the track, collect our stuff, and get ready to go. Once we were convinced it wasn't just a bad joke, we headed down there as quick as our stiff legs and blistered feet could carry us. We gathered up our kit, relaced our boots, got our jackets on, and slung our rifles. Things were looking up and our spirits soared as the trucks came into view down a muddy track to take us back to camp. Apparently the exercise was cut short for logistical reasons, and that was just fine with the troop. We had a few nice days on camp to look forward to, much of which would be spent trying to nod away in a lecture room.

CHAPTER 11

MARKSMAN

The next task for the troop was to learn how to shoot with live ammunition, and in late November (Week 11) we headed out for a full two weeks to a shooting range a few miles from CTC. It was a top-notch range, perched up on some high cliffs next to the English Channel, and we were going to sleep there so that we could shoot from dawn till dusk every day, and get in some night shooting too. The troop would set up shop in a large underground bunker that was very damp and smelled like piss, but we didn't mind. We called it the bat cave, and at least we had mattresses, even if they were thin and flimsy, and we were out of the rain. The bunker was a luxury suite compared to Dartmoor. And we were close enough to camp that we would have hot food sent out to us three times a day.

Things were pretty easy-looking as we arrived at the ranges but we all knew that looks could be very deceiving. Beside the range was a very steep track that led down to a secluded beach where the waves were constantly pounding the sand and rocks, and there were sandbags all over the place. The potential to get thrashed was all around us, and we knew damn well we would be visiting that beach. We had heard rumours around camp about that beach, and as we carried our bergens down into the bat cave we got a good look at it. It was nearly winter now, and the water of the English Channel looked dark and foreboding. You can imagine what was going through our heads as we looked at the foamy waves hitting the beach.

The troop was sent down to the bat cave for the evening, and we were in fine spirits as we sat there cleaning our rifles, laughing and joking. Even with the thrashings, this was going to be a comfortable couple of weeks. Tom had brought his guitar and was taking requests from the lads. It was amazing how many songs he knew off by heart, but the troop still always requested "The Nod Song" over and over. The team left us alone, and we were in our bags and getting to sleep by nine-thirty. We were warm and dry and going to get a full night of sleep. This was unheard of, and we were loving every second of it.

We started shooting the next day. We slid into a good rhythm the first week, working our way up from shooting from fifty metres all the way out to four hundred. It was encouraging to finally be getting a lot of rounds down, and for the most part the troop was enjoying itself. We were developing towards the final few days of the shooting package, when we would all have test shoots out at various distances and from various shooting positions. It rained and blew constantly but we expected nothing less. It was tricky to fire out at long ranges in strong cross winds, but with a bit of practice we learned to aim well wide of the targets and hit them with some degree of consistency.

The troop still had a high fitness standard to maintain, and every morning we were up at six to head out for an early-morning session. Often we went down to the beach to do fireman carries on the sand. Running and carrying weight on the sand was very difficult and used up a tremendous amount of energy. Our PTI showed up most days too to take us for long runs out along the cliff tops. Every time we ran nowadays we were in full rig with boots and jackets, webbing and rifles. There would never again be an "easy" phys session, and week by week we would add weight to our webbing. The PTI loved to have us carry each other up steep hillsides as fast as we could, and every time he would be there yelling, "It pays to be a winner!"

The troop was progressing well, and most of the bullshit that had made the previous few months so horrible was put aside. True, the phys was difficult, as always, and produced all sorts of blood, sweat, and tears, but we knew that that was the currency we had to pay for our coveted green berets. We focused on the shooting, and as long as we were all safe and paid attention to the instructions of the pros we were doing well.

We had our first shooting test midway through the second week and most of us passed with no problems. Those that didn't just kept on taking the test over and over until they did. The sergeant had dreamed up a number of different physical challenges to pass the time, and recruits were getting hurt. It was almost as if that was the sergeant's plan. He still figured the troop was too big and wanted to cull the herd. One guy failed to put his safety catch on, and soon enough he was running up and down the ranges with a forty-five-pound jerry can of water in each hand. The sergeant told him he could stop when he started crying. Shortly afterwards, the young lad was crying, and the next week he put in his notice and left the Corps.

We spent a lot of time cleaning our rifles, and one evening the team came down to the bat cave to see how we were getting on. The troop had only done a cursory cleaning of their weapons and the team got upset. So in the dark we got kitted up and headed down to the beach for a motivational speech, Royal Marines–style. The team yelled at us about slipping standards as we did push-ups and sit-ups in the surf. The waves broke over our heads and tossed guys around like dry leaves. We dragged and carried each other up and down the beach and were often thrown back in the water to do another set of push-ups. It was a very tough session, and believe me when I tell you that the North Atlantic is not a nice place to swim in early December. The North Sea sweeps down into the English Channel, and I think the only thing we needed to make the atmosphere complete were a few icebergs for visual effect.

We also spent time practising walking towards targets and engaging them with automatic bursts, pumping magazine after magazine of rounds into them from close range. It was good action and I was very happy to finally be making a lot of noise with my weapon. In the end, I shot well enough to get top shot in the troop and marksman status. I was issued with a badge of crossed rifles that I got to affix to my best drill uniform. It is still on there today.

CHAPTER 12

DIVIDENDS

The next several weeks at CTC went quickly for the troop. We were doing a variety of exercises, and we became well acquainted with our new physical training regime down on the bottom field assault course. All of the phys that we had done up to this point would prove to be a cake walk compared to what we were being subjected to now on the assault course. Everything we did was done with webbing and a rifle on, and the weight we had to carry increased day by day and week by week until we reached the regulation thirty-two pounds. There was plenty of mud for us down there because the grass on the bottom field was pounded out of existence by the winter rains and the boots of hundreds of recruits. It was a good thing we had spent so much time climbing thirty-foot ropes back in the gym days, because we met them again out on the assault course, with the twist that down there we had to climb them while fully rigged and kitted. I saw ambulances show up at the ropes more than once to collect injured nods who had lost their grip and got creamed falling to the ground.

Each day we'd all get a sick feeling when we formed up in our kit to wait for the PTI to lead us down to the assault course. Some of the nods were so nervous about the pain they were about to endure that they would have vomited all over the place long before we had even started the session. Nobody laughed at them, though, because we were all on the verge of getting sick ourselves.

We always practised for the final test we would face in Week 22 to graduate from the bottom field. We did full run-throughs, and there were no breaks in the final test, so it was straight into a few rope climbs to get started. We would then line up in pairs and get ready to go around the assault course as fast as we could. The course was composed of walls to get up and over, trenches to jump, nets to crawl under, hills to sprint up, tunnels to crawl through, and ropes stretched tight to crawl across on. Even though it was all over in five minutes or less it seemed to take much longer. I never struggled with any particular obstacle on the course, but it was a lot of work to force your legs to keep moving when you were so tired. At the very end of the course you would scale a twelve-foot wall with the help of a knotted rope and then yell out your name at the top so the PTI could record your time. The rule was that your time had to be faster than your last attempt or you would get punished. It was some amazing motivation and worked for the most part. The troop's times kept getting faster and faster and the PTI was pleased.

A moment after completing the assault course you'd line up for a two-hundred-metre fireman's carry. You would try to pair up with someone who was roughly your same weight, then you'd pick him up and get him onto your shoulders – both of you still wearing your kit and carrying rifles – and sprint for two hundred metres. If you made it in ninety seconds you passed. I have always been a very light guy with little chicken legs and there weren't many guys in the troop the same weight, so it was hit or miss that I'd match up with someone similar when I got to this part. By the end of the fireman's carry you would usually be covered in a bit of puke, and lots of mud, spit, and snot. It is amazing how much crap will pour out of your face when you exert 100 per cent effort. It was pretty disgusting really, but considering we were all looking the same, it didn't really seem like a big deal.

After the fireman's carry, there was one test left, the regain, and this was done out over a large tank of water. The tank measured about thirty feet across and about six feet deep and was brimming with dirty, stagnant water that was so cold in winter that it often had a thin layer of ice on it. Ten feet over the tank there were four parallel ropes stretched across the length of the tank. The idea was to climb up a ladder on one side of the tank, crawl out on top of the rope to the middle of the tank and do a regain. This is where you drop down until you are hanging by your hands and swinging freely beneath the rope. Then, tired and still wearing all of your kit, you are expected to get yourself back up on top of the rope and crawl off to the other side. If it sounds easy, I can assure you it is not. But it is certainly easier to try and get it done on your first shot, because if you fail you will inevitably be doing it again in a moment. Only, on the second attempt you will be absolutely freezing and drenched, which means you will weigh a whole lot more.

Live HE (high explosive) grenades were added to our list of toys during this period, and after a lecture and a bit of hands-on practice with them we went up to the local grenade range. We tossed grenades at various targets for a few hours and had a good laugh. Everyone loves tossing grenades. It is very satisfying to hear the WHOOMP! as a fistful of high explosive peppers the targets with shrapnel. They are useful around water too, as we would later prove in Afghanistan. It is the lazy man's way to get fish to come to the surface.

The field exercises that we would be doing later in training would involve helicopters, and before we could fly in helicopters over water we had to learn how to escape from them in case they ever had to ditch.

One day the troop headed up to a Royal Navy facility where there was a helicopter chassis hanging from the ceiling on cranes, suspended over a large swimming pool. The idea was to get strapped into the airframe, and then it would be dropped into the pool and you would have to make your way out. Helicopters are top heavy because the engines and transmissions are above you, so usually when they land in water they roll over after a few seconds. The simulator did that as well, so that as the pod hit the pool it rolled through 180 degrees, and then there you would be, still sitting in your seat with your seat belt done up, but upside down in a fake helicopter underwater. It was a neat experience, and we went through it in both the light and the dark. Some guys panicked a bit and had a hard time popping out the windows and getting through the hole, but as long as you just stayed calm you learned that one breath of air can last a very long time. Of course, this was in a relatively warm pool. If we were to ditch in the North Atlantic, I don't think that breath of air would last nearly as long.

To complete Week 15 and the first half of training, we had one last short trip into the gorse fields to polish up our basic soldiering skills. For once the weather was dry as we headed out and the forecast called for clear skies. It was a nice change to be dry, but unfortunately we were in the middle of a cold snap and the temperature had been going down to minus seven Celsius at night. When you are forbidden from wearing warm clothes that can get a little uncomfortable. When we got out to the fields we got cammed out and yomped all day around the training area with our bergens, going from hill to valley to practise our skills in target indication, stalking, judging of distance, navigation, and observation. We stomped around the gorse day and night, and froze on sentry duty. The skies were clear and the stars were brilliant but a little cloud cover for warmth would have been appreciated. One night, though, getting warm was not a problem. One of our sentries fell asleep and a member of the training team crept up on him and stole his rifle. A moment later the alarm was sounded and we were all up and packed in the blink of an eye. The team told us what had happened as we all sat there shivering in the crisp night air, freshly out of our warm sleeping bags. The team was righteously pissed off, and noticing our shivering they told us to put on our fleece jackets, combat jackets, warm winter pants, and toques. Once we were all toasty warm and dressed like snowmen we assembled on the road for the inevitable thrashing. The team got us sprinting off around distant trees and crawling up and down the hard gravel road. It was murder on the knees and elbows, and the team didn't let us off easy. We spent half of that night in the push-up position, and after only a very short while the sweat was pouring off us. We were learning first-hand why we weren't to sit around in all of our warm kit. If you have to move off quickly and with no warning, you will pay the price.

We were in a world of hurt by the time we were finished. We all had to ditch our warm clothes in our bergens and then the entire troop had to stay on sentry for the rest of the night. It was around midnight by this time, so that meant we'd be sitting in silence in our wet clothes, staring out into the darkness, for seven hours. It was agonizing, as the troop just lay there, quietly shivering.

The morning eventually did arrive, and the normal kit muster was carried out. The team had no intention of letting even the most minor infraction pass after what had happened, but to brighten up the occasion they had me sing "O Canada" at the top of my lungs for the troop while the inspections took place. You might expect one or two run throughs of the anthem to suffice, but you would be wrong. I sang continuously for nearly half an hour, and the troop appreciated it, as I could tell from the laughs and taunts.

After the final kit inspection the troop learned that a few guys had taken too long to complete the navigation exercise the previous night and would be back-trooped, along with one who had failed a speed march. It was a very tough blow for the originals that had to leave the troop and it was sad for some of us to see that blob cover up their faces outside the office. It wasn't as if we would never see them again. They were still on camp, but they would have to experience all their hardships with brand-new people, which is never as easy as with old friends. Two of my best friends in the troop (luckily not Tom or Steve) both went to a special section for injured nods called Hunter Company that week with stress fractures in their feet. We weren't the only troop losing members, of course. We had ourselves received some back-troopers just before this exercise, and with them and the new departures our numbers were now at 26, down from 55, and of these 26 only 20 were originals. That was a casualty rate of 63.6 per cent in our troop. It was a higher than average number, and our training team was thrilled.

We had our final drill inspection for phase one, where one of us in each section was presented with a white stripe to wear on our uniform to indicate we were now the section commanders. I got a stripe and was proud that all of my hard work was being noticed. I had received the highest overall mark in the troop up to this point. This of course only meant that I would now be the shit shield for the section when the team was unhappy, but for the moment I tried not to think of that. I celebrated with the troop by cleaning the accommodation and getting ready for another set of rounds.

CHAPTER 13

TACTICAL

Training was getting more advanced now and we were moving into a phase where we always had simulated enemy around, with the training team pretending to be the bad guys. Ambushes were the flavour of the day, and my section was laid out in the edge of the trees along the top of a small hill, about twenty metres away from and over-looking the track the enemy would be passing along. We were arranged in a textbook ambush position, the machine gun in the centre with five other rifles alongside it, and two of our lads a bit farther off, at each end of the fifty-foot line, to act as cut-offs. The cut-offs were there as a last resort to shoot any enemy that had managed to slip out of the main kill zone. We had been lying in wait for a few hours and were getting edgy. The heavens had opened up on us and the wetness was bringing a chill with it, but the rain was a blessing in disguise. Poor weather often makes the enemy less observant, and at the same time it would help to mask any noise that we might be making. I checked my watch and looked up and down the line to make sure everyone was still covering their areas and paying attention. The enemy had been going up and down this track unmolested for days, and it was time to set things right.

I checked the magazines I had laid out beside me for the hundredth time, making sure they were fully bombed up and the springs felt strong. I had learned that nothing you could control should ever be left to chance, and I knew my section members were checking their magazines too. And it helped to pass the time. I checked with my cut-offs to make sure there was nothing visible coming up the track, then made a call on the radio back to the troop HQ. I had to keep them in the loop.

I was starting to get settled down and comfortable again in my little depression in the cold dirt when I got the call from my right-hand cut-off that we had enemy approaching. There were only two of them, but that was just fine for my section. I heard over the net that they were coming up the track on foot, and their ETA in the kill zone was thirty seconds. Word was passed down the line and everybody immediately forgot about the cold and how lifeless their limbs felt. Safety catches were quietly taken off and triggers gingerly fingered as everyone settled their weapons tightly into their shoulders.

We had been waiting there for a long time, and it was nice to know that the shit was about to go down any second. That familiar rush of adrenalin started to course through my veins, and I loved it. Adrenalin is a natural high, and if it is a drug, then you can call me an addict. These guys didn't know what was about to hit them.

The enemy was coming into my view now, and I was pleased to see that they were not much of a threat. They had their rifles slung and were hunched over in the foul weather, looking miserably at the ground. They were chatting to each other quietly and I imagined they were complaining about the lousy weather and being sent out on a useless patrol on such an ugly day. One of them had a cigarette lit and

I wondered if he had any more in his pockets that I could get to take back for the troop. As the two baddies wandered into our kill zone I lifted my hand to hover over the shoulder of my machine gunner. The gun was always the first to shoot, and once he opened up everyone else knew to engage their targets.

When they were right in front of the six of us, I tapped my gunner on the shoulder and he immediately let rip into the pair of them. Everybody jumped in the game a split second later, and the enemy went down hard. They didn't have a clue what had just hit them, and as quickly as the firing started it stopped. We had just made a shitload of noise, and it was time to search the dead and get the hell out of there as fast as we could. We couldn't be certain how many more enemy were nearby and we didn't want to sit around to find out. I quickly sent two men down to see what intelligence they could gather from the dead, and got my cut-offs to start making their way in from the ends to the centre. My search party came straight back with the enemy's weapons and ammo, and although they hadn't found any maps or documents, they did get a nearly full pack of Marlboros. A great success!

We moved off in our order of march, and weaved our way back through the trees towards our troop location. I got on the net and troop HQ answered up right away. I gave them a quick sit rep (situation report) and told them to let the sentries know that we were hauling ass back towards their location. Headquarters responded with an unexpected message. They told me to proceed back to the enemy we had just shot up because they wanted their smokes and weapons returned. I confirmed the message and halted the section. I told them what was up, and off we went to the ambush site to give back the Marlboros and weapons. By the time we got back to the track we had just left, the enemy had moved and were standing up under a large tree. As we headed over to them they told us that we had done a good job of not being seen and that we had sprung a very effective ambush. They were pleased that we were taking on board what we had been taught so far, and even got a bit of a chuckle out of the troop's attempt to steal their cigarettes. We gave them back all of their stuff, and the two training team members headed off down the track the way they had come as we headed off back to the troop harbour for our next tasking. We had only been firing blank rounds, but it was still exciting.

We had been in the field again for a few days and this exercise in ambush tactics had moved us into the much more tactical and interesting part of training. It was Week 17 and we had been inserted into the exercise by two blacked-out Chinook helos that had picked us up right outside CTC. We had gone for a quick five-mile speed march early one morning and then got straight onto the helos and taken out to the field. We had been yomping a lot this exercise and gotten very little sleep. It was a big difference, though, from what we were used to. Instead of getting no sleep because of getting generally fucked around by the team all night, we were getting no sleep because we were up all night setting ambushes, conducting recce (reconnaissance) patrols, and setting up OPs (observation posts) all over the place to keep tabs on any enemy movement.

The weather was characteristically abysmal, and I can remember one night I was nearly broken. I hadn't slept in days and was moving about like a zombie. We were harboured on a steep, muddy hillside in among a dense patch of forest and it was pouring. Earlier in the evening it had been snowing, but it had warmed up around midnight and turned back to rain. I was freezing as usual, and soaked to the bone. We were on strict light discipline, which meant no lighting of fires to cook, so I had my dinner cold. I remember kneeling in the mud, wearing all of my kit and my helmet, and staring at the ground. Everybody else was off on tasks or hunkered down under their shelters, but I had been busy moving about to ensure the rest of the section was doing what they were supposed to and had everything they needed. I had no shelter up and didn't care. I was past that point. I just kneeled there, sinking into the mud, staring down at my open foil bag of stew, and watching the water pour from my helmet into my food, just having a few quiet, miserable moments to myself.

Before I could find my way back to a happy place my radio crackled to life. Any thoughts I had of getting some sleep were put aside as I clambered into the centre of the harbour to find out what was up. My fire team (four men) was being tasked to go out on a recce patrol, and as the team went over the map and gave me some quick orders the life seeped back into me. I had a job to do, and once I was certain I knew what it was, I crept up and down the line and gave the lads the good news. As the guys got up and got their kit together I stared at our map and plotted our route in my head. I jotted down a few bearings and distances in my notebook, put fresh batteries in my radios and night vision goggles (NVGS), picked up my rifle, and assembled the team. We headed off in single file into the gloom, careful not to step on the sentry as we shuffled past.

Our job for the night was to recce a route that the troop would take to an enemy objective a few kilometres away and attack later that week. We had to determine if the going was easy or hard, if there were any obstacles, how long it would take the troop to get into an attack position, if there were any paths or tracks that weren't on the map, where the troop would stop short before moving into position, where we could put emergency rendezvous points, where the line of departure should be and from which direction the attack should go. We also had to recce the position itself from the south and make notes on any enemy activity. There was a lot of work for us to do and if we wanted to be done before first light we had to get a move on.

We found the going to be pretty good, and moved quickly in the direction of the target. We marked on the map the fences that were missing and a small stream that actually turned out to be a big mud pit. We got to within 150 metres of the target and went firm on the ground. We all lay in a star on the ground facing outwards, with our feet touching in the middle. It was an effective way to cover all directions with your rifles, made it easy to move a bit and whisper to each other, and in this position you could keep kicking each other's feet to stop from falling asleep if you had to stay for a long time. We lay there for about ten minutes to listen for any movement in our area, but with the heavy rain we couldn't hear anything. The rain would cover our noise as well, so it wasn't completely unwelcome. I left two guys at the RV (rendezvous) and two of us crept up towards the target to confirm the line of advance and get eyes on the building.

We got right up to the edge of the trees and starting confirming what we'd thought we had already observed through the NVGs. As I described it all, the other nod with me was sketching it. He drew out the paths and tracks at the target, fences, walls, and the building in detail. Noting the doors and windows of buildings is very important when doing sketches on a recce. All exits and entrances are paramount. We made note of where the troop could best set up their machine guns, and took bearings and distances to key features. We didn't see any enemy that night but guessed where they would have their guns set up if they had any.

There really was no limit to the amount of info you could gather on a recce, and all of it was important. Time spent on recce is rarely wasted, and I am sure those unfortunate boys at Dieppe in 1942 would have agreed. They would have been pleased to find out days before they actually hit the beach that their tanks couldn't drive on that loose shingle and gravel.

We pushed back into the bush and slithered around to a few different points to get a look at everything from a different perspective. Distances change when judged from a different angle, and new positions often reveal themselves. We had arranged a cut-off time with the two guys we had left behind at the RV, and we had to leave to get back to them. We had plenty of information, and if we managed to get out of there without being compromised, it would be back slaps all around with hot tea and crumpets. Well, maybe cold water and a hard brown biscuit. We got the team reassembled and went firm again for a moment to see if we were being followed. It was as quiet as it could possibly be so we headed back the way that we had come and stopped again after a few hundred metres. The two of us that had been on the recce passed on all of the most important info to the others so that everybody knew the best bits. We do this so that if we got in the shit, it wouldn't matter which one of us made it back to the troop. We could all pass on the relevant information.

We arrived back at the troop harbour and my fire team got straight into their slugs. The rest of the section was covering the sentry and wouldn't rope any of us into it for a few more hours. I still had a lot of work ahead of me. I had to write up a patrol report in the dark, and it can take a very long time depending on how detailed you make it. I got up a shelter and went head-first into my Gore-Tex sleeping bag cover so that I could use some light. It was hard to breathe in there, and a little bit cramped, but at least it was dry and warm. I finished up my report, and realizing there were only a few hours of darkness left, I took the liberty of exempting myself from the sentry rotation for the rest of the night. The exercise wasn't over yet, and I needed some rest.

CHAPTER 14

STOPPAGE

After a quick trip home at Christmas to see Jennifer and the family it was straight back to CTC to carry on. The troop spent the first two months of the new year in the field, one way or another – either out on actual field exercise, or furthering our learning through thrashings galore on the bottom field at camp. During these weeks I also experienced one major setback, which ultimately turned out to be a blessing.

There was no let-up in the training schedule, and if anything the training team managed to cram more and more stuff into it. We spent a lot of time with the AES (assault engineers), who taught us all sorts of useful skills. We learned all about area defence weapons such as the claymore. The claymore is really an anti-personnel mine, but since the U.K. doesn't use "anti-personnel mines" we had to change the description. We studied big anti-tank mines and nasty little ones that just take off your foot. Believe it or not, some of the best little ones out there are Canadian-designed. Now, I'm not suggesting that Canada still manufactures and exports land mines. I am just saying that back in the day, Canada came up with some very nasty ideas.

We started to work with the Corps' newest vehicles in mid-January (Week 21). They are light armoured personnel carriers called Vikings, and we went out on a four-day exercise to get acquainted with them. They are tracked, articulated vehicles. They are not nearly as heavily armoured as a tank, because they are designed to swim and spend a lot of time in Norway on the snow. They carry four guys in the front section and a section (eight guys) in the rear. One of the guys up front stands out of the top and works a GPMG. The Vikings were brand-new and provided a much better way of getting around than yomping with our bergens. To begin the exercise, the troop headed to the Royal Tank Corps training area where the Vikings were based, had a few familiarization lectures, and inspected the vehicles.

We drove around that training area for the next couple of days, setting up troop harbour locations at night near the vehicles. We still had to put out sentries, and we still had to send out patrols every night and recce targets, but it was a nice change to have warm vehicles to crawl into in the morning, and to strap our heavy bergens to their outside rather than our shoulders. We often practised de-bussing in a hurry from the Vikings as they drove down the tracks with constant enemy contact. It was tricky to keep any situational awareness in the back of the Vikings, and when we heard shots being fired outside we never really knew what was going on until the alarm sounded for us to get out. The driver manning the radio would tell us what direction the contact was in, but until you jumped out you couldn't be sure if you were in a field, amid trees, or near buildings. In spite of the constant stream of updates from the drivers and the little window in the rear door (which would be covered in mud after a few seconds of driving), we were still pretty much blind coming out of that Viking every time.

But we practised nevertheless, swinging the heavy door open and tumbling out of the backs of those Vikings time and time again. Typically we would come out and form a long line off to a side, facing the threat. The gunners up on top of the Vikings would be hammering away at the targets while we sorted our shit out, and then we would roll into a section attack, covering and moving our way up to and through the objective. Once the enemy was eliminated, we would all move back to the vehicles, clamber into the back, and roar off to do it all over again.

As much as I liked being driven around, I have to admit that I preferred dismounted ops. The vehicles were bullet and bomb magnets, and I wouldn't have liked to have to pile out of the back into a hail of gunfire when you didn't even really know where it was coming from.

We had our Week 22 bottom field tests after the exercise, and all of the hard work we had put in was about to pay off. Once these tests were out of the way, there would be a more relaxed physical training regime until the Commando tests, just to keep us ticking over. We were getting plenty of exercise out in the field anyway, and that was where we were spending most of our time now. Just a few painful minutes down on the assault course and it would be smooth sailing until the final show.

The warm-up before we got started was much more tame than usual. The PTI didn't give a shit about how well we performed moments before the tests – he just wanted us to pass the tests and so was giving us a better chance by letting us go up the ropes with fresh arms. We were told to get our kit on and to line up in front of the ropes for the thirty-foot climb. There are eight ropes altogether down there, so even if you try to get to the back of the queue to hide for a bit it won't take long for your turn to come around. I was at the front and grabbed the rope, just waiting for the word. The PTI looked at us and said, "Well, what are you waiting for?" Off we went. I was so nervous as I started that I felt a lot weaker than usual. I had doubts for a split second, but once I got into the rhythm with my legs and arms, my nervousness faded and it was all business. I have never been the fastest up the ropes, but I have never been the slowest either, and before long I had both hands on the white tape at the top of the rope. I shouted down to the PTI and he had a glance up to make sure I wasn't cheating. As he looked back down at his clipboard and shouted out my name I descended under control, so as not to let gravity kick my ass. I moved off to the side once I was down and shook out my arms. One test down, three to go.

The assault course was next and the PTI called out names in the order he wanted us to run the course. The fastest guys were at the front so they wouldn't overtake the slower ones and confuse things. I was in the middle of the pack. The first guys were off and running, heading around the course two at a time. We were set off at one-minute intervals, so I had five or six minutes to watch the racing snakes zipping over and through the obstacles. Soon enough it was my turn and I sprinted off the line, jumping the tank trap filled with water with good distance. Then the thirty-metre sprint, at the end of which I somehow got up and over a six-foot brick wall. I crawled under the scramble nets, jumped over the leaning fence, swung across the monkey bars, pulled myself up onto the top of a zigzagging wall, ran down the length of it and jumped off, climbed up onto the rope obstacle, crawled out on the rope and did a regain, crossed the swinging bridge, sprinted up the long, lonely hill, threw myself over the five-foot wall, and again up over the fence at the top of the hill, crawled through the tunnels, scrambled up the twelve-foot wall and was done! It sure sounds quick and easy when I type it.

When I was running up the hill I knew I was going to make it. I knew what a pass felt like and I was sure that I would have plenty of time to spare so I let off the throttle a bit. My scrawny legs needed all the help they could get to power their way through the fireman's carry, which was the next test. That was my nemesis, and I only passed it about 75 per cent of the time. I finished the assault course with more than thirty seconds to spare out of the allowed five minutes, and joined the rest of the troop walking in a big slow circle on the field, trying to get some air into my lungs. But we only had as much time as it took the last of the troop to finish the assault course, and that wasn't long. Without any hesitation the PTI got us all lined up at one end of the field by a big white post. Two hundred metres away we could all see the other white post. The only thing separating us from it was a little over a minute of the most intense output of energy that we could muster. I knew what it felt like when you got to the other end, and that knowledge, combined with the sight of the other few guys who were spewing, made me take a few steps back and join them. I retched onto my boots until the PTI told us it was time to get on with it, then wiped my mouth with the back of my hand and blew my nose, getting most of it on myself. All aboard the pain train.

I got my partner up onto my shoulders and he curled up into as tight a ball as he possibly could. The more compact he was, the easier it was, and he squeezed me with his legs so that he wouldn't move around as much. Everybody was ready to go and the PTI told us to get on with it. Off I went, leaning forward to try and let gravity pull me along as I pumped my free arm and drove with my legs. The first one hundred metres always went smoothly, but as I passed the halfway point the crushing feeling on my chest became acute and painful. Between my kit, his kit, and his body I had about 240 pounds on me. I am a meagre 148 and I had to give it everything I had to keep up with the pack. At the 150-metre mark I felt a wave of relief flow over me. Yes, I was firmly in the hurt locker, but I was having a good run and knew I would make it. My partner was encouraging me along, telling me to push hard and not to give up, and as I crossed the line with ten seconds to spare I dropped him to his feet and went for a walk to compose myself. I walked to the fence and bent over, content but feeling fucked. My chest was heaving and I just wanted this all to be over. But only half the troop was finished, so I wandered back and gave my mate the luxury of carrying little old me two hundred metres the other way. He made it with no problems, as he always did, and as we walked back towards the tank we prepared ourselves for the final test of the day.

I was confident as I queued up at the bottom of the ladders that led to the regain ropes. I was good at regains and hadn't failed to do one at the end of a session as short as this for a long time. I usually put on such a good display of how to do a proper regain that the PTI had started to call it the Vancouver Manoeuvre. As long as I did what I always did I would be fine. Everybody in front of me was completing their regains to the shouts of the PTI and I was determined to get it done as I climbed the ladder and gripped the rope. I slid out onto the rope and crawled along until I was halfway and out over the icy water. I dropped down until I was hanging there with my arms straight, and with plenty of strength lifted my feet all the way back up and got the backs of my knees over the rope. For most people who struggle with regains that was the hardest part, but I found it the easy part. The hard part for me was getting my armpit up on the rope and then flipping myself around until I was back on top. I had the technique pretty well mastered though, so I went through the motions, but found I was struggling. I just couldn't get my armpit up, and every time I did I would fall back down before I could reposition my other hand and get ready for the flip. I tried again and again but it was getting harder with each attempt as my strength drained away. The troop was cheering me on, but after a few more attempts I was spent. I had to choose between hanging there upside down for the next few minutes and then going in the tank, or just going in straight away. So I let go, and with a tremendous sense of disappointment failed the test.

The next day four of us had another go at it. It wasn't just the regain we had to be tested on – all four tests had to be done back to back to qualify as a pass. So we went through it all again. Up the rope, around the assault course, a quick fireman's carry, which was just as dreadful as all the others, and back up over the tank. Would you believe it, I failed again. The scenario was identical. I got my legs back up on the rope with ease, and then powered out after that. I couldn't for the life of me figure out what was happening, and after my latest trip into the tank I was in a bad state in my head. I really didn't want to leave the troop and couldn't understand why I was failing something that had come so easily to me before. I had no explanation, and the PTI offered plenty of advice but I had trouble taking it on board. I didn't know how to change my technique when it had worked so well before. The next morning I woke up knowing it was now or never, and the troop gave me plenty of pep talks as I got on my kit and headed off for the assault course. The troop wouldn't be coming to watch as they had some lectures to attend, but they all wished me luck and told me they would see me on the other side.

I headed down there knowing that it was do or die, and went about my third bottom field pass-out test of the week. Lucky me. Ropes, assault course, carry a guy, and out over the tank. As I hung there for the third time I was all over the place in my mind. I couldn't let the idea of failure creep in there, but I was fearing the worst. As usual my feet found their way up again, but I just couldn't close the deal. I was more tired than in the past, having been subjected to this test three times in as many days. I found my way straight down into the tank, and as I crawled out for the last time, my PTI spoke. "I am disappointed, Olafsen. You are a good lad, but that was a fucking embarrassment." He walked off to start the paperwork to get me out of the troop.

CHAPTER 15

ALONG THE WAY

I moved into Hunter Company over the weekend, and as I passed by the old team office for the last time I saw that the infamous black blob had covered my face and body on the troop photo. It was official. I was out of the troop.

Hunter was not only for injured nods. It was also a place nods were sent when they needed some extra help to pass a criteria test, and I was going into Hunter to get extra help with my regains. Hopefully, if I could pass the bottom field tests with them right away, I would be able to join the next troop along. Hunter was divided into two sections, one for those with injuries and the other for those who just needed to pass a criteria test before being slotted back into circulation with a troop. I headed for the second section and reported to the sergeant major. He welcomed me to Hunter and looked at my file before telling me that he hoped I would be out of his hair in less than a week. I agreed with him and moved into my new room. I hated it there right away, as I was surrounded by a lot of guys who were full of defeatism. I wanted to prove that I shouldn't even be there, and found my new PTI right away to schedule some time down on the bottom field.

There was a session scheduled for the very next morning and I told him that I would be jumping in with the group. He was cool with that, and told me he would help me square away my regain and get ready to pass the test. I chilled out that night with a few cold pints, and in the morning I was ready to meet the challenge. We went straight down to the tank at eight o'clock, and the PTI first made me remove my kit and go up on the rope to show him a regain. I got up there and did a perfect regain with no hitches. He told me to do another one so I did, and then one more for good measure. I came down and after getting my kit on he sent me up on the rope over the tank to show him what I had. I did a regain without a problem, and then another at his request. He asked me to give him a third regain, and again I executed one flawlessly, just like I had been able to do before the test. When I climbed down off the rope he confronted me. "You are a fucking idiot." "Yes, staff," I replied. "You shouldn't have failed that test," he said. "No, staff," I agreed. "Would you like to redo the entire test right now?" he asked me. "Yes, staff," I said.

The PTI rounded up one of the other guys who was getting some extra help down there that morning and made sure he would be available for me to carry across the field in a few moments. He then weighed my kit and we got on with it. I went up the rope with no problem, made it around the assault course as fast as always, carried that stranger two hundred metres in the allotted time, and climbed up onto the rope over the tank and did a textbook regain. With that my time in Hunter Company came to an end. I took my stuff out of there and moved in with my new troop, in time to watch them all doing their bottom field pass-out tests the following week.

While I had been messing around with Hunter and watching my new troop get thrashed around the bottom field, my old troop had been out in the field again. My old faithful companion Tom, the brick musician, had gotten an infection in his knee and had to be pulled off the exercise. That got him back-trooped as well, and sure as shit he ended up in my new troop with me. It was great to have a familiar face around, and together we discovered just how much of a cock our old sergeant had really been. The new troop we joined was run very differently from the old one, and it was for the better. The sergeant addressed the nods like they were people, and never once gave them ridiculous speeches in the middle of the night while they sat in bizarre stress positions. It was an amazing transition for me, and one that I was happy to embrace. The recruits were still very dedicated and had to work their asses off, but they did it with far more smiles than I was used to. There was also a fellow Canadian in the troop, a guy from Hamilton who had also been in the Canadian Army Reserve. He was a funny bloke, and very switched on. He was into his snowboarding and surfing, and took his soldiering very seriously. He is now a sniper in the Corps, and has spent plenty of time in Afghanistan. I was put in the same section as him in my new troop and was pleased with that.

It was still Week 22 for me, and the first real thing that I had to do with my new troop was to head out into the field for an eight-day field exercise. Normally I would have dreaded an undertaking like this, but with the new troop and updated regime I was looking forward to it. The exercise would span a weekend, so we would be able to kill two weeks of the training program in one shot. It was two exercises combined into one. The first was to test all of our defensive location and NBC (nuclear, biological, and chemical) warfare skills, and the second was all about assaulting buildings and clearing houses. There was a lot of potential to do something cool for a change. It would of course involve a lot of hard work, but chucking grenades and firing on fully automatic always brought a smile to my face.

It was still only February and the weather up in the Welsh hills was notoriously unpleasant at this time of year. We all settled down for the long bus ride and grabbed the last bit of sleep that we could bet on. Along the way we even stopped for a burger, something that my old troop would have never even considered. When we finally arrived we stepped off the bus into brilliant sunshine, with not a cloud in the sky. It was very cold out, somewhere around freezing in the warmest part of the day, but the air was crisp and clear, and most importantly we were dry.

We stepped off in a long troop snake, moving around wood blocks and following old tracks across the barren hills. The area we were in was similar to Dartmoor but with more wood blocks and structures around. It was still very exposed to the wind and the elements and would be an unpleasant place to live when the weather turned sour. After a few miles we approached our defensive position and were pleased to find some permanent trenches already pre-dug for the troop. For practice, the troop would have to dig one large trench with a roof on it, but that would be done in section shifts. We were now into a tactical exercise, so the troop put out some four-man standing patrols in wood blocks around the position. We lay down among the trees, keeping our eyes peeled for enemy. If we saw any enemy creeping about we were supposed to initiate a contact by firing at them with our blank rounds. We rotated through the different positions to keep things interesting and got among the trench-digging party as well. The trench was going to be big enough for four men to live in and fight from. Half of it would have a cover and half would be open to the heavens. There was a lot of digging to be done, and even with fresh hands on the shovels at all times it wasn't done for nearly twelve hours. The troop also had to construct barbed wire entanglements and obstacles all over the place and lay mine fields to protect our flanks.

On this NBC test exercise the threat of a biological or chemical attack was ranked "high" so we had to wear our large protective suits. It was very cold just standing around waiting for an attack, and the NBC suits were nice and warm. It was great to stand around in those, with our overboots on and the hood up underneath our helmets. Even with all that kit on it was quite chilly, and in the morning when we went to fill up our water bottles from the jerry cans we had to break up the ice in them to get any water to flow.

At first light we were all stood to as usual, and as we started to heat up our breakfasts we came under a simulated gas attack. There were explosions all around and large gas clouds started to form and drift across our position. We all scrambled to get our respirators on and waited behind our guns for any enemy to come at our trenches. After the gas had all drifted away we went through the routine of decontaminating ourselves and helped each other rub powder all over ourselves to absorb and neutralize any chemicals. We came under attack later that day and some of us had fake liquid agents sprayed onto us as if they had been delivered by an enemy aircraft, so we decontaminated again. We were all a little tired from hardly sleeping at all the night before, but overall this exercise was a piece of cake. No rain, no thrashings, no yelling and screaming, and no streams.

As the afternoon wore on they decided that our NBC skills were up to scratch and we filled in the trench we had dug. We packed away our NBC kit, got under our bergens, and yomped off to start Phase 2 of the exercise. Hours and miles later, with tired legs and aching shoulders, we arrived at a house built for FIBUA training (fighting in built-up areas) and the whole troop set up our roll mats and sleeping bags *inside*. We were told that we were in a secure area, that there were no enemy around, and that we would only have one sentry position of one man for the whole troop to rotate through that night. That meant that from 9:00 p.m., when we had finished receiving our briefs for the FIBUA phase, to morning, each man would have to do approximately twenty minutes of sentry inside a dry house. The house was just a concrete box with no windows or anything, purpose-built for attacking with grenades and rifles, but this was a luxury that I could barely even begin to explain to the rest of the troop. It seemed to me that failing those regains was the best thing that had ever happened to me. I got in my warm sleeping bag at nine, and between then and seven I got up only once for half an hour. I was in good spirits.

The next day the troop sent out recce patrols to check out our first target, a cluster of farm buildings and a tall water tower about a kilometre away across the valley. The exercise took on a pattern for the rest of the week. Each evening and morning we would send out recces to observe targets, then later that day the troop would attack them and occupy the new houses. The next day we would simply repeat the process, moving from building to building. The sections that weren't on any recces that day would maintain a sentry and practise our FIBUA drills on the buildings we had occupied. We spent hours stacking up outside doors in four-man teams. Four guys would get into a tight line right up against the wall outside a door that we were going to enter. The first guy would toss in a grenade, and once it had gone off, the team would pour through the door, heading in specific directions and covering specific parts of the room as they advanced. Sometimes we would toss in two grenades, spaced a few seconds apart. We were told that in 2003, to protect themselves against the grenades that always preceded a violent entry, some Iraqis had hidden in armoured boxes inside the buildings; then, once the grenades went off, the Iraqis would spring up and hose down the guys as they came through the door. We would toss two grenades sometimes, so that, should the enemy spring up after the first one had gone off, instead of being met with juicy targets coming in the door, he would get a face full of shrapnel.

Once the recce section had come back, we would all receive orders and look at maps that we drew on the walls in chalk. We usually set off at last light and attacked just after dark. One of our sections would always peel off to a flank and set up a fire support team to suppress the targets as the remaining sections moved onto the objective. Very simple drills, but also very effective. Looking back on it all now, it is amazing how important all of this basic training was. Exactly one year after this exercise, I would be doing it in Afghanistan with real grenades, real bullets, and real enemies. For now, though, we were getting plenty of excitement just throwing practice grenades. They didn't really explode but had a charge in them to make a tremendous BANG! when they went off. It was fun, and the troop was having a blast.

I loved being in the first team through the door. There would be rifle fire going off all around the location as the fire support team suppressed in-depth targets, and some enemy would be shooting here and there – you could see their muzzle flashes in the windows. Our four-man team would stack up outside the door we were going to breach, and grenades would be prepped while the rest of the team kept an eye out up above and to the rear. The grenades would be hurled through the door and after a few seconds, BOOM! That was our cue to move. One after the other we would go through the door with our rifles held high in the shoulder, ready to fire on anything. You would be completely focused on what was happening as you came in and the smell of burned gunpowder filled your nostrils. You quickly followed your wall, shouting out what you were seeing and how many doors and windows were present, so the team commander could get a picture of the building layout in his mind. Room by room you would storm through the house in set-piece plays. Rifle fire would crackle from other rooms, and when a target presented itself you didn't hesitate for even a second – *bang bang* and move on. One in the head as you go by, then the rifle back up in the shoulder. If you found it necessary you could toss grenades into rooms as you advanced, but you would have had to be careful if you had been doing it with real grenades. There were lots of your guys in the house, and drywall isn't known for its ability to stop shrapnel.

As you cleared your sectors, the next team would usually move in and leapfrog through to carry on. Going up stairs was always particularly dangerous because the enemy might roll grenades down at you. Speed was key, and as we practised all that week we got faster and faster as our drills got slicker and slicker. It was exciting work and demanded a lot, and my hat goes off to the boys out there who wrote the book on this stuff by doing it for real.

It was a great week of training, and after our final big assault on a cluster of four large buildings we yomped off for about six miles to a building where we would spend the night. It was early in the afternoon when we arrived and the trucks wouldn't be showing up to collect us until the morning. Rather than just fuck us around and thrash us like the sergeant would have done in my old troop, the team told us that the exercise was over, and our time was our own. We got a full night of sleep with no sentry routine, and in the morning when the trucks showed up we loaded our bergens with grins from ear to ear. On the final morning of an exercise we were well rested, well fed, warm and dry. It was a good morning, and the best part of it all was that we were two weeks closer to getting our green lids.

CHAPTER 16

ICE PIGS

Slowly but surely we were nearing the end of training. It was Week 24. There were still a lot of hurdles ahead, and they would certainly only continue to get higher and higher, but at least now we were to a point where we could actually count them in one sitting. The rest of training would be full of variety, which helped to speed things up, and many of the old pains in the ass were simply a thing of the past; kit musters in the field, random midnight thrashings, change parades and stress positions. We were deep enough into training now that the team understood none of us was going to quit no matter what they threw at us. The only thing that could back-troop us now was an injury, and with this in mind the team had no reason to test our mental resolve. Much of our focus from here on in would be learning specialist skills such as amphibious and cliff assaults and preparing for the final Commando tests.

But before we could get all warm and fuzzy about graduating out of that hellhole, there were still a few cold hands and feet to deal with.

The first of the final Commando tests was called the Endurance course and it was exactly as advertised. It was a six-mile obstacle course across the moorland and woodland of our old familiar gorse-filled training area on Woodbury Common about four miles from camp. The trail had a lot of steep hills to run up, large mud pits to plough through, ponds to wade across, tunnels and pipes to crawl through, and an underwater culvert, this portion requiring that a guy be stationed at each end of the culvert so that when someone went through they could make sure he didn't get stuck and drown.

After this first part, there is a four-mile run back to camp as fast as you can; just you, your snotty face, and your thoughts. Once you are back on camp you have to quickly make sure your rifle is in good working order after dragging it through the mud and get ten shots on target on the range. This must all be done in seventy-two minutes, and when you finally arrive at the ranges before you shoot you are panting and heaving with the best of them. I hate running long distances being fully rigged in wet clothes and boots filled with water. The course is designed to test your determination, and at that it excels.

We headed up to Woodbury Common one cold afternoon to get introduced to it all. It was snowing, there was a fairly strong wind ripping across the training area, and the tunnels had ice in them. The troop had a little warm-up session to get the old blood flowing, and then we went racing off after the PTI. This was our first practice run-through and the PTI had to make sure that we followed the correct path and knew which obstacles to tackle and which to avoid. There were tracks and walking paths criss-crossing the area and plenty of ponds that we didn't have to go through. A guide on the first day was handy.

We all took turns crawling through each tunnel as we got to it, and in many places there were two tunnels side by side so that on the day of the race you wouldn't get completely stuck behind somebody who was much slower than you. The tunnels had plenty of water and ice in them, and as we went from tunnel to pond to tunnel around the track my hands began to freeze. My body was hot from all the running, and my feet were toasty, but my hands were in a world of hurt by the end of the first run-through. I couldn't feel them at all, let alone move them. Submerging them over and over was agonizing. I am still missing some feeling in my fingertips as a result of this experience.

After the initial tour, we had to go through it all again, this time at speed and on our own. We would be running back to camp as well, since it was a complete practice. The only thing being left out was the shooting. We were sent off in groups of three or four, and ploughed through the ponds and up those steep hills as the snow came down and the wind blew. My body was leaving a trail of hot steam in the air behind me as I ran, and everyone had a steaming head. The only cold part was my hands, and they were pretty much useless. Our knees took a pounding as we crawled through those tunnels over the rocks and shale (on the final test a few weeks later, many guys would secretly wear knee pads under their pants). After a pleasant four-mile run back through the country lanes to camp we got ourselves undressed. I couldn't untie my boots with my frozen fingers, and most of the other guys were having the same problems. We took turns undoing each other's boots with our teeth and then finally got a hot shower.

The next day, after a twelve-mile yomp, we got onto buses and headed off down to Poole on the south coast. This was the home of the Royal Marines' amphibious training wing, where we would get introduced to all the different landing craft the Corps used and learn how to get from ship to shore to assault the beaches.

At daybreak our first morning at Poole, the troop headed down to the docks in full fighting order. We had inflatable Zodiacs to use (IRCS – inshore raiding craft); larger jet-driven, rigid-hull boats, which hold nine guys and are bristling with machine guns (ORCS – offshore raiding craft); LCAS (landing craft, assault), which could hold a vehicle or about thirty guys; and LCUs (landing craft, utility), which were much larger and could hold about ten medium vehicles or as many as 150 guys. The LCAs and LCUs were flat-bottomed and jet-driven and each had a large ramp that came down at the front. They were designed to get right up onto the beach so that men and vehicles could storm ashore. To keep from getting stuck on shore, they would drop an anchor on their approach so that they could winch themselves backwards if need be to get off the beach.

The troop started the amphibious assault drills with the smallest craft first. Section by section we practised coming into shore in the Zodiacs. They couldn't get right onto the beach, and the bootnecks driving the boats loved to get nods wet, so we had to go over the side in chest-deep, freezing water to wade ashore before running up the beach. So we were wet and cold from the start, and wouldn't be dry again until very late that night. We slowly moved up into bigger and bigger boats until the whole troop was assembled in an LCA offshore. We all easily fit in an LCA as the troop was hovering at around twenty-five people with the constant intakes of back-troopers. We headed for the beach, and as we got close the LC operator at the ramp (there were two of them – one was driving) would let us know how long until the ramp went down. When the LCA ground up onto the shore and the ramp dropped we all came storming out of there in two files and headed up the beach. We got up towards cover and assumed firing positions, covering all the angles. Once we had finished getting up onto the beach, the troop would peel back into the LCA, and as we headed back out to sea, the team would talk to us about how we could do it better, where the guns in the troop should be, and how we should react to enemy fire out on the beach. We kept coming back in and hitting the beach until the team was satisfied with our drills. We would have to do it all again once it got dark, but for now we were done. It was well past lunchtime, but we drove out into the middle of the harbour to practise cross boarding at speed.

When the LCA was cruising along in a nice straight line, the smaller ORCS pulled up alongside and wedged their bows in against the LCA's side. Then, while we were moving, we would take turns piling over the side of the LCA into the ORCS. The coxswains of the ORCS would then go tearing off around the harbour. The ORCS are very quick, powered along by big twin Rolls-Royce diesels, and can easily crack forty miles per hour. With that engine power, they could have gone a heck of a lot faster if they hadn't been weighed down with so much armour and weaponry. The drivers of the ORCS had a great time ripping around out there and they got us soaked in the swells, but we were having a great time too, and for a few moments during the wild ride we'd completely forget how cold and miserable we should be. We went back and forth between the LCA and the ORCS a few times before heading back to shore for supper. We would have a hot meal and get out of the cold for a bit before we had to head back down to the docks to do it all over again in the dark. The drills that night were essentially the same (including cold and wet), but doing them in the dark was a little different and required more concentration.

With the amphibious training behind us, we looked ahead to our final field exercise looming on the horizon, which we would have to pass before we could tackle the Commando tests. But before we headed out into the field one last time we had an introduction to one of the Commando tests. Known as the Tarzan Assault Course, this was the shortest of the four tests that we would have to do. The whole thing lasted a maximum of thirteen minutes and was sort of an expanded version of the five-minute assault course that we had done on the bottom field. It was a series of rope obstacles and climbs, each about thirty feet up and in among the trees, and done without safety harnesses and with very few safety nets down below. You started by climbing up a very high tower and then doing a steep slide down a long rope to the ground. They call it the death slide, and you just grabbed a short rope in one hand, flung it up and over the long rope that stretched down to the ground, grabbed the other end in your free hand and went for it. Losing your grip was a bad idea. Then you sprinted off and climbed up a rope ladder into the trees. There were plenty more ropes to crawl along, ropes to swing on, and cargo nets to scramble up. It took a lot of concentration to get cleanly from one obstacle to the next and was a serious phys session with all of the customary kit on. Once you had gotten through all of the high rope sections and were back on the ground you had to sprint about four hundred metres to the start of the original assault course. Then you went through the entire, familiar assault course, sprinted back towards the Tarzan section a few hundred metres away, and scaled a very steep thirty-foot wall with the help of yet another rope. Once at the top you would call out your name and collapse.

The troop went through the Tarzan course a few times, practising our transitions between obstacles, and did our final practice run at speed. I managed to finish in the allotted time, but the old familiar mixture of snot and spit attested to the intensity of it.

CHAPTER 17

FINAL EX

Week 26, and we were heading into our final field exercise of training. All the troop cared about was getting it done, whatever the cost.

In the accommodation, the troop received orders for the upcoming attack and were issued blank ammunition and practice grenades. We cranked up the stereo and laughed back and forth as we smeared our faces with cam cream and stuffed our webbing with the tools of our trade. Underneath our joking around was the awareness that this was serious business, our final ex, and it was a test. This exercise would be the troop's last chance to convince the training team that we were ready to join a Commando unit, and we knew that it was not uncommon for nods to fail final ex.

At noon we moved out to the football field with all of our kit and met up with a pair of Royal Navy Sea King helicopters. The troop was split in half, and once our bergens were stowed away in the helo we jumped up and took our seats. The helos increased engine power and we were off and running. We flew low and fast for nearly an hour across Southern England and as we neared the LP (landing point) we got the signal to prepare to move. We were out over Dartmoor somewhere, flying over an area that I didn't recognize. The sky was covered in broken clouds and the air was crisp but dry. Things were starting off well. The helos touched down and we all leapt out with only our fighting order on. We left the bergens on the helos, and as the helos took off we fanned out into a defensive position, scanning for the enemy and covering our arcs. We cocked our weapons and prepared to move off. We already had our orders and knew what we had to be doing. I dug out my compass to ensure that I had my bearings; as we stepped off in half attack formation I stuffed it away and got my rifle up into its comfortable position in my shoulder.

We went about a mile at a medium pace until the old mine complex that we were going to attack came into view over the grassy hills. We went down onto the ground and section by section moved into our attack positions. We had a fire support team setting up off to the right flank, and my section and another were going to assault. When everyone was in position, we gave the signal for the attack to start. The enemy were milling about in several different positions, and as the fire support team opened up with their guns they took cover and started to return fire. Our attacking sections started to fire and move towards the targets, breaking into smaller and smaller teams as we got closer and closer. We were basically in a flat gravel pit with large gravel mounds all over the place and a few old derelict buildings. We took cover behind the gravel piles and lads started prepping grenades for the final show. We tossed our grenades on target as other rifles forced the enemy to stay in cover, and with the WHOOMP! of the grenades we followed them up with a final push, some automatic bursts, and a few bayonet thrusts for good measure.

With these spots neutralized we started to move forward, looking for and attacking rear positions as they appeared.

We swept through that mine complex fast and furiously, and the fire support team had to switch their fire quickly as we moved into their kill zones. With the last of the enemy killed we took up defensive positions and sorted out our ammunition among the section. The all-clear was passed up the radio net to HQ, and just as quickly as we had arrived we were heading out of there, back up to where we had been dropped off to rendezvous with the helos and carry on with the exercise. As we got to the correct grid, the helos turned up right on schedule. We piled on board and headed off to Plymouth, where we met up with some trucks that took the troop and all of our kit deep into Dartmoor before dropping us off on the dripping hills.

We shouldered our heavy bergens, and as the trucks roared off into the distance we yomped into the cold, misty twilight of Dartmoor. Night was quickly overtaking us as we yomped along, but that didn't stop us from covering a lot of distance that evening. We carried on for mile after mile, not really knowing how far we had gone or how much farther we had to go. We stopped for a few quick breaks, huddling around barren rock features, and then were off again, snaking into the night. We had all heard that there was a lot of yomping to do on final ex, and we were learning first-hand that the rumours were true. We kept on moving all through the damp night, and when there were only a few hours of darkness left we started to climb a large hill. At the top was a large rock feature, like an old broken tooth protruding from a grassy gum. There were a few outcroppings that could provide shelter for the troop to huddle under, and it was here that we set up shop.

We all needed some sleep, and as we tucked in beneath the outcroppings and got out our sleeping bags we initiated the standard sentry routines. We found out which direction the main enemy threat was from, and placed our guns up among the boulders to meet the threat. These guns were manned twenty-four hours a day, and with most of the troop quietly getting a bit of rest I sat behind one of the guns, scanning the misty hillside with my night vision goggles. By now it was morning, very quiet and peaceful, with no movement anywhere. The fog muffled any noise there was, and it seemed the action of the whole world had been paused. It felt like the calm before the storm. The troop stayed up on that hilltop keeping out of sight for the whole day, and when the fog lifted around lunch time we could see into the valley below us. It was a few kilometres away, but down below, tucked in among some trees and next to a stream, we could make out a small farm complex. This was our next target, and when last light fell we would be sending out recce patrols to gather intelligence on it. We spent the whole day just keeping out of sight and trying to stay warm. It was still only early March. Talking and movement were kept to a minimum, and other than the odd sentry shift, there was very little for us to do. We were all just waiting for darkness so we could get the show on the road.

As the light began to fade late in the afternoon, the recce patrols started to shake out, and soon they wandered off into the growing fog towards the farm complex in the valley. Most of the troop was still tasked to stay behind in the troop harbour, and once again I found myself behind the gun up there. The night was just as peaceful as the early morning had been, and as uncomfortable as it was sitting in the cold rocks blowing on my fingers, it was so peaceful that I couldn't help but appreciate it. It hadn't rained in nearly twenty-four hours, and I was well rested and well fed. So far so good.

The recces came back late that night, and after we had all received orders for the attack we packed away all of our kit and got ready to move off. It was 0400 when we started, and we wanted to time the attack to start just a few minutes before first light. We wound our way down the hill and into the trees on the valley floor, where we found a good spot to ditch our bergens. In fighting order we crept through the trees, steadily advancing on the farm complex. The standard routine followed. Fire support peeled off to a flank and got in a good position to provide suppressing fire, and the rest of us moved into an assault start line. We could see a few enemy moving about near the complex, and as our guns opened up on them we all started to move forward, covering each other and moving in turn. We had done this numerous times now, and as we leapfrogged through each other I was pleased with how smooth it was all going. The first guys were up to the entrances of the buildings, and without any hesitation they tossed in their grenades. Meanwhile, some of us were ensuring the enemy in the yard were well and truly dead and others were putting rounds into the upper-storey windows. Our boys were into those buildings and out the other side in no time. We pushed beyond the buildings and out among the stone walls to search for in-depth positions, but there weren't any this time. The fire support section came lumbering up with their guns and ammo, and joined us in providing an all-around defence. The section commanders were having a chat with the troop boss in the complex, discussing what our next task was now that this farm was firmly in our hands.

We carried on like this, day after day out on the moor. The weather turned foul as we expected, and our bergens got heavier and heavier. We slept out in the barren, sopping wastelands each night, recce'd positions and sent in attacks each morning. Most times when I should have been able to get a few precious hours of sleep, I found myself head-first in my sleeping bag cover writing up patrol reports, or cleaning up sketches of buildings and complexes. Our rifles needed constant attention. Weapon, kit, self. We yomped incredible distances each day, and everyone's shoulders, backs, and legs were being rubbed raw and chafed from straps and wet clothing. Our bodies were screaming in pain.

After several days of this routine, it was time to start the final phase of the exercise. We yomped off again, this time a few miles to a road junction, then tossed our bergens up onto some trucks that were waiting to take us away from Dartmoor and back to Plymouth. About an hour later we had arrived in Plymouth, then went across on a ferry to a peninsula. On a prominent hill at the end of the peninsula was our final target for attack. The hill overlooked the entrance to the main harbour, and on it was a massive fort that had been built in the early 1800s to protect the harbour during the Napoleonic wars. The fort was shaped like a huge octagon, was several stories high, and had extensive underground passageways and rooms. Those sides of the fort that weren't protected by steep slopes running away from the walls were surrounded by old-fashioned moats. It was a formidable defensive position, and in reality, because of the hundreds of rooms and miles of passageways and tunnels, it would have taken far more nods than a single troop to storm it, but we were set up for a great time nevertheless.

The day after we arrived in the area of the fort we sent out numerous patrols to check out the approach routes and lay out the plan of attack. The idea was to attack at last light and enter the fort by sneaking in through different routes. One section was going to scramble down a slippery slope to the base of the wall, get through some windows into the lower passageways, and hide out until H-Hour. My section was going to rappel down a thirty-foot face into the moat, wade across, and get into the lower levels through some windows as well. The third section in the fire support role was going to scale the walls with some lightweight assault ladders and set up their guns to fire down into the fort. We were going to try and time everything perfectly, so that just as the guns cleared the top of the wall and got into position we could come storming up the stairs and start clearing rooms. Because of our limited numbers we would only clear the rooms around the lower, inner ring of the fort, but even this was a huge task. We were going to go through a huge amount of ammunition and a ton of grenades.

At 1700 hours we dumped our bergens and patrolled off to our various start points. We wanted the attack to kick off as the sun dipped and needed to keep up a steady pace to meet our deadline. The troop broke up into three separate patrols and ours headed off to get ourselves waist-deep in the stagnant moat. We crept up through the trees to the edge of the moat (everything was overgrown – it was two hundred years old, after all) and tied up our harnesses for rappelling down. We had two ropes going, and as the lads descended them two by two the rest of us kept up a defensive watch for the enemy. This was our most exposed moment and we had to be very aware of our surroundings. As quietly as could be we all got down into the water and hid away the harnesses and ropes. We pressed up to the wall of the fort, and slowly moved off in search of the windows we were supposed to get in through. We found them a little ways down the wall and propped up a lightweight ladder. One by one we got up into the window, then dragged the ladder in after us. We found ourselves in a pitch-black room and had to feel our way along the walls as we followed the section commander down the passageway. He had the only set of NVGS and was the only one who could see where we were heading. He led us along the corridor a little ways and then we went firm. We were near the stairwell that we would use to break out into the main courtyard and now had to wait for the guns to get into position above.

It seems that everything went to plan with the other sections, because right at the designated time we heard the guns start their work up top. That was our cue, and as we headed up the stairs we could see the night sky getting nearer and nearer. We saw an enemy zip across the opening of the stairs up top but he didn't see us creeping up out of the blackness. We reached the top of the stairs and went straight into action. I looked across the courtyard and saw the other section pouring out of their stairwell about one hundred metres away. They immediately started clearing rooms to their left and right and we were doing the same. We moved quickly and methodically with guys peeling off into rooms as we passed. Grenades were going off all around and the guns were going through belts of ammo like they were trying to get rid of it at the end of a long exercise. There were numerous enemy firing at us from rooms all around the ring, and as we cleared rooms and approached their positions they scooted into new rooms. Some of the enemy were going down, and many refused to die until we had tossed a grenade into their room and put a burst into them.

I was having a blast and loved engaging targets as I moved with purpose, rifle in the shoulder, constantly scanning over the top of my rifle. Whenever I turned my head to look, my rifle and upper body swivelled with it. Targets popped out of entranceways and our quick snap shots would have dropped them if it had been real. Parachute flares were fluttering down above the fort and trip flares were going off all over. The fort was lit up like day and explosions were echoing off every wall. It was chaos to an outsider, but to us it was all very organized and going smoothly. We rapidly advanced around the diameter of the courtyard, going from room to room, covering the next fire team's move, with them doing the same for us. The air was filling up with smoke from the flares, and the smell of battle was thick. Gunpowder, dust, and smoke, mixed with the sweat and stink of a long exercise, filled my nostrils. We were rapidly nearing the end and the targets seemed to have all been neutralized. We cleared the last few rooms, and then sent a few guys back to check the enemy again and make sure they were down for the count.

Fire support came down from the walls and joined up with us in the courtyard. The troop consolidated our remaining ammunition and started looking up at the walls, thinking about where to place every-one to establish a good defensive perimeter. We didn't know if the enemy was going to mount a counterattack and wanted to be pre-pared. It was right at this moment that we all heard the magical words that every bootneck loves. The troop sergeant called it out loud and clear. "End Ex!" The troop cheered, and our final exercise was over.

CHAPTER 18

END EX

With the final exercise out of the way I only had two difficult things left to do before I could leave CTC with my green beret. Only the four Commando tests and another live-firing exercise in the field remained. For several members of our troop, things had not gone nearly as well. Four lads had been injured on the long yomps and sent to Hunter Company. Two more guys just straight up failed the exercise – the team had decided their contact drills weren't good enough and they were sent back a few weeks in training to get some more practice and have another go at it with a different troop. But the rest of us had cleared a huge hurdle and now only had to face two weeks of live-fire contact drills and the four Commando tests in Week 30 before our final parade where friends and family could come and watch us looking our best.

We did the live-fire contact drills up on Dartmoor, and the two weeks were typically lousy. As each wet and dreary day slipped by we inched closer to the end of it all. As cold and miserable as we always were up there, this time we left happy with one more important tick in the box. All we had left to conquer were the Commando tests.

We didn't have to wait long. They started the very next day. First up was the Endurance course, and in the morning before we left camp we packed our webbing to the standard twenty-two pounds, picked up our standard ten-pound rifles from the armoury, and had as big a breakfast as we could squeeze into our butterfly-filled stomachs. We got on the buses that took us up to our favourite gorse plantation, and in the crisp morning air we went for a little run with the PTI to get ourselves warmed up. The sky was clear and the weather was co-operating with us. Naturally we would be soaked once we went through the tunnels and waded across the ponds, but on the four-mile run back to camp we would get a chance to dry out a little bit.

With our warm-up over, the PTI picked up his clipboard and began to call out the names of recruits in the order we would run the course. As usual, the fastest went to the front, and as usual I was in the middle of the pack. The first group took off running down the track and disappeared around a bend. Group 2 stepped up to the mark and waited. A few minutes later they too were unleashed and my group moved up to the pole position. I was very nervous and felt like I always had before a session on the bottom field. I felt sick knowing how I would be feeling in about ten minutes. I wasn't afraid of failing the test; I had never even come close to failing it on any of our run-throughs, but the sickness I would feel as I tried to power up and down the hills with all my kit was never welcome. We waited as calmly as we could while the minutes ticked by until the PTI told us we had ten seconds left. My heart raced like anyone's does at the start of the big race, but with the word "Go!" all nervousness left me.

My group went tearing off down the track, trying hard not to sprint too quickly. Completely burning yourself out at the beginning was to be avoided, and for the first five minutes or so we had to go around the course as a group. This was for the underwater culvert. We needed at least three guys there at once to push and pull each other through the tight space. But once we were past that culvert it was a free-for-all. The pipe itself wasn't very long (less than ten feet), but it was a few feet underwater and barely big enough for a medium-sized nod to get through with all of his kit on. I am a pretty skinny guy so sailed through with no hang-ups, and once the last of our group was safely out of the water, we headed off on our own. Within minutes we were well spaced out, each to our own fitness levels.

I was in my own little battle the whole way around, fighting my burning lungs and trying to get my legs to move. It felt as if I was in one of those dreams, where no matter how hard you try you just run at a ridiculously slow pace. I dragged myself through the long tunnels with my rifle clanging off the inside of the pipes, and waded through thigh-deep mud. I was struggling to keep myself moving, but every-body was at this point. All I had to do was make sure I kept on moving and it would be fine. As I crested the last big hill and broke out onto a gentle track in the trees I knew I had done it. Four miles to go, much of which was downhill. I broke into a natural stride with my rifle firmly held in my right hand and settled into it.

There wasn't much to do on the way back but lean forward to try and let gravity help a bit and think about the end. Step by step, minute by minute I was getting closer to my green beret, and the thought of finally getting there drove me on. As I covered the last few hundred metres to camp I started to think about my rifle and whether it had sur-vived the beating I had given it in the tunnels. I hoped the sight was still secure and hadn't been banged off line. I entered the gates of camp and headed for the ranges grinning, as I knew I was at the end. As I arrived at the range the PTI was there and recorded my name and time and told me to quickly get on with the shoot. I sat down on the ground, heaving and shaking from the run, and cocked my weapon. I had a plastic bag in my pocket with a string and cleaning rag to pull through my barrel, so I gave it a quick clean and grabbed a magazine from the pile. I slotted into an empty lane, chambered a round and took aim. My sight was all over the place as I struggled to catch my breath, so I stopped, took a few deep, slow breaths, and opened my eyes. I had settled down a bit and had no more time, so I cracked on and squeezed off my ten shots. All of them were well on target, and as I unloaded my rifle I was already starting to think about the next test. This was all business now, and I wanted to get the hell out of CTC! I moved to the rear and watched the others come panting into the range hut to collect ammunition, and those of us who were already done had a chuckle and slapped backs. Today was over for us, and tomorrow was a whole new challenge.

Early the next morning we climbed onto some buses with our webbing and rifles and drove out to the gorse plantation yet again. Today we would be doing the nine-mile speed march, and this test was done as a troop, running in a tight formation. In less than ninety minutes we would do nine miles over hilly terrain and wearing all of our kit. After our customary warm-up to get the blood flowing we fell into three ranks on the track. A quick pep talk from the PTI, a right turn, and we were off. We walked very quickly with huge strides for the first few hundred metres to get into it, and then broke out into a jog. You had to carry your rifle in your right hand and pump with your left the whole way. We jogged on any flats or downhills, and any uphills we walked at the ridiculous pace. I preferred the jogging to the walking part because I naturally take small strides and found it painful on my calves to keep in step.

The whole troop was going along very strong and fed off each other. Nobody wanted to be the first one to quit. Eighty-five minutes later we arrived at the gates of CTC. There we stopped for a moment. It was tradition that when a troop finished the nine-miler they would get led into camp by a drummer from the band. So as we cleaned the salt and snot away from our faces, the drummer took up his position at the front of the troop, then we triumphantly marched into camp. As we marched down the main drag, I was watching all of the newest recruits lining the sides of the road. I could remember when I was in their boots, as jealous as could be and wishing I was among those marching by. And finally here I was, and it was magnificent.

There is no rest offered during the Commando tests, and we had our third test bright and early the next morning. The Tarzan Assault Course was waiting for us as we headed out with our fully loaded kit. There was no rain, and we were happy to have dry ropes to grip instead of slippery ones. This was by far the shortest of the tests, but in my opinion it was the most tiring of them all. I was hoping to be done in under the allowed thirteen minutes. One hundred per cent effort – everything you have – for thirteen full minutes. Take my word for it; it is hard core. As we lined up to climb the tower, I felt like I always did: sick. But of course, when the PTI told me to go I gave it everything I had for what turned out to be eleven minutes and twenty seconds. I got up the ladder and out onto the high ropes obstacles with a fury. I climbed and shimmied thirty feet in the air as I had been taught, and when my boots finally hit the ground I was off and running for the old assault course. This four-hundred-metre sprint was where the fatigue really started to set in, and I started to feel the standard leaden feeling in my legs. I pushed and drove as hard as I could and carried myself down to the start of the assault course with everything I had. I went across the obstacles for the last time. I powered up that long hill at the end, and after heaving my body over the final fence there was one last one-hundred-metre sprint to the thirty-foot wall.

I grasped the rope dangling down at the bottom of the wall, and hand over hand I started to climb. The wall is nearly vertical, and has protruding stones to step on and push off from, but after everything I had just done my arms were threatening to give way. I clung to that rope and pulled with all of my strength. My lungs were on fire and I couldn't get enough air into me. But on I went, up and up until finally I dragged myself over the top and onto the metal platform. I yelled out my name for the PTI to record, and collapsed in a heap. I was spent, well and truly, and have never been as fatigued as I was at that moment. I sat there for a few minutes staring at the ground down below and retched as I struggled to catch my breath. There were others doing exactly the same thing as I on that platform, but I knew I had passed, and when the official times were announced after the last man was done it was merely a formality. I was nearly there and only had one last little walk to complete.

The next day we woke up very early at a small military camp on Dartmoor. This was where we would start the longest of the tests, and of all the tests this was the one people were most likely to fail. It was called the thirty-miler, and just like the name suggests we would be travelling thirty miles that day. Thirty kilometres would have been a challenge in its own right, but no, this was thirty *miles*. We would set out in sections to tackle this one, and in addition to the twenty-two pounds of webbing and the ten pounds of rifle we had carried on all of the other tests, we would also each take a backpack filled with warm kit, extra food, and light shelter just in case the weather turned very nasty very quickly and we had to stop wherever we stood. This was the ultimate test of endurance, and all of the thirty miles would be done over the rough terrain of Dartmoor. Many people failed this test because of injury. There were plenty of twisted ankles and wrenched knees to be had. Every five miles or so there would be a checkpoint where we would be able to have a drink and a snack: we would need every calorie we could get. A medic would also be present at every checkpoint to help out the lads and patch them up if he could, to keep them in the game. The section had eight hours in which to finish the test, and by first light we were lined up at the gates of the camp getting ready to go. We showed the training team that we all had the necessary safety stores, repacked it all, and with no fanfare set off into the early morning light.

The first mile was all uphill and we walked up the track at a fantastic pace. The strides were long and very quick, and after all the work my little legs had done in the last few days I was in agony after a few minutes. My calves were burning and starting to cramp up and I was afraid that if we kept up this pace the whole way I wouldn't be able to do it. But once we crested the first hill and broke out into a jog over the grass-covered flats, my legs began to warm up and feel a lot better. As with the nine-miler, we took flats and downhills at a run, and uphill terrain we walked at a brisk pace. A few miles into it we had found our groove and we carried on with little or no pain.

By the third checkpoint we were all starting to get tired and had a good crust of salt forming on our faces. My hands had begun to swell from swinging them down by my side for hours on end, and my feet were beginning to get sore. But my lungs and legs still felt strong, which was paramount; everything else was just a luxury. One of the members of the section had started to fall way behind and as we prepared to leave the checkpoint he came limping up. We only stopped for about four minutes and had to leave again before he had even had a chance to sit. We didn't expect to see him at the next checkpoint. The next time we eventually did see him was back on camp after the test. He had a broken foot and would have to heal up before he did all of the tests over again at a later date.

As the day wore on, Dartmoor wore on us. Mile after mile we ran over hills, up mountains, and through valleys. Hour after hour we kept up that crazy pace, and hour by hour we felt our strength slipping away from us. We were well into a serious epic, and it was taking its toll. At the late checkpoints we were all collapsing to the ground when we arrived and had to use every bit of strength to get off the ground again when it was time to move off. By mile 25 I was firmly planted in the hurt locker. The only thing that kept me going was visions of a green beret.

We had been going for well over six hours and were nearly there. It was amazing that some of the guys were thinking of calling it quits so close to the end, but they were. At some points we nearly had to push guys along and then, a few minutes later, they would be running as if they were fine. There were some intense inner battles being fought that day and our endurance and determination were being tested. I couldn't feel my legs any more as we got to within a quarter mile of the end, and even though we were so close I wasn't smiling. Nobody was. We were simply too fucked. As we came across the final stone bridge most of the training team was there, clapping for us as we crossed. The company commander was there, and some other people I didn't know had a few cameras out. When we had made it over the bridge we stopped running, and staggered over to a nice patch of grass, in a daze. We had finished the thirty-miler, and my body was aching. I slumped to the ground and lay on my back, staring up at the overcast sky with my chest heaving and feet burning. I couldn't believe it, but it was true. It was over.

With everything wrapping up at CTC there wasn't much to do other than finish some paperwork, pack up all of our kit for forwarding to our unit, and prepare for our final parade. We spent a lot of time marching around camp in our best uniform, our blues, and every night we polished our boots and brasses for the next day's inspection. My family was coming over to see me on the big day, and I couldn't wait to see Jennifer, who was travelling with them. I had hardly seen her at all in the last nine months. I had seen her for two weeks at Christmas when I had flown home, and for two weeks again at Easter. A total of four weeks together in nine months wasn't a whole lot and we missed each other tremendously.

Then the big day was finally upon us. It all started early for the troop. We had everything packed away that we were going to leave camp with. We'd left out two dress uniforms and a set of civilian clothes for the end of the day. The families had showed up in the morning, and the first time they would see us was when we were up on stage in our smart, dark green dress uniforms. The curtains parted and there we were, the whole troop on display and looking proud. One by one we marched out to the front of the stage to receive our green berets. From that point on we were entitled to wear the coveted green lid, and as the crowd cheered and clapped we marched off to go and get changed into our blues for the big parade.

The weather that day in May 2006 was perfect, and although we had practised an indoor routine in case of rain we wouldn't have to use it. All of our families were sitting on the bleachers when we marched onto the parade square. We headed out into the centre of the square in front of everybody and halted for our final inspection. This was the last time at CTC we would have to stand still for some high rank to wander up and down our ranks looking us over and asking us pointless questions, like "How are you enjoying training?" or "Where are you from?" We stood to attention with our rifles shouldered, scanning the bleachers for our families. I found my mother, my father, and my stepparents sitting with Jennifer. The inspection seemed to take forever, and as the feeling in our fingers drained away we wiggled our toes inside our boots and tensed all of our muscles to try and get a little blood flowing. With the inspection finished the troop closed rank, and as the band started to play we stepped off into our arms drill routine. We snaked around the place, broke into small groups, reformed into large groups, and flipped our rifles about for our families. Everything went as smoothly as could be, except for one moment when Tom's magazine slipped off his weapon and somebody kicked it as they marched past, sending it skidding across the pavement.

With the good part of the show over and our bayonets stowed away we formed up into three ranks to be formally marched off. The big moment was approaching. Nobody in the stands realized the significance of what was about to happen, but we recruits were boiling over with pride. All through training we had been referred to as "troop" or "recruits" when ordered around on the parade square, but this time would be a little different. As the adjutant of CTC took his place at the front of the troop with his sword drawn and held high, I heard the words I had longed to hear for all those horrible months. His voice thundered out across the parade square.

"ROYAL MARINES! To your duties! Quick march!"

PART 2

PAY ATTENTION

Overleaf: At another settlement in the "Desert of Death." We called this one "Star Wars."

CHAPTER 19

45 COMMANDO

As I rode the train north up the English coast my mind was racing. I was heading into the unknown again. Yes, CTC had been a terrible place, but it was familiar and we had mastered it. Just as I had reached the top rung of the ladder I had been cast back down to the bottom. I was off to join my unit and was totally unsure about what was awaiting me.

After the big parade back at CTC I had gotten a few days of leave and spent some time with my family and Jennifer. My parents left before Jennifer did and we were alone in the U.K. We travelled about on the trains and drank lots of wine as usual. She rode the train with me up to Scotland before I reported for duty, and as usual she shed a few tears when we had to part ways. The only difference this time was that it was she who was going to the airport to fly away.

I had been drafted to 45 (pronounced four-five) Commando, which was based in a small town called Arbroath on the southeast coast of Scotland. The camp was on an old World War II airfield and was obviously very flat. I showed up there on the Sunday evening the day before I was to report for duty and was given a place in the guardroom to sleep. Before long all of the other guys from my troop who had been drafted to 45 began to show up too, and of course Tom, the musical brick, was right there with me. Tom and I had started training together, been bricks together, got back-trooped together, and were now drafted to 45 together. There was definitely a pattern being set, and luckily for the two of us it continued along like that for the next eighteen months or so.

First thing in the morning we were all up and ironing like mad, intent on making a good first impression with our very first sergeant major in the Corps. We polished our boots and shaved with new blades before heading off to try and find the movements office in the maze of unfamiliar buildings. The camp was very empty as the unit had recently returned from a long exercise in Norway and was away for a few weeks of leave. There was the odd bootneck walking about, and even though we were all dressed the same as them and wearing the same beret it felt as if we stuck out like a bunch of sore thumbs. After everything we had been subjected to at CTC it just didn't seem possible that we would be able to rub shoulders with and eventually fight alongside seasoned old bootnecks. Eventually we found the office we were looking for and lined up outside the movement senior's office. When it was my turn I smartly stepped inside, stood to attention, and presented myself as we had always been taught. "I am Marine Olafsen, PO63754V, reporting for duty from CTC." Well, that was my intention anyway, but before I had even gotten halfway through my address the old sergeant major just waved his hand to signal there was no need for any of that crap. He asked my name, told me which company I was to report to, and gave me an accommodation key. I headed outside to wait for Tom, and as he came out we both found that we had been assigned to the same company, Zulu, and believe it or not we were going to be living in the same room as well.

Tom and I found our accommodation, which was in a different company's block. It was reserved for Zulu Company overflow and had nobody else living in it. We had a six-man living space for just the two of us, which was good, but even better was the fact that we would be off of the company's radar when it came time for weekly rounds. We picked our beds, dropped our bags onto them, and headed off to search for Zulu lines. We found them after wandering aimlessly about the empty camp for a while, and also the sergeant major we needed to report to. I started with the official introduction again but he wasn't too interested in any of that. For now we simply represented some paperwork for him and he got us straight into the process of officially joining the company. We were issued with some basic kit, like magazines and rifle slings, and then sent off to familiarize ourselves with the camp.

There really wasn't a whole lot for Tom and me to do for the next few weeks, as the program was at a standstill until the bulk of the unit got back from leave. Each morning Tom and I would report to our company and be sent away for most of the day to do some phys and keep out of sight.

The unit was going to be deploying to Afghanistan in late September and it was already the middle of May. We had a shitload of training that needed to be done between now and then, and I for one knew I needed some insight into where we were going and what we had to do when we got there. Pre-deployment training was to be the name of the game for the next few months, and I needed to focus. I was aching to get on with it.

CHAPTER 20

GET ON WITH IT

Once the unit was back and Zulu Company had reassembled we all settled in to camp life at 45. We spent our days working hard and our evenings playing hard. We drank a lot of beer in the grots (accommodation) at night and had barbecues in the courtyard. Tom and I were getting to know the lads in our new troop (yup, Tom and I were in the same troop too) but getting to know the whole company was a bit more tricky. There were around 120 guys in Zulu Company, and if there is one constant in the Corps, it is that you spend half of your time just trying to learn people's names. As with every troop I would ever eventually serve in, my nickname was soon established, and again it was simply "Canada." I would also find out that every Canadian in the Corps got the same nickname.

We explored our new surroundings, going for long runs to learn the area and attending many pub crawls in Arbroath. Arbroath had just one little nightclub and three or four decent pubs, which wasn't much to support an entire unit of bootnecks. On weekends most of

Yomping off into Dartmoor under heavy pack. Dartmoor is a huge area of high hills covered in wet, knee-deep grass and separated by marshlands. The troop would come to hate it.

My section during training getting comfortable under a rocky outcropping in Dartmoor.

Up on a mountain near Camp Bastion to get a look at our area of operations. My sniper friend, on the left here, was badly wounded shortly after at Jugroom Fort.

A large, well-marked mine field just off the main highway in Helmand Province.

Keeping in touch with Camp Bastion out in Dasht-e Margow (better known to us as the Desert of Death).

A desert patrol in our Wimiks mounting a .50-calibre heavy machine gun on top.

Tom and me shortly after arriving in the Garmsir DC.

Our section bedroom in the DC. The sandbags in the windows are to keep Taliban bullets out.

Viking armoured vehicles gathered in the Garmsir DC before we attacked Jugroom Fort.

One of my holes in the desert with my lucky flag proudly displayed.

My section, my GPMG (general purpose machine gun), and me after a night patrol south of the DC.

Our five-star restaurant in the DC.

A section of mortar men load up onto a Chinook for a daylight insertion.

It was nearly time for some R&R and I was tired of dealing with Taliban.

Playing with our new grenade machine gun at the Eastern Checkpoint.

Passing through Kandahar for R&R, this was the best iced cappuccino and Boston cream donut I have ever had.

Part of my section around a Wimik, with me in the driver's seat, before we head out on patrol.

The heavily armoured Mastiff truck I was in on MOG North.

The guts of MOG North getting ready to move out.

A typical scene at the barnyard mortar line.

My mortar pit at the barnyard, filled with plenty of high explosives.

A Chinook comes in to land inside FOB Gibraltar.

Me (bottom right) and my section at FOB Gibraltar.

Out on patrol near FOB Gibraltar with a crazy attack dog named Tsar.

A landing craft backs out of *Mounts Bay* to ferry troops ashore.

Mounts Bay with the stern down and a Merlin coming in to land.

A large landing craft on the beach in Cyprus.

My mortar set up on a beach in Turkey.

This dhow became our OP after we couldn't insert on the shore.

Chilling out on the Ganges on a cockroach-filled dhow.

the guys actually went home, and because 45 is based so far away from most people's homes we had a special schedule up there. Every Friday we were released by noon at the latest so that the lads had a chance to travel home that afternoon, and on Monday we never started work until noon so that nobody had to use up an entire Sunday trying to get back to work.

Throughout that summer the unit was very busy with our pre-deployment training. Every day on the news we were hearing stories about the stiff fighting that the Paras (Parachute Regiment) were encountering in the Helmand province of Afghanistan, and considering the fact that these were the guys we would be replacing in just a few short months we paid very close attention. The Paras were involved in gun battles with the Taliban on a near-daily basis and were paying the price by taking fairly heavy casualties. We constantly received intelligence briefs on the situation on the ground and it was obvious that we were going to have our work cut out for us. But for now we just had to pay attention to what we were being taught and take everything on board.

Pre-deployment training was very thorough and it made for long days throughout the week. The company received a lot of lectures on a whole range of subjects, from general Afghan culture and their history to basic language courses. These lessons were all taught by Afghans who had fled the Taliban and moved to the U.K. and were now on the payroll of the MOD (Ministry of Defence) to pump soldiers full of first-hand knowledge. We practised speaking basic Pashtu to each other and learned some very basic commands, like how to say "Stop," "Hands up," and "Don't move." These were obviously the most important, because if someone approached us we could at least get them to stop and chill until we could bring up an interpreter. We learned how to use interpreters effectively and practised speaking through them to Afghans. Most of the interpreters we would be working with had been royally screwed by the Taliban and hated them much more than any of us did. Most of them came from Kabul, the Afghan capital, which had always been a fairly liberal city where higher education was widespread and women could be employed as doctors and professors. The interpreters were mostly from well-off families and had learned to speak English in the universities. But when the Taliban rolled into Kabul in the early 1990s they and their educated families had been targeted. Many of their mothers were forced to quit their jobs because women weren't allowed to work outside the home in a Taliban utopia. Their fathers were murdered for being too bright, and the interpreters were beaten for being young men who wanted to wear jeans and tee-shirts. Many had been forced to cut all their hair off and publicly denounce those very things that they held dear. When enough was enough and an opportunity presented itself, many of these guys had fled to Pakistan with whatever family they had left, and now they were working for the MOD. I have since met many brave interpreters in Afghan, and it is nice to work with people who are as passionate about our cause as we are.

Specialists and engineers came to teach us about improvised explosive devices (IEDS) – things like roadside bombs, trip wires, and mines that the Taliban were deploying against friendly forces – and how we could try to counter the threats. Suicide bombers were a big problem where we were going and we had to know what signs to look for. Any advance warning, even if only a second or two, was better than none. Even women, children, and donkeys were exploding over in Afghanistan, and it would be very hard to avoid exposing ourselves to the risks. All we could do was try to minimize it. Roadside bombs and other IEDS were the larger threat, however, and were claiming far more lives than the suicide bombers. The Taliban were tricky with these and constantly coming up with new ways to trigger the explosions. They set these bombs off remotely or with long command wires, or sometimes with a combination of the two. They used lasers that shot across the street, like those on your automatic garage door that can sense when someone is beneath the door and will then stop shutting. Sometimes pressure sets off the devices, and there is a whole host of other possible triggers. Most of the bombs were anti-tank mines that they would often stack six or seven high and then supplement with a bunch of old artillery shells. The enemy adapted very quickly to any of our countermeasures and was importing knowledge and expertise from the Iraq insurgency.

We learned all about the enemy weapons and how to use them, how to identify coalition vehicles and aircraft, how to answer to and deal with the media, and how to set up a host of different vehicle checkpoints. Sometimes we set these up on foot patrols and other times we were dropped in by helo. We practised detaining individuals and preparing them for transport and interrogation. We practised urban navigation, kept our signalling skills up to speed, and learned about different radio reports that were in frequent use in theatre. We spent time at the ranges to ensure our weapons drills were on the ball and fired off thousands of rounds from all of the different guns we would be taking with us. We practised patrolling with NVGs and infra-red flashlights and lasers. It was a long and intense package, and as much as we complained about the lack of time off, I was happy to be getting the training.

Some of the most fun we had that summer was riot control train-ing. It was bootneck versus bootneck, no holds barred. Half of us would get into pads and helmets and line up out in the streets with the big plastic shields like you see on television. Then the other half would form up into a big rowdy crowd that was about to explode out of con-trol. Those of us in riot gear would have to try and control the crowd and make them move where and when we wanted. It was their job to resist and to aid their efforts they had huge piles of potatoes heaped up along the roadside that they could chuck at us. They also had real

Molotov cocktails to smash on the road at our feet. On our side, we had batons and a few attack dogs. The recipe for some good Marine carnage was written and all the ingredients laid out. From the word "Go" it was controlled chaos. That crowd would come into us, trying to kick the shit out of anyone they could pull away, and we in turn tried to beat them down with our batons. When things got a little out of control we would open up a path down the centre of us and the dog handler would come charging through with his German shepherd snarling and lashing out at anyone nearby, even us. We got pelted with potatoes and it fucking hurt sometimes. You would try and take them all on the shield of course, but the odd one would get you in the face or crotch. Tempers flared as we battled it out and it didn't take long for real blood to flow. As guys fell over and got knocked on the head the ambulance had to make an appearance. The riot was called off and all of the guys started to chat and have a good laugh about it. There were no hard feelings. There was no need. Tomorrow we would switch sides, we would be the rioters with the potatoes, and everything would be fine.

In the last few weeks before we flew I was made the RO for my troop (radio operator), and would double as a machine gunner with a GPMG. I would be carrying the radio for the troop boss and following him around wherever he went. It wasn't a bad job, other than the fact that you had to carry a radio. I would constantly be in the loop and know more than everybody else about what was really happening. I sought out the signallers and spent some extra time trying to get my head wrapped around all of the different radios and different antennas I would have to set up to try and get comms when out in the desert. Once we arrived in theatre we would be issued with different types of radios anyway, but for now I learned what I could about the kit we had.

We got our desert kit issued one day and from then on we wore desert camouflage instead of our normal green. There was a shitload of kit tinkering to do over the next few weeks and we all modified our new combat vests and webbing to our liking. I chopped off the three clips that did up our vest across the front and sewed on a big, heavy-duty zipper. The pouches were crap and never stayed closed so I sewed a bunch of Velcro all over it – nobody needs their magazines flying out all over the place as they run around. We started to break in our new boots, changed our helmet covers from green to desi (desert), and started the long process of packing for a six-month deployment. There was a shitload of paperwork to be done before we left. Sign for this, sign for that. Fill this in, fill that out. It was all done in fine military fashion: at a snail's pace and in total disarray.

Slowly but surely, however, things began to fall into place, and as the middle of September rolled around I was as ready as I was going to be. We all watched the news every night to see the Paras scrapping it out in dusty villages and living in dirty little holes in the ground. Place names were becoming known to us from the intelligence briefs, and they were starting to be mentioned on the news with more and more frequency. Sangin, Kajaki, Musa Qal'eh, Gareshk. The unit would become intimately familiar with these names, but for now we could only wait in suspense. These were exciting times.

CHAPTER 21

BASTION

CENTRAL HELMAND PROVINCE, SOUTHERN AFGHANISTAN
SEPTEMBER 26, 2006

I flew into Camp Bastion in the back of a Hercules transport aircraft and wasn't sure what to expect. The plane came in to land at a very steep angle, twisting and turning to make itself a hard target until the very last second, when it levelled out and hit the dirt runway with a bump. As we walked off the tail ramp the heat hit me in a dusty and dry wave. It was stifling and I could hardly breathe. We were told to hurry along because a dust storm was on the way. We could see this enormous wall of dust towering on the horizon, and within an hour the visibility was down to about twenty feet. The wind was blowing in every direction and sand was swirling about in great whirling tornados. All afternoon this went on, and we cowered in the tents listening to the racket outside, wondering if this was normal. Luckily, in the thirteen months I would eventually spend in that province, that turned out to be the only dust storm I would ever encounter. I guess it is fitting that it happened on the day that I arrived.

Before I left the U.K. I had grabbed my little Canadian flag that I had hung on the wall beside my bed and stuffed it into the front pocket of my combat shirt. I wanted to bring any little bit of luck that I could along with me, and I felt that a Canadian flag to hang wherever I went was certainly a good thing. That flag eventually became a part of me and was in my front pocket every time I went on patrol throughout the tours. It became filthy, sweat-stained, and tattered, like my uniform. Strange things happen when you get attached to simple things, and by the end of my time in Afghanistan I was convinced that it really had brought me good luck and I would refuse to go out the gates without it.

Zulu Company had been split in half as we deployed. Half had gone to Kabul to provide security on the large NATO base up there, and my half had been assigned to Force Protection at Camp Bastion. Within days we were calling ourselves the STG (Shit Tasking Group) and were foreseeing a long and boring tour.

Our two troops had been combined with some army platoons to form a company that was going to be in charge of security around Camp Bastion. Camp Bastion at the time was big, but nothing compared with what it is now. It was a massive square camp in the middle of the desert, well away from the Helmand River and any populated areas. Each side was about one and a half miles long, and the perimeter was made up of a large dirt pile and a shitload of barbed wire in front of it. Half of the camp was just empty wasteland, ready for future growth, and the other half was a sea of large, interconnecting tents. There were all sorts of helicopters based there, both supply and attack, and just outside the perimeter was a dirt runway carved into the desert that we had first landed on.

Our company tasking was threefold. First, we had to provide a small quick reaction force (QRF) in case anyone tried to attack the camp, which was exceptionally unlikely considering its location. In the five years it has existed (since 2005) Bastion has never once been seriously attacked that I know of. Next, we had to help provide manning for the sentry positions around the camp perimeter and help out with the front gate, checking vehicles that came and went and searching locally employed people. Finally, we had to patrol outside the camp to maintain a presence in the area and to keep any would-be attackers thinking that they might bump into a British patrol at any second.

When we found out what we were going to be doing we felt massively let down. Here were two troops of kick-ass Commandos being paired up with some random army reserve platoons to protect Camp Bastion while our bootneck brothers were getting in the shit up and down the province. We immediately began to fight for better jobs, but someone upstairs in the good ideas club felt Camp Bastion needed some bootnecks on board just in case the shit hit the fan. Looking back on it I suppose it makes a little bit of sense, but at the time we felt abandoned by Brigade. We complained up the chain of the command again and again to get re-tasked, but at the end of the day we were told to shut up and get on with the job.

The troop had been issued with a bunch of Wimiks for doing our patrols. These were stripped-down Land Rovers that were bristling with firepower. All of the sides and doors and the roof had been removed. The back had a big steel frame welded into it with a hand-cranked turret that we could mount a wide variety of weapon systems on. The guy riding shotgun also had a GPMG on a mount. We had ballistic panels that we strapped all over them to give some protection from small-arms fire, and attached ILAWs (84 mm rocket launchers) and grenades to every bit of leftover space. The back where the gunner stood was filled with radios, water bottles, and ammunition. Since I was the radio man for the troop I became the boss's driver and really enjoyed screaming about in the desert on a taxpayer-funded 4×4 session.

Our vehicles took a beating and we were always trying to strap more and more guns to them. I had a bit of experience working with metal and building brackets and things so I started wandering over to the bootneck workshops on camp and bugging the welders and armourers for favours and parts. There I found yet another Canadian in the Corps named Dolf. He was an armourer and had been in for a few more years than I had. He was from Ottawa and it was awesome to be able to chat about hockey in the middle of an Afghan desert sur-rounded by Brits. He was a Senators fan, but nobody is perfect. I went over to visit and chat with him when I could, and over the next few years I bumped into him all over the place, including in Malaysia and on a ship in the middle of the Indian Ocean.

We usually headed out in patrols of four or five vehicles and cruised around our desolate box. There were nomads walking about here and there with their camels and dogs, and the odd little cluster of abandoned buildings, but for the most part our area of operations (AO) was empty. Empty of people anyway, for there sure were a lot of minefields around. All up and down the thirty-kilometre stretch of Route 1 that ran through the AO there were massive minefields. Some of them were clearly marked and as large as several football fields, and others weren't marked at all. Any time we were travelling near Route 1 we had to be extra cautious. The locals had marked out some of the danger areas by painting little stones red but these weren't always easy to spot when you were driving along.

One day as we were cruising along I spotted a red stone beside me and hit the brakes. We stood up in our seats to get a better view of what was up ahead and sure enough there were little mounds all over the place to our front. We gingerly backed our way out of the danger area and boxed around it a few kilometres. It was dusk as we finally turned back in the direction we wanted to be going and after a few minutes the boss screamed out, "Stop Stop Stop!" I locked up the brakes, nearly toss-ing the top gunner right out of the vehicle. "What the fuck?" I shouted over, not sure what the hell was happening. "Mines," he said. "We just drove past a red rock. An old one, faded, but red for sure." Without moving the vehicle we began to scan the ground very carefully around us for any sign of the obvious. The boss stood up on the hood of the Wimik for a better look and that was when he spotted it. "Holy shit!" he exclaimed. "Gimme your camera!" He lay down on the hood and took a picture of something just in front of us. I crawled up beside him and had a look. What I saw sent a chill up my spine. About one metre in front of the front right wheel was a large, partially exposed mine. There was no doubt that we would have driven straight over it, and it was only by sheer chance that anyone had even spotted that little rock in the fading sun. As slowly as I possibly could, and half hanging out of the vehicle to see what I was doing, I backed out of that place taking care to keep my wheels in the tracks I had just made. Once clear we made a very large detour around that area and drove back slowly and carefully. We only had so much luck issued for each day.

These patrols were a good way to get familiar with our new surroundings and used to all of our new kit, but after a few weeks it was getting old. The other three troops of Zulu Company had since moved down from Kabul and were preparing to head south into a very active area called Garmsir. We were very jealous and were hoping to get attached to our old company. But in the meantime we just had to keep on our toes and train when we could. We spent a lot of time on the ranges just outside of Bastion and practised firing every weapon we had. Everything from pistols to .50-calibres. We became acquainted with the little 51 mm mortar and did section attacks up and down the ranges under the hot desert sun.

A week later the troop was patrolling along the edge of a canal in a well populated area and we were looking for a fight. We had been in theatre for six weeks already and hadn't seen any action. This was the first foot patrol we were on in an area where there were known to be Taliban and we were hoping they would have a pop at us. A lad from 45 Commando who was on a liaison team working with the ANA (Afghan National Army) had just been killed in the area by a suicide bomber and we all had a little revenge in mind.

I was carrying the radio for the troop and patrolling along near the troop boss. The locals were all around us but wisely keeping their distance. The whole point of the patrol was to reassure the locals and remind them that we were still a presence in the area, but what we were really looking for was a contact. The rest of 45 and 42 Commando were getting among it up and down the whole province and were in contact with the enemy daily, but so far for the STG it had been boring. The troop had been transported down from Camp Bastion in Vikings and dropped off a few kilometres from the canal. We had cut across the farmers' fields that were full of last year's opium poppy leftovers and were now heading northeast along the canal. It was hot out and I had on a ton of kit. The new body armour we had recently been issued was very heavy and very uncomfortable. It stopped bullets and would prove its ability to do that over and over again, but it made you overheat and slowed you down a lot. There is a fine balance between protection and mobility and I wasn't entirely convinced we had achieved it yet. The radio wasn't getting any lighter either as we patrolled along, but it didn't bother me because of what I could do with it. Apache gunships were just a call away, and the flying time from Bastion where they were based was a few minutes. But the enemy isn't stupid and they knew how quickly we could summon help.

The boss stopped along the way to talk to locals with our interpreter a few times, and when he did the troop fanned out to take up good defensive positions. Some guys went firm at the corners of buildings while others preferred to stay on their feet and keep moving to present a harder target. Each to their own. The locals all fed us the same bullshit that we had been getting from them for the last six weeks. Nope, no Taliban around here. We love the British. Can you bring us some water? And food? And ammunition? And can we have some vehicles and gas too? Of course we will tell you if we see any Taliban. No, we don't grow opium. It is someone else's farm. Over and over we heard the same crap. According to the locals there weren't any Taliban in the country, yet the Canadians, Americans, Aussies, Estonians, and Brits were fighting them daily.

We carried on with the patrol for a few more kilometres up the canal. I was constantly chatting to the Viking crews who had moved out of the built-up areas and were wondering when and where they would be returning to pick us up. The kids kept running up and asking us for candy and you really had to be careful around them. First, the odd one explodes, and second, they are mostly little thieves. They will claw at your watch and tug on your bootlaces if they get too close. Many soldiers over there have been mobbed by kids only to find later that their pouches on their webbing had been opened and things were missing. We were careful not to give the kids anything for a few reasons. If you handed out even one bit of candy you would be immediately mobbed and would have exposed yourself to attack. You would often cause more harm than good.

We were all on edge as we moved along that canal. There were plenty of areas on the opposite bank from which the enemy could fire on us, and the troop was doing its best to stay alert. The sweat was pouring into my eyes as we walked along and I wished we didn't have to wear our helmets. But I kept my rifle at the ready in my shoulder. I had been training and waiting for far too long to let my guard down. As we approached a bridge going across the canal I got on the net and let the Vikings know where we were and that we would need a pickup in five minutes. They began to move back into the area as we veered away from the canal and headed out between the compounds and into the fields to meet up with our ride home. As the Vikings pulled up next to the troop and the guys all piled in, the patrol came to an unexciting end. No contacts. No action. The STG was going back to Bastion.

Things picked up a bit as we started to get roped into convoy protection duties. There were a lot of convoys heading from Bastion to the giant airbase in Kandahar and they all needed a shitload of guns to try and keep the Taliban at bay. Suicide bombers were hitting nearly every convoy as they made their way through the city of Kandahar, and just east of Gareshk in our province was a stretch of road that was being called IED alley. This quaint little piece of highway was strewn with vehicles that had been attacked and destroyed and at the time was known as the most dangerous stretch of road in the world. The first time the troop sent some Wimiks as escort they got hit in Kandahar.

As they were making their way back through Kandahar city one of our Wimiks was targeted by a suicide bomber. He drove into them with his shitty little car loaded with explosives and blew himself up. The Wimik was tossed up and over a central meridian and our three guys were in a world of hurt. The two up front had shrapnel in their faces and struggled to get out of the vehicle to prepare for an armed assault. The guy that was up on top cover took the worst of it and got a large piece of shrapnel through his throat. It tore his larynx out and he was barely able to breathe as the Wimik that was following behind pulled up to offer assistance. They loaded up the wounded as the convoy disappeared into the crowded streets ahead, and went off to try and find a secure location. They made it to the nearest ANP base and called in a helicopter to get the guy with half a throat to Kandahar for treatment. Everyone survived, but they were lucky indeed. Canadian soldiers turned up very quickly to secure the blast site and upon inspecting the car that had exploded they found about a half dozen artillery shells that had failed to go off. Only a fraction of the explosive power in the car had actually worked and my three friends were only saved by Taliban incompetence.

That night when the last Wimik returned to Bastion we had to clean up the weapons of the guys that had been hit. They were all in hospital at Kandahar and wouldn't be coming back to the troop. The lads sealed off the bathrooms and for the next few hours washed blood out of their rifles and scraped bits of cartilage off of their kit. It was a sobering experience for me, knowing that these were little bits of my friends that I was washing down the sink. But the show had to go on, and the next week I found myself up on top of a Wimik heading through IED alley.

The convoy was a mix of British and Estonian vehicles. We were going to deliver some construction equipment to a drop-off point just north of Kandahar where a bunch of roadblocks were going to be constructed. We had a large fuel tanker with us to top up all of the vehicles at the other end and a few replacement trucks for the roadblock-building crews. Altogether, the convoy on the way out had about twenty-five vehicles in it. All of the larger vehicles stayed grouped tightly together in the centre with a screen of Wimiks around them, zipping about like bees protecting their nest. We had a pair of Lynx helicopters to escort us through the most dangerous areas, like the large town of Gareshk and IED alley. I was up on top of one of the Wimiks manning a big .50-calibre machine gun.

My convoy was lucky enough not to get hit by any IEDs or car bombs that day, and we had the added security of Whiskey Company being on the ground in Gareshk as we passed through, which certainly helped. There had been no action for me but I was content. I had gotten away from camp for a day, and roadside bombs were not the type of action I was looking for.

The rest of Zulu Company that had gone down south was clashing with the Taliban and starting to take casualties. One lad had been killed already and a number had been injured. They were starting to need BCRS (battle casualty replacements) and beginning to draw manpower from our troops up at Bastion. Any new guys that were coming from the U.K. were joining the troops on Bastion to fill the gaps created by us moving south. Nearly everybody wanted to go and join the company down in Garmsir, so every week we put our names in a hat to see who would get to go. In the middle of December my name was drawn from the hat and I was told to start packing my kit. The fighting troops had returned to Bastion to reorganize before heading south again, and with a farewell and a giant grin I moved across camp to join them. Tom, the musical brick, was over there and I was coincidentally put in his troop, his section, and given a bed in his tent. We were reunited once again and I was quickly brought up to speed by the guys on what I had been missing.

Tom had had a close call very early on in the tour. When they had first arrived in Kabul they went out on a patrol at night. As they were moving down a tight street someone had opened fire on them from straight ahead. A bullet had grazed his head, leaving just a little cut that required two stitches. He was a very lucky boy. Back in our grot in Scotland there was a third lad who had moved in that Tom and I had gone through training with. I learned that he had just been shot through the arm in a big contact the previous week while fighting next to a guy who was, tragically, killed by an American F-18. My friend was in hospital on Bastion and would soon be heading home. That meant two out of the three of us from our room had been shot. All of the guys reminded me of this on a daily basis, told me that I was from a cursed grot, and that I was certainly next on the list. It was all very reassuring as we prepared to move south again.

We were very busy throughout the closing days of 2006. I was the GPMG gunner for the section and went through a ton of link on the ranges. The engineers had recently built a large compound on the ranges, with huge sand-filled walls, for live-fire exercises. We practised clearing through the compounds with bullets zipping everywhere and lots of live grenades. It was all good fun but the purpose behind it was deadly serious. The next time we did this it would be for real. We attended many ramp ceremonies on Bastion, standing with our heads bowed in the crisp winter air as flag-draped coffins were loaded onto Hercules. These ceremonies were happening all too frequently. But there was little time to dwell on any of that. As we got closer and closer to the day that we would leave for Garmsir we tinkered with our kit to no end. We were issued with a tremendous amount of ammunition and I had never thought that I would be expected to pack so much weight. We had no idea how long we would be away from Bastion – a long time was all that they could tell us. There was no room in our bergens or webbing for the small comforts we would have normally liked to pack. I had a few tins of chewing tobacco and some small bottles of Crown Royal that were coming with me and that was it. Most of our warm clothing was left behind to make room for bullets and bombs, which was a shame because the weather had gotten much colder than I ever would have expected. There were light dustings of snow from time to time and there was plenty of freezing rain.

On the day that we were scheduled to fly we packed everything away for the last time and laughed and joked about in our rooms, tunes blaring as we worked. We were about to get stuck in the shit and we all knew it. There were endless bad guys where we were headed, and intelligence was telling us that we would be very busy. We packed the kit we were leaving behind nice and neat by our beds in case something happened to us, and some people wrote death letters that they handed to the sergeant major. I have to admit that I wrote one, but don't ask what was in it. That is just for me to know.

As darkness fell the troop started to get its kit on and put the massive bergens in neat rows so that we could grab them in the dark and make our way to the helicopters in order. I could not believe the kit I was going to carry. Between my GPMG, ammunition, grenades, 51 mm mortar bombs, webbing, body armour, and bergen, I had well over two hundred pounds strapped to me. All I could do was pray that we didn't have to go far once we got off the helos, and that there was nobody to shoot at me once I had my bergen on.

CHAPTER 22

GARMSIR 1

GARMSIR DISTRICT, SOUTHERN HELMAND PROVINCE
2350 HOURS
JANUARY 2, 2007

I was on board one of the two massive Chinooks carrying Zulu Company members and thundering towards the LZ in the dark. The helicopter's interior was lit only by low-powered red lights, and I strained to see out the windows. In between the rhythmic thumps of its huge rotor blades I could hear the other lads chambering rounds in their rifles, just as I was doing. We would be on the ground any second, and about one kilometre south of where we were going to land there was a scrap taking place. As the helicopter twisted and turned in the blackness at treetop height we caught glimpses of red tracer arcing off into the night from unknown and unseen positions. The crew told us to be prepared to get off the helicopter as fast as we could. We could be in for a hot reception and they didn't want to be on the ground any longer than they had to. I could hear my heart thumping along with the rotors as I clutched my GPMG. There was no way we were getting off this thing in a hurry once we hit the deck. We had too much kit to do anything quickly. Our bergens were piled up high down the centre of the helicopter and I could barely see the guys sitting across from me over the stack. We got the signal to be ready to move, and as the helicopter flared, the tips of the rotor blades lit up with millions of little sparks from the sand, creating two large, dim halos overhead.

The helicopter touched down heavily as the pilot forced it to the deck. The ramp was already down before we hit, and the crew immediately started heaving our bergens out the back and into the darkness. Our guys were helping to throw shit out of the Chinook, and slowly but surely we all started moving out the back. I stepped down off the ramp, grabbed a random bergen to get it out of the way, and got into a defensive position around the helo. As the last man stepped off into the deep dust the helo powered up and lifted off. We were in a hurricane of sand and dust as the Chinook gained height and banked away out over the river. The noise of the engines slowly disappeared as the sand settled down on top of us, and apart from the ongoing gun fight just to our south, everything became deathly quiet. Zulu Company had arrived and it was time to get a move on. Half the troop at a time, we found and struggled to get on our bergens. Mine was just too heavy for me to be swinging it up onto my back. I had to sit on the ground to feed my arms through the shoulder straps, roll over onto my hands and knees, and then, little by little, with every ounce of strength I had, I stood up. The company was ready to move off. We wanted to get away from the LZ as fast as we could, and with my gun slung I fell into the troop snake that was already disappearing into the darkness in the direction of the tracer.

The weight that I was carrying was crushing me. I could hardly breathe because of the pressure on my frame and I had no idea how far I would be able to go. But everyone else was carrying just as much as I, so until everyone else started falling over I was determined to

crack on. The company picked its way down between some compounds and moved into a series of small, walled streets typical of
Afghanistan. We had a guide with us that had come out from the compound we were going to help occupy, and to my relief we didn't have
far to go. The LZ was only about five hundred metres from our new
home, but it was more than enough to put me straight back into my
familiar corner of the hurt locker. As we crossed one final field I could
make out some sandbagged sentry positions up on top of some compound walls and knew we were there. We got into the compound and
grouped together in sections and troops to do head counts and make
sure everyone was where they were supposed to be.

We were only about four hundred metres north of where all the
shooting was taking place when we were pointed towards a corner of
the compound where we could drop our bergens. For the first time I
heard artillery fire being called in on targets, and as we gratefully took
off our kit and poked around, the sky was filled with the long, slow
whistle of friendly artillery shells. The loud explosions that followed
sounded reassuring because they were our guns firing. We were shown
a place to lay out our roll mats and sleeping bags and quickly given a
"Welcome to Garmsir" speech from the company commander, to the
background noise of automatic weapons firing and artillery crashing
away. My world had changed drastically in the last hour, and it was all
very exciting. There was little time, though, to just chill and take it in.
The boys on the sentry positions were seriously undermanned and had
watched us enter the DC (district centre) happily. We represented manpower and that meant that they would be able to get some sleep.
Sentry lists were quickly written up and straight away we were up on
the compound walls for quick briefs on the direction from which the
enemy usually shot at us and what sorts of assets we had to counter
any attacks. We couldn't make out too much in the darkness and
couldn't wait for first light when we would really be able to take in our

new surroundings. We had plenty of night vision capability, but you can still only see so much with that.

Through that first night we rotated through the sentry positions and listened to the show that started and stopped every hour or so. From up on the walls we could see the flashes and bursts from the artillery and could make out a large hump that our guys had obviously occupied and were firing from down onto the Taliban. Our job wasn't to stare at the action to the south, but it is hard to take your eyes off of it when you have only just arrived. For once I was actually doing something useful in a sentry position. There were real enemy around and they had attacked these positions on numerous occasions. Nothing else can make you take a sentry shift seriously quite like some bad guys creeping around with AK-47s and RPGs.

At first light we all got some breakfast on as we took in our surroundings. The DC we had occupied was about fifty metres square and had only recently been wrestled from the enemy. The bullet holes and bomb blasts all around attested to the intensity of the fighting. The walls were literally plastered with bullet holes from top to bottom and had much to be desired in the way of being properly defendable. The sentry positions up top were little more than a few sandbags piled up in front of you with no overhead cover yet. Much of the outer edge of the compound was lined with rooms that we were going to be living in and they all had doorways and windows that were still open to the outside. As we quickly learned, the odd bullet came zipping through those openings and all that first day we filled sandbags and stuffed them into the holes to offer some protection. The rooms were all up to a standard Afghan level of cleanliness. The floors were literally covered in several inches of old dried-out shit, and not all of it was from four-legged animals. We spent all morning clearing this away as we took turns filling sandbags and soon we had bare concrete floors to live on.

That afternoon we were taken out on a familiarization patrol to learn our way around the bazaars. For the most part the DC was plopped right on the front line that separated us from them. Facing south from the DC, the Helmand River ran along the right side. About two kilometres to the left was the canal I mentioned in the prologue, which ran parallel to the river, from north to south. Three hundred metres south of the DC was a main road that ran across the front, coming across the river on a large bridge and running straight across until it hit the canal and ended. That road was the front line. Everything north of it was relatively friendly. Everything south of it was enemy. It was all very simple. Along that two-kilometre stretch of road we had three checkpoints that all faced south over no man's land. The farthest one from the DC was at the junction of the canal and the road and called Eastern Checkpoint. We had a Central Checkpoint midway, and farthest west and next to the river was the hilltop position that we had seen all the action coming from the night before. This was known as J-TAC hill (joint tactical air controller) and offered a dominating view of no man's land to the south. The ANP had a small checkpoint at the near end of the bridge and helped to man J-TAC hill. Before we had arrived in the area J-TAC had changed hands several times between the ANP and the Taliban. A lot of blood had been spilled on that hill for its strategic and observation value.

The area north of the crossroad was filled with streets of markets and bazaars and used to be a bustling place. But now there was nothing – the odd person could be seen trying to salvage something from an abandoned shop but that was about it. There was a small ANP station in the area and a few families still farmed a kilometre north of the markets, but for the most part the people had been driven away by war. We threaded our way east through these abandoned streets, heading for the Eastern Checkpoint. A few hundred metres from the checkpoint the buildings stopped and there was open ground to cover, so as we came out from behind the buildings we separated ourselves and jogged, trying to keep ourselves as low as possible. We were within a few hundred metres of Taliban now and the only things between us were some open fields. The checkpoint was about fifty feet from the canal and was made up of three small single-storey buildings. On top of each building was a small pile of sandbags that our sentries could lie down in, and around the back there were ladders up to the buildings' roofs.

We scurried across to the back of the buildings and crouched down. Our guide told us this checkpoint took fire from the south and the east and from northeast across the canal. In pairs we crawled up the rickety ladders and slithered up behind the sandbags to have a look at the situation. Our guide pointed out various compounds that the Taliban occupied and showed us firing positions that they frequently used. Some of the places they shot from were no more than one hundred metres from our position, and the guide told us that they fired at it daily. Immediately south of the checkpoint was a large cotton field stretching back to a treeline and a system of irrigation ditches, behind which were some compounds obscured by the trees. Across the canal to the southeast, about one kilometre away, were some large compounds that we would later get to know very well. They were called Vodka and Strongbow.

Once we had our bearings we headed back down the ladder and went west to the Central Checkpoint. This was also up on top of a building and provided overwatch across much of the open fields that separated us from them. It really was a no man's land to our front, and anything that moved out there was enemy. This location also took fire daily and sent a lot back in return. We continued on our front-line tour and headed over to J-TAC hill. This was a prominent little knoll that sprang up out of the surrounding flat terrain. It was about eighty feet high and a couple of hundred feet across the base. The dirt track that led up to the crest was exposed to the enemy and we had to hustle to get up there. There was a series of bunkers dug into the face of the hill and these were used for sleeping in and storing kit. There were a few sandbagged firing positions along the top, and like the other two checkpoints, it looked out over no man's land. There were far more compounds just to the south of this one that the baddies constantly used as cover for launching attacks against the hill. All of the compounds had names for quick reference: Frog Eyes, Four Cigars, Lone Tree, Spindly Tree, Gold, Bronze, and Platinum. The Taliban had tunnels dug in among these compounds and could move up to their many firing positions with near impunity: many of these were only two hundred metres away. These tunnels and holes offered great protection, and unless an artillery shell or bomb fell right into their holes, they could often survive bombardments. It was into this warren of activity that the artillery had been firing the previous night.

We headed back north to the DC after we had seen enough to take over the sentry duties so that other members of the company could head off on the same tour we had just had. Within minutes of our leaving J-TAC the enemy started to throw some mortar bombs and a few high-angle RPGs up our way. J-TAC started to fire into the Taliban firing points and we hustled on to get behind the walls of the DC. They had obviously seen us leaving J-TAC and wanted to catch us out in the open. Some of the bombs landed within fifty metres of us, but other than that it was a weak attack. But it was very thoughtful of them to remind us that they were still there. Around dinner time they decided to remind us again. They probably were aware that a new company was in town and wanted to inflict some early casualties on us. A number of large 107 mm Chinese rockets, mortars, and RPGs were sent over towards the DC but luckily none of them landed in the walls. The nearest hit was about twenty metres outside the DC.

We rotated through the sentry for a few hours and then my section was off to man the Central Checkpoint for the evening. We gathered up all of our kit, a bunch of extra ammunition and food, and headed off into the fading light. It was about eight hundred metres to get to the checkpoint and we arrived in good time. We took over from the other guys moments after there had been a quick RPG attack on them. We settled into a routine, taking turns observing no man's land with our thermal sights and NVGs. We had boxes of parachute flares that we could send up whenever we wanted to light the area, and if we really needed a good light show there was an 81 mm mortar line set up beside the DC that could illuminate an entire square kilometre.

Shortly before midnight the Taliban started to fire on Eastern Checkpoint off to our left and a little battle flared up. Our guys answered the call of the RPGs with machine gun fire and a few ILAWs (84 mm anti-armour weapon). Soon mortars were called to help out and explosions were echoing across the valley, ensuring nobody was getting any sleep. As that was all happening J-TAC off to our right started to get contacted too. They had a FOO with them (forward observation officer) who could call in the artillery, and he started to do just that. The gun line was about ten kilometres out into the desert and the rounds took over a minute to reach in front of us. You could hear the distant bang of the guns firing long before the low whistle of the incoming rounds, and then CRASH! The shells would strike with enormous ferocity, lighting up the night with brilliant flashes. Mixed into this was a constant stream of red tracer heading south both to our left and our right. RPGs were arcing from out of the darkness to both sides. Two out of three checkpoints had just been hit and we all expected to catch it up any second. Everybody was up and ready to fight. We heard over the radio that we had an F-16 in the area that had some weight to shed, and a moment later we could hear its powerful engine circling overhead looking for a target. I was standing behind my gun with a long belt of ammunition draped down my left side. I glanced at my watch and noticed it had just gone past midnight. My first full day in Garmsir was over. This is what I had come to Afghanistan for, and I was ecstatic.

CHAPTER 23

GARMSIR 2

0100 HOURS
JANUARY 6, 2007

The troop silently crept south along the river past J-TAC hill. The air was still and although it was well below zero we were already sweating heavily. We had to drink from our Camel-Baks constantly to keep the drinking tubes from freezing solid but the extra weight we were carrying kept the cold out of our bodies. We had our backpacks on and they were filled to the brim with plastic explosives and massive anti-tank mines. The sky was clear and we had all applied cam cream to keep the shine down on our sweating faces. I was in the middle of the slowly moving troop snake and had brought my GPMG and a thousand rounds for it. With its weight added to that of the explosives I realized I was carrying too much link, but it was too late to ditch any kit now. We had crossed the line and were moving into the Taliban's playground.

Tonight we were escorting four assault engineers to the enemy's best firing positions so that they could dismantle their cover. The troop methodically pushed on down along the riverbank for another one hundred metres, constantly scanning for any sign of the enemy with our NVGs. Our point man had a thermal sight on his rifle and would have a good chance of seeing any heat sources out to a great distance. But the area near the river was criss-crossed with drainage and irrigation ditches, waist-high grasses, and low dirt banks. It was possible we could walk right up on the enemy before we knew they were there, and this was an area where the Taliban often posted their own sentries. We had comms with the lads up on J-TAC hill and they were covering our patrol with all of the tools of the trade: Javelin heat-seeking missiles, machine guns, mortars and artillery. If the baddies wanted a scrap we would be more than happy to accommodate them tonight. As we passed our first checkpoint we turned east and pushed up a path away from the river. We were quickly in among the compounds that the Taliban used as cover from J-TAC and had to focus completely on the task at hand. It was likely there were booby traps and mines laid for us, and every small room and doorway that we passed had to be checked and cleared before we could move on. We passed though the first large compound and turned south again, pushing deeper into Taliban territory.

Across the vast majority of the Helmand province the British forces were operating on an ROE (rules of engagement) called Card Alpha. This ROE allowed you to protect yourself and others with lethal force if you believed that there was an imminent threat to human life. Loosely translated, it meant that you couldn't fire unless fired upon. But down here in the area we were in, things were a little bit different. We were pushing into a large box from which all of the civilians had fled long ago. This was a huge area where "429" reigned supreme. 429 was a much more robust ROE that allowed us to fire on virtually anything that moved. 429 said that we could fire into likely enemy positions and assured us that there were only enemy forces here. The enemy were deemed to be irreconcilable, which left us with only two options when we were dealing with them: kill them or capture them. Negotiation was out of the question.

As we moved south we heard from our big brothers up on J-TAC that we had enemy moving just to the south of us in the next cluster of compounds. We weren't sure if they had seen us or not, but we moved on with extra caution and focus. This was no longer a game. Training was over and we were getting paid to do the job for real. We pushed on towards the next compounds and the point man looked in for any heat sources. Everything seemed to be clear and we carried on as before. Scanning, looking, sweating. I wanted to watch my feet the whole time to see what I was about to step on, but at the same time I had to keep looking for the enemy. I tried to make myself as light as I possibly could and to only tread in my friends' footprints. The lead section made it to the target compound and quickly ensured it was clear of enemy. The troop slowly and silently moved out among the ruins to set up a defensive perimeter and I pushed up to the front to get my machine gun where it was needed. We created a ring of steel and set the engineers free to do their thing.

It was easy to spot the Taliban's favourite spots. They had blankets on the ground so it was more comfortable to sit there and brass casings were spread all about. There was one wall in particular that the engineers would be removing this evening, and it was big. The wall was about thirty feet long and seven feet tall. At each end it was about a foot thick, but it got fatter towards the centre, and as we would be able to tell from the ruins, it was nearly four feet thick in the middle. Anyone who has been out to Afghanistan will agree with me that the mud walls of those compounds are a lot tougher than you expect. It takes a lot of explosives to completely knock one down. A little further south from where we were there was a very small building that was only about 50 per cent damaged, even though it was perched right on the edge of a twenty-foot-wide, ten-foot-deep crater that had to have been made by at least a 1,000-pound bomb. This was exactly why every one of us had a backpack full of explosives.

The engineers moved around that wall setting up charges and spooling out det cord. They were working quickly and professionally, setting it up to be detonated remotely. In no time at all they were propping the last of the charges in place with lengths of wood they had brought with them. We all kept an eye out for any sign of enemy movement, and luckily it seemed that nothing was moving our way. J-TAC was giving us the all clear as well. The last thing we needed in our little area was a shitload of tracer bullets whipping around. We were sitting next to 240 sticks of C4, eight bar mines, and a mountain of det cord, all of which was primed and ready to go. The engineers gave us the signal that it was time to move. "Okay, lads, unless you want to be fucking vaporized, we suggest you piss off."

The troop began to peel out of the compound we were in and hustle back the way we had come. If the engineers were hauling ass north, we all had every intention of keeping up with them. We could go much faster now as we were fairly certain that no baddies had snuck in between us and J-TAC. We went for about one hundred metres and took cover behind another large compound wall. Once we had all done a quick head count, the engineers got on the radio. They told HQ it was about to go down, and a second later the Earth heaved. The explosion sounded as if the sky was being torn apart and the air around us shifted heavily, sucking the air from my lungs. We were all facing away from the blast, and in the clear night sky I could see the flash travel the whole depth of it, from directly overhead all the way to the horizon. We were much closer to a blast of that size than is recommended by any safety standards, but I wouldn't have changed it for the world. The debris started to rain down on us and we were all soon coated in dust and dime-size pieces of dried mud. Obviously there was no need to go back and see if everything had gone according to plan.

The engineers were well pleased with themselves. There is nothing they like better than blowing shit up.

We all got back onto the riverside track and hauled ass up to the safety of our own lines, moving easily with empty backpacks. As the lead section began to pass by the base of J-TAC hill, the boys up top began to engage targets only two hundred metres to our south. As we had moved off, the Taliban had immediately begun to follow us up. With luck some of them had even been caught up in the blast as they followed our trail. Whether that was the case or not, I guarantee that explosion scared the shit out of them, because they couldn't have been very far from it. With J-TAC covering our withdrawal we carried right on past them, past the ANP checkpoint at the end of the bridge and on to the DC. The Taliban were always up for a scrap, and J-TAC was well equipped to deal with it. Before they were finished answering the Taliban's RPG call, they had retaliated with Javelin missiles, machine guns, and artillery. We always carried a much bigger stick than they did and were smacking the baddies with it in the exact compounds that we had been sitting in only moments before. And now there was one less wall for them to cower behind.

0030 HOURS
JANUARY 10

The troop was cammed out again and pushing south from the Eastern Checkpoint. We were under clear skies with millions of stars visible. There was no moon and it was very dark, just the way we liked it. All of the troops took turns each night to push down south into bad guy territory and do some damage. Sometimes two troops would push south, and sometimes even the whole company, but usually we left guys behind to man the three checkpoints and help out on the sentry routine back at the DC. Tonight it was our turn to form a fighting patrol, and we had a good task. We were going to push down into the Taliban compounds, draw them into a fight, and then quickly withdraw. As they fired on us while we made our getaway we would have a massive B1 bomber circling 20,000 feet overhead, and once we were clear of the baddies they would be on the receiving end of a few 2,000-pound bombs. It was a good system and worked well to kill the enemy while keeping our exposure to a minimum.

We pushed south under the guns and missiles of the checkpoint along the sunken track beside the canal. We were well spaced out to avoid many casualties from any one explosion and were staggered down both sides of the track. As we pushed beyond the treeline and neared the compounds we were heading for, the lads on the checkpoint let us know that they would have trouble keeping an effective overwatch from here on in. We acknowledged and continued on our way. There were deep ditches all around that were half full of water and plenty of other hiding places for Taliban to be lurking in. Smashed compounds provided ideal cover.

We carefully and quietly cleared each compound we passed and spaced out sentries to maintain a protective screen facing south. Our job was to continue pushing on west until we reached a large compound that had a high tower in one corner of it. This tower had been shelled by our artillery many times in the past but had never been brought down. We suspected the Taliban were still able to use it as an observation post, and the big boy circling up overhead was going to bring it down. But we didn't want to waste such a heavy piece of ordnance on just any tower. We wanted to use that bomb on a tower that was filled with Taliban. As we approached the target compound we heard reports from Eastern Checkpoint that there were definitely heat sources moving around the area, and we fingered our safety catches as we went firm in the shadows along the track. I was sweating heavily again as I always did when carrying one hundred pounds of gun and link. The cam cream came off with my sweat and rolled into my eyes in brown, green, and black drops and it stung. For any boot-neck it was a familiar feeling, but one that you never got used to.

The lead section began to move forward again, faster now and with a new purpose. They wanted to draw some fire and start a fight. We needed the Taliban to crawl out of their holes and expose themselves. As the point section moved towards the compound the rest of us pushed up to support them. The other gunners and I moved off to a flank to get in a good firing position with a clear line of sight. Our guys up front announced our arrival by sending a flurry of ILAWs slamming into the compound walls and through the compound doors. Then our guys hurled 40 mm underslung bombs into the compound, and we began to let rip with the guns. Bad guys began to pop their heads up here and there and fire with wild bursts from their AKS. From the south and south-west we could see distant muzzle flashes that were sure to get closer and closer as they moved up to meet the challenge. The troop were anxious to use up all of their rockets so they didn't have to carry them back, and all around were the ear-splitting WHOOMPS! and sharp vacuums that sig-nalled someone had pulled the trigger on 84 mm of rocket-propelled kick-ass. A fraction of a second later the air was split with a massive BOOM! as a warhead struck home. RPGs began to sail through the night towards our positions and explode in the fields and ditches around us. Shrapnel was whistling and whining through the air around us as we stitched the tops of the walls with tracer. The Taliban that were brave (or stupid) enough to expose themselves for even a second were instantly painted with a dozen infrared lasers, guiding everyone else onto the target. It was like a game at an amusement park, with targets popping up at close range and disappearing just as quickly. The lads we had spaced out along the track were helping to suppress and hold up the targets that were advancing from the south and there was no doubt that the second we left, this area would be crawling with baddies. That was exactly what we wanted.

The troop knew it was time to get out of there. Not that we couldn't have taken them on, but there was a B1 bomber circling overhead, fully loaded with heavy bombs and with pilots who had probably been airborne for at least eight hours. If they had itchy trigger fingers and were dying to get back to their distant base, I didn't want to be standing around in their shooting range any more. Most of the troop began to peel out of the contact area, with the rest of us giving covering fire as the lads nearest the enemy ran back through our positions. The guns were among the last to move because we could put down the heaviest weight of fire, and as I got up to move I realized that my webbing was much lighter than when I had arrived. The barrel of my gun was smoking hot and smelling of burnt oil. When I was moving after some action it was a constant battle to keep from accidentally touching it.

One by one and section by section we moved back the way we had come and the incoming fire dropped in intensity as they continued to fire at our old positions. There was no requirement to patrol slowly any more, and we moved quickly to make room for the big show. Our rear guard and their GPMG maintained a weight of fire when it was needed as we moved, and much faster than the Taliban would have expected we were nearing the checkpoint. The guns up on the roof were firing over our heads with long streams of tracer as we moved into cover behind the buildings. As always, the last thing we did was a quick head count to make sure we were all out of the kill zone, and then we made the call. The Taliban were crowded around that compound, still sending the odd RPG our way and probably congratulating themselves on the great victory they had just achieved repelling the British invader. Little did they know the climax was yet to be played out.

We let HQ know that the B1 was free to unload, and in return we heard that the eyes in the sky were watching the Taliban collect at least three dead or wounded guys from around the compound and move them towards the tower. This tower was exactly what the bombardier would have his cross hairs focused on. About a minute later we heard the standard "Splash three zero" message, and a few seconds later we heard the freight train approaching. It starts quiet, like a distant, rumbling train, but gets very loud until it sounds like thunder directly overhead. The unusual thing is that the transition from quiet to loud only takes about a tenth of a second. Before you even realize that you are hearing something approaching, it has hit and the detonation takes over your senses completely. BOOM! The sky lights up in every direction, and a sparkling mushroom cloud instantly climbs hundreds of feet into the sky. There is a shower of sparks and red-hot shrapnel that bursts out from the impact like a violent volcano. It is an awesome spectacle, and that night, immediately after the first bomb hit, we were lucky enough to hear over the radio for the second time "Splash three zero." The show was repeated for us, and the sounds and shock wave that hit us in the face was just as awesome as it was the first time. There were smiles all around as this was one of those few times when civvies literally would pay thousands to be there with us. Two more times in the next few minutes we watched smaller 1,000-pound bombs do their best to outclass their bigger brothers. Sadly, after that, it was the end of the bombing mission.

As we patrolled back to the DC all was quiet to our south. It seems the Taliban hadn't enjoyed the end of the evening's show nearly as much as we had. We got into the DC, got some tea on the go, and settled down to clean our guns, still wide awake with our veins pulsing full of adrenalin. Nobody had even gotten a scratch and we had been in a decent gun fight. This was exactly the way things were supposed to go. Well planned, well trained, and well armed hit-and-run operations.

We got the rest of the morning off so that we could catch up on some sleep, and were happy to learn when we were up for lunch later that day that the observation tower was no longer a part of the landscape. The B1 had reported that the base of the tower was surrounded by enemy when the first bomb hit the bull's eye. Overall it was a well-executed mission that resulted in many enemy killed, and we were happy to learn that there were many more opportunities in the pipeline.

CHAPTER 24

JUGROOM FORT 1

DASHT-E MARGOW (DESERT OF DEATH)
0600 HOURS
JANUARY 14, 2007

woke up in a hole in the desert with the early morning sun in my eyes. The ground was lumpy and full of stones beneath me and my body was aching. For the last few weeks I had been sleeping on a concrete floor, and now this. I sat up in the cold morning air and could see other people's breath coming up from other holes dotted around mine. A few people were milling about their vehicles, smoking and drinking tea, while others climbed from the back of the Vikings, rubbing their eyes after another shitty sleep. It was a lot easier to just sleep in the vehicles with no digging required, but I figured I had more room and felt safe in my hole. I had a nice little drainage ditch full of rocks at the base, which had helped to ensure it didn't even rain, and a wall of sandbags around the forward edge to protect me and my gun. The sandbags also helped to break the biting wind that swept across the desert, completely un-hindered. The locals called this part of southern Helmand the Desert of

Death, and for good reason. If you were ever lost out here on your own, you wouldn't last long. There was nothing around for miles and miles, and if you headed west you would be alone all the way to Iran. It froze all winter out here and baked in the summer. There was the odd gentle dip or fold in the ground, and the great expanse was covered in small flat pebbles. But other than that, there was emptiness.

We had driven out here the day before in preparation for a large-scale raid that we were going to be carrying out that night. We had packed up all of our kit at the DC and brought it with us, not knowing how long we would be out in the desert. We had grabbed as much ammunition as we could possibly carry, and then stuffed a bunch more into every nook and cranny of our Viking. The entire company had loaded up onto a dozen Vikings and gone tearing off from Garmsir into the desert to the west of the river, with a number of Wimiks in support. It was not a very comfortable ride for those of us stuffed in the back. We were all massive with our body armour and webbing on, and then when we crammed all of our daysacks, weapons, guns, ILAWs, food, water, and boxes of ammunition inside with us it became ridiculous. Our knees were up around our chins and there was no hope of moving about to get some blood flow. Every time we got out for a piss break or anything, half of the lads nearly collapsed as they jumped down onto legs that were fast asleep. It was smoky and hard to breathe in there. Sometimes we could open up the hatch to get some fresh air, but this only forced a constant flow of choking dust into the cab and into our lungs. You could barely talk to each other when you were moving because of the roaring tracks beneath you, and with only the one little dirty window at the back you had no idea where you were. Long periods in the back of one of those were a nightmare, and over the next few days we would end up spending more time in than out of them.

We had driven out of the DC and across the bridge, and headed straight through farmers' fields to get into the open desert and off of the mined tracks. For mile after mile we had meandered up and down the edges of the valley and through the wadis leading up out of it before finally breaking into the open desert. The armed convoy tore across the gravelly plain, cutting across random tire tracks and leaving an enormous cloud of billowing dust in our wake. Our destination was about twelve miles out into the wasteland, southwest of the DC. We were aiming for the gun line, and would set up shop next to the big 105 mm howitzers that we used to lob shells in support of our ops in Garmsir.

As we choked on the dust and the cab filled with smoke we arrived at the gun line and piled out onto weak legs. We gingerly limped about on pins and needles and looked at our new surroundings. There wasn't much to see. Four guns were lined out facing back towards the east with their crews milling about their large piles of ammunition. There were a number of supply trucks, a fuel tanker, and a front-end loader that was beginning to construct a large dirt wall that would eventually surround the area. The Light Dragoons were also here with their armoured reconnaissance vehicles facing outwards all around. These vehicles were called Scimitars, resembled small tanks, and had a crew of three. They were armed with a machine gun and a 30 mm chain gun and could move quickly.

The company Vikings had formed up into parallel troop lines with about thirty metres between each line. Everything was organized this way so that if vehicles had to move abruptly in the night they could follow set paths without running over sleeping bootnecks. We were told to start digging shell scrapes (fox holes) next to our vehicles and so spent the next few hours hacking away at the tough ground. This was not a nice sandy desert that we were in, and digging a hole was anything but easy. A pick had to be used for much of it, but at least with solid ground the sides of your hole tended to stay fairly square. We had the whole afternoon to chill out and get comfortable in the dirt and we sat about laughing and joking. I took my beloved Canadian flag from my front pocket and decorated my nice hole with it. It looked fantastic there against the sandbags and I always felt proud to have it on display. It was nice to be able to relax a bit after the high tempo we had been working at for the last couple of weeks. We had been under fire every single day since we had flown down from Bastion, and a day off was appreciated by all. As it got dark we pulled on what warm clothing we had and settled into our holes to catch a bit of sleep in between the inevitable sentry shifts.

And now, with our breath clearly visible in the morning, we clustered around the vehicles and stamped our feet to get a little blood flowing. We got our cookers fired up and the water on, speculating all the while on what our big task was going to be. We suspected it was going to be a long day, and in this we were right: it would prove to be one of the longest of my life. For a bunch of the lads it would be their last day in Zulu Company, and for one guy it would be his last day alive.

Throughout the morning the officers and stripeys were all over at HQ, huddled around maps and taking notes on what the company commander (OC) was telling them. They were getting a rough idea of what our job was going to be, and just before lunch the whole company received a formal set of orders. We stood or sat on the ground in troops and sections, with our atts and dets (attachments and detachments) in groups among us. There were a lot of people involved besides Zulu Company. There were all of the Vikings with us, BRF (Brigade Recce Force), the Light Dragoons in their Scimitars, the artillery, B1 bombers, A-10 ground attack aircraft, F-16s, Apache attack helicopters, and a British Nimrod surveillance plane that would record all of the action from above. It was a fine ensemble of firepower, and we were anxious to find out exactly what it all would be aimed at.

The target was a massive compound complex that had fifteen-foot walls around it with towers and defensive positions built into the walls.

It was an ancient fort on the eastern side of the river. The outer walls of the fort were about 250 metres back from the riverbank, with a low, flat flood plain separating the two. The fort had been under aerial surveillance for a long time and was a hive of Taliban activity. It was heavily defended in an area that had been virtually untouched by the current conflict. Taliban ruled supreme in the fort and in the surrounding areas to the north, south, and east. Cultivated areas, treelines, and ditches swept away from the walls in most directions with a large system of compounds one hundred metres to the north. Up until now the Taliban had used this place as a base of operations, unmolested and uncontested. It was believed that much of the activity we were seeing five miles to the north near the Garmsir district stemmed from this area, and most of the fighters moving north into Helmand from Pakistan had to pass through this bottleneck. It was going to be our job to smack them around a bit and show them that we could reach out and touch them where they felt the safest.

There were multiple phases to the pending attack, and tagged on the end of a very detailed set of orders was the possible Phase 4. In a sentence or two the oc told the company group that if conditions were favourable we might breach the fort and shoot up the place, but because the orders for Phase 4 were virtually non-existent we suspected it would never happen. Nobody would throw an entire company of bootnecks into a very complex attack, against a well-organized, well-armed, and dug-in enemy, across an obstacle as formidable as the Helmand River without a proper set of orders. At least that's what we thought.

After orders were finished we all headed back to our troop areas and prepared for the task at hand. The plan as we understood it, excluding Phase 4, was simple enough, and with this in mind we got our kit on and jumped into the Vikings to head off for rehearsals. All of the Vikings, with the whole company on board, went thundering off into the desert in our order of march. The oc had his way with us all afternoon, getting us in and out of the Vikings over and over again. We practised piling out and shooting our way out of ambushes like we had done in training, and then piling back in just as fast. The company went through the motions of how they would drop off certain elements along the way, and certain troops peeled off in order to occupy different positions. There were a lot of moving parts to this one, and any practice the HQ could get at moving us around in an orderly fashion was time well spent. With rehearsals finished, we headed back to the gun line to get some food down our necks and tinker with our kit. I went through every bit of link that I had, checking each bullet for damage, adding as many tracer rounds as I could to the belt and ensuring they were all properly seated in the link. I folded it all away nice and neat in my webbing and double-checked my personal medical kit. There wasn't much to it, just a few field dressings, a tourniquet, some ibuprofen, and a bunch of morphine. I filled my Camel-Bak, put a few fresh IR glow sticks in my pocket, fresh batteries in my personal radio and NVGS, and cleaned my gun again. The gun felt reassuring, ready to go with a heavy dose of oil and all of the working parts sliding smoothly and easily. I admired it as I put the end of a link of bullets into the gun and slammed home the top cover. Sweet.

The last thing I had to do was strip the Canadian flag from the side of my hole and stuff it back into its pocket over my left breast. There was no way I was going out on this patrol without my lucky flag. With my battle prep finished and a meal in my belly there was nothing left to do but sit and chat with the troop. At last light we all began to mount up in our Vikings, and as we moved off towards the assembly area, the Light Dragoons headed south to their own firing point.

We arrived at the assembly area a short while later after it had turned completely dark. We moved at night so that any Taliban who might have been watching our dust clouds and reporting on where we were headed would have lost sight of us. We had a few hours to wait before we were going to head off again, so we all got as comfortable as we possibly could in the cramped vehicle and tried to nod off. Most of us were having trouble sleeping with the anticipation of a large fight and just chatted about home and what we would do when we finally got back to the real world. We fantasized about seeing our girlfriends and heading down to the local pub for a beer. Many of us had vacations planned and some had children that they were going to be seeing for the very first time. I just thought of getting home to Vancouver Island and how I was going to do as little as possible when I got there.

We were waiting to coordinate our attack with a diversion that elements of 42 Commando were going to be delivering a few miles to the north. They would be moving south from the Garmsir DC and clearing through a few large compounds with 81 mm mortars in support. We wanted to move into position as their attack was going in, so that by the time we unleashed our fury many of the Taliban would have already been drawn into the open and be on their way north to meet the diversionary attack. At around midnight, with our legs fast asleep and our bodies sore from being stuck in the Viking for nearly five hours, we headed off to our position.

The plan was very similar to what we had done with the B1 bomber on the tower four days earlier, but on a much larger scale. The company group was going to push up towards the fort without crossing the river. While this was happening, the B1 upstairs would drop some heavy ordnance on the fort to make the Taliban think that they were softening it up for an actual assault with troops. Once the bombs were finished falling the company would move as close to the river as possible, and when the Taliban came out to meet the attack everyone would unload on them. The Scimitars were up on a piece of high ground looking across the river and could fire on heat sources with their powerful 30 mm cannons. We had a lot of .50-calibre machine guns to hammer the complex with and GPMGs set up on tripods so they could fire long, sustained bursts with great accuracy. The artillery would get in the game and hammer targets whenever the FOO called it in, and our boys would go to work with their Javelin missiles, picking off targets of opportunity. The Apache gunships would be up there engaging targets that would surely converge on the fort to join the fight, and once we were finished unloading on the baddies, the jets would swoop in to continue dropping bombs on and strafing the enemy. My troop was going to be dropped off a little bit to the north to act as a blocking force, to bar any enemy that tried to outflank the company along the river. We were a security net and wouldn't be firing on the fort. All in all it was going to be a massive display of modern weaponry, and there was no doubt who was going to come out on top.

My troop peeled off from the main body of vehicles as we neared the river and jumped out of the Vikings as we reached our blocking position. The sections spread out into a line, hiding among the trees and ditches, waiting to give the enemy a wonderful reception if they tried to attack down this route. We crawled into our positions and began to wait. And wait. And wait some more. We lay there for hours waiting for H-Hour, and froze while we were doing it. A layer of frost was settling on everything and I was continuously blowing on my hands so I would be able to use my gun. As we wiggled to try to keep warm we finally saw, well off in the distance to the north, the diversion attack going in. We could see long streams of tracer seeking out their targets and hear the mortars going to work. They were putting in a massive fire for effect, and the explosions were so numerous it just melted into one long, continuous rumble. Other than the distant battle, everything in our area was quiet and still. The cold was penetrating my entire body and I was in the familiar position of balance on my toes and forearms. We lay perfectly still, listening for any movement. We were waiting for the big show to start to our rear, and a few minutes later and right on schedule the first of the big bombs began to strike the fort.

Instead of just one or two bombs coming down like we were accustomed to, this was a major air strike. The U.S. Air Force had spent a small fortune in fuel to get the bombs all the way there, and they had no intention of flying back with them. Numerous bombs were slamming into the fort. Again and again the air reverberated with the shock of thousands of pounds of high explosive going off. They were really giving the fort the good news, and I was disappointed that I was facing away from the show. As the bombing run began to taper off, everything slowly grew quiet again. The rest of our company would have already been in position with their fingers on triggers. All they were waiting for was to see heat sources moving in and around the ruins and for the Nimrod up above to send word that the area was target-rich. And as expected, the Taliban began to crawl up out of the ground and man their positions to meet a frontal assault on their stronghold. But instead of a frontal assault, they were met with a flurry of bullets, shells, and missiles.

The world erupted to my rear, and I couldn't help but keep glancing back to see a steady wall of red tracer advancing across the river to the fort. Javelins were sailing off into the night with their customary scream and striking individual heat sources. The Scimitars off in the distance were pummelling their targets with a slow, continuous beating of 30 mm rounds. There were Apaches off to the south and east, and way off in the distance I could make out Hellfire missiles flashing up out of nowhere in the night sky and streaking down to unseen targets on the ground. I had never witnessed such an awesome display and seriously struggled to focus on covering my arcs. Way off to our front we could see that the diversionary attack had ceased and we had no way of knowing if it had helped significantly. All that we did know was that there were a lot of Taliban up and about, gauging by the number of Javelins that were being fired. A tremendous amount of money was being spent on the most expensive firework display I had ever seen, and it was of course impossible to keep it up indefinitely.

The baddies began to realize that they had been duped into thinking they were exposing themselves to meet a full-on assault, and they began to disappear again. Many of them had simply been obliterated by the weight of fire coming their way, and others were crawling back down into their holes and tunnels to wait out the storm. The firing from our company tapered off as the targets evaporated, and soon things were deathly quiet again. The only sound I could hear was from our section's radio, crackling to life to give us some instructions. Phase 2 of the attack was complete, and it was time to get on with Phase 3, the withdrawal back into the desert. The rest of the company was already packing up their weapons and piling into the Vikings, so we got up from the cold ground and did the same. We hadn't fired a shot and were a little disappointed, but we had carried out a vital task, securing the company's exposed flank.

As the Vikings and Scimitars moved off towards another assembly area out in the desert, the air strikes and strafing runs started up again. The Taliban were coming out to say goodbye and were getting smacked for their hospitality. Our vehicle trundled back out into the open plains with the section complaining about not getting a better role to play in the big show. Everyone felt let down, and I was no exception. It was five in the morning and we all just wanted to head back to the gun line and get some sleep. But the bright-ideas club was having different thoughts, and events were about to spiral out of control.

CHAPTER 25

JUGROOM FORT 2

0630 HOURS
JANUARY 15, 2007

The rear door of the Viking clanged shut and the section looked around at each other with their mouths hanging open. What had just happened was beyond belief and I wasn't sure if I had heard the boss right, but the looks on everyone's faces said it all. My hearing was fine. An hour ago we had arrived at the assembly area, and the troop boss who was riding in the front of our Viking had headed off into the centre of the vehicles to have a chat with all the other officers. They had talked for nearly an hour while we sat in the Viking, wondering why we weren't heading off to the gun line to get some sleep. We had no orders for Phase 4 and the sun was already coming up. We almost always attacked at night to make use of our technological advantage, so it was obvious that we wouldn't be heading to the fort for any action. What was the holdup? But soon enough we got our answer.

While we had been sitting there with the hatch open, the heater cranked, and the cab filled with smoke, the boss had come up and opened the back door. But he didn't tell us we were heading back to the gun line. "Phase 4 is on," he said dryly. "All three troops are going across the river. The first troop will dismount at the walls and attack through some large breaches that the bombers made. Our troop will be in for close support and reserve, and the final troop will park a little further back as a fire support base and reserve. Be ready to move in ten minutes." With that he closed the door. We were about to launch our most ambitious attack yet, in daylight, and our orders consisted of four or five sentences.

It is true that the company commander probably had a lot of information that we didn't. He was in touch with the Nimrod surveillance aircraft circling high over the fort, and he probably was taking orders from the unit or brigade commander. But that still didn't explain the complete lack of orders. We were going into the attack with very little information and we would be heading off to do it in only a few moments. With the anticipation of certain action filling our bodies, the company moved off towards the fort.

As usual we couldn't see much of anything as we headed east towards the river, and through the internal intercom system we got some updates from the vehicle commander who was standing up out of the top of the forward cab manning the Viking's GPMG. He told us that the lead vehicles were already entering the river and that the water was about a metre and a half deep. This was just at the limit of the depth that a normal Viking would float in, but with all of the extra armour and RPG cages attached to the Viking we would certainly be heavy enough to keep traction on the river bed. As we got closer to entering the water ourselves we could hear gunfire and explosions through the open hatch. The Scimitars were firing at the fort again to help cover our crossing, and with the lead troop halfway across the river their top gunners had started to engage enemy targets. Our Viking was soon in the river too, and the water quickly got deeper until we could see the waterline at the bottom of our rear window. The Helmand

River was wide at our crossing point and slow moving. It had to be, or else our vehicles could have easily been washed downstream. There was a shitload of activity outside our steel box, with explosions and automatic fire filling the air. We got a member of our section to stand up and bring his Minimi into the fight out the top hatch. He had only been up there for a few seconds before he started letting rip with long bursts out across the river. We were all yelling up at him to try and find out what was happening, but he was too busy up there to give us much info. He kept screaming down to us to keep digging into his pouches and handing him up sections of link to feed his gun.

The main crossing point was well over one hundred metres wide, and as we crawled up and out onto a very wide sandbar we came under fire. Rounds were pinging off the side of the vehicle constantly, and it was entertaining to watch our guy. All we could see was his legs, and he was dancing, bobbing, and weaving about like a boxer caught in the corner. Our Viking commander was firing heavily and it was difficult to hear anything over the wall of gunfire. Over and over again the commander and our man yelled "RPG!" as the Taliban fired into the company. Empty brass casings and link were pouring down through the hatch onto my legs and the acrid smell of gunpowder was thick. Things were getting mental up top, and even with the number of enemy rounds hitting our Viking I was dying to get up there and have a look. A second later I got my chance.

The Viking commander's GPMG jammed. I was clutching my gun and yelled at our Minimi gunner to get down so that I could get up and swap guns with the Viking gunner. As he came down I went straight up and was into the thick of it. I dragged my gun up after me, and screamed over the gunfire and explosions to the gunner to hand me his gun. I popped my gun open and poured a ton of oil into the working parts as he was disconnecting his from the turret. I crawled out of the hatch as he handed his gun back to me and I passed mine forward to him. He was totally in the zone, and quietly and methodically mounted my gun in his turret, took aim, and started firing again. Slow is smooth, and smooth is fast when in a gunfight.

I went to work to try to fix his gun and couldn't find anything wrong with it. All the working parts seemed to be operating just fine, so I gave it a fresh dose of oil, cracked the gas plug open a few more turns, and put on a fresh belt of ammo. As I got the gun settled into my shoulder and watched where everyone else's tracer was going I got my first look at the scene.

We were right at the eastern edge of the sandbar and had stopped just short of a twenty-metre-wide branch of the river. We were directly south of the leading edge of the fort and there were vehicles all around. One hundred metres north of us there were six or eight Vikings parked up on the flood plain in front of the fort and some of them were pretty much at the base of the wall. To the north, east, and south of the open area we were all in were numerous ditches, irrigation canals, treelines, and dirt piles. The bootnecks in the Vikings closest to the fort were pouring out the back of them and taking cover in the ditches and among any other bits of cover they could find. The high wall had collapsed in a few spots and some of the lads were making their way towards these breaches, obviously getting ready to try and break into the fort to shoot up the place. There was enemy everywhere. All of us were taking fire from the north, east, and south, and the air was thick with AK-47 rounds and RPGs. Enemy mortar bombs were starting to whistle in among the vehicles and out on the sandbar to our rear. I figured they were ranging our escape route so that they could bring some accurate fire on us when we left.

There was red tracer coming from the tops of the Vikings and singing off in every direction. The area to the front of the fort where the lads were trying to move was engulfed in explosions, and a flurry of bullets were hitting the ground. Because we were in the kill zone now all of our big guns had stopped firing in support of us, except for the Scimitars on the other side of the river, which kept engaging targets about one hundred metres to the southeast of me. Above all the noise of the ensuing battle I could still hear the slow and methodical *thump, thump, thump* of the 30 mm cannons and their high explosive rounds finding targets off to my right. The targets nearest to us were about one hundred metres away and kept popping up from behind large mounds of earth. I could see them scurrying around in among the trees and made out more than one baddie running about with an RPG launcher over his shoulder. As I tried to take all of this in I started to fire into the edge of a stand of trees and along the tops of the dirt mounds.

With bullets flying around everywhere and targets clearly visible, I worked my gun up into a frenzy. The belt of rounds was being sucked up from down below at a fantastic rate as brass and link poured from the bottom of the gun. For every enemy I fired at, another one immediately appeared. There was too much activity to be sure if I was hitting any of them. Did they drop because they had been shot or because they had ducked down under their own steam? Clearly some of them were being hit, but there were so many guns blazing from our vehicles, it was impossible to tell who was hitting what. I didn't give a shit anyway. If I could stop even one RPG man from letting off his round, then I was doing my job. The gun was firing nearly flaw-lessly for me, and as I tore through my link I yelled down below for more. Hands appeared all around me from the dark cab, all draped in 7.62 mm link and I greedily gobbled it up. The roof of the cab was becoming carpeted with the leftovers of a good shoot with the gun. Smoking brass, expended link, and short pieces of usable link that had been torn off were all around me. My hands were dripping with black, carbon-stained oil that was pouring out of the bottom of the gun, a good sign that it was well lubed. Several times as I loaded in a fresh belt I gave it a good drink.

I hardly had any time to even glance to my left to see what the rest of the company was up to. I was in my own world and they were in theirs. I had my personal radio stuck to my ear, and my section commander from down below was relaying whatever updates he got over the company net. In turn, I radioed down what I could see. Strange to have to talk on a radio to someone who is only a few metres away, but it was that loud outside where I was standing that I couldn't hear a damn thing. My ears were beginning to ring from the constant hammering of the gun. I heard that we had taken some casualties off to my left and I wasn't surprised. There were just too many rounds in the air for nobody to get hit. The explosions from mortars, RPGs, friendly ILAWs, 40 mm bombs from the UGLs, and hand grenades were constant and violent. I wanted the vehicle to move. We were just parked in a static location and attracting bullets, but we had to stay firm. We were in a perfect spot to suppress the southern targets and there really wasn't any more room on the flat area directly in front of the fort. It was already congested and we just would have made things worse.

Off to our right there was a pesky enemy that kept popping up from behind a dirt pile and then quickly dropping down again. He had an RPG launcher in his hands and was just trying to get a decent shot off at us. I told the guys down below what was going on and four of them quickly popped open the back door and came out in a flash. They all had UGLs on their rifles, and once they had identified the mound I was talking about they began to lob 40 mm bombs back in behind the enemy's cover. They all quickly got off a few shots on target and piled back into the vehicle. Apparently we were getting ready to move off back to the other side of the river. As the partial updates came in over the radio I kept on firing at what I could see, and even when the targets were all out of view I carried on firing at points where they were likely to pop up again.

A few Vikings were already making their way across the river with the company's wounded, and with the last of the dismounted lads back in the Vikings near the fort we all started to head back. We had only just entered the river when the first of our artillery shells began to whistle overhead and slam into the front yard of the fort. As we moved farther from the fort we could start to use bigger and bigger weapons on the exposed enemy. I came back down from the hatch as we headed across the river. I couldn't fire with any accuracy as the vehicle bumped along the riverbed so there was no need to expose myself to the bullets that were still striking the sides and back of the vehicle. But once we were all across the river the Vikings formed up into a long line facing towards the fort and began to fire across the river. Enemy mortar bombs were still falling around us but having little effect. There weren't that many of them, and the ones that did come close buried themselves deep into the soft, damp sand before exploding and sending plumes of dirt straight up in the air.

With all of the troops safely on the west side of the river the fort started to take the full brunt of modern weaponry again. The artillery was hard at work already, and the Scimitars had moved up onto a piece of high ground about six hundred metres to our rear. They were firing over our heads relentlessly and I was very glad that the Taliban didn't have some 30 mm cannons with advanced sighting systems of their own. Our air assets began to go to work on the fort again. We were much closer to the big bombs than I had ever been before, but the river was such a clear dividing line between the bad guys and us there was very little chance of the pilots dropping their loads on top of us. I then got the best show I have ever had. We were all still firing out across the river, adding to the chaos and destruction when the big bombs hit. This time there was no freight train approaching as there was too much gunfire filling the air, but the explosions were certainly heard . . . and felt. From only five hundred metres away and across open ground, there was an unbelievable amount of movement in the air with the blast concussions.

Again and again the bombs found their targets, and the fort quickly became completely hidden from view. Numerous mushroom clouds were stretching hundreds of feet up into the clear sky. The tops of the mushrooms were being pulled sideways by the wind and forming one long, dirty cloud of dust and debris. New mushrooms were constantly being forced up into the air to mingle with the old ones. The enemy knew when it was time to go underground and with our accurate air strikes the enemy fire tapered off until it was almost gone. One by one the Vikings stopped firing, until there was only the odd burst coming from our end when somebody spotted something. It certainly wasn't quiet, as the artillery, heavy bombs, and Scimitars were still doing their thing, but we were able to have a breather and enjoy the show.

We were still receiving conflicting reports over the net about who had been injured and how many people required a Casevac (casualty evacuation) back to Bastion on the inbound Chinook. Some reports were as low as two, and others said up to six. Either way, there were no reports of any deaths. The troop commanders and stripeys were then called into a central area behind one of the Vikings for a quick meeting, and as they scurried around from vehicle to vehicle frantically opening doors it became apparent that something was wrong. The radios were a flurry of activity with everyone saying the same thing and asking the same questions. A Marine was missing and couldn't be found anywhere. I refused to believe it when I first heard it. Surely he just jumped in a different Viking and was sitting there, laughing and smoking with a different section. We don't leave people behind, and carry out numerous head counts to safeguard against crap like that. But as the troop boss came running up to our vehicle I could tell that the reports were deadly serious. Everyone was looking for him, checking and rechecking vehicles. They confirmed he wasn't with the injured heading up to the helo pickup point, and he certainly wasn't in any of the Vikings with us. After a few more minutes of panicked searching and repeated head counts it was official. We had a Marine left on the other side of the river, and as my gaze fell back to the east I felt sick to my stomach. The area he had been in at the front of the fort was an absolute cauldron of high explosive, shrapnel, and large-calibre shells.

CHAPTER 26

JUGROOM FORT 3

1000 HOURS
JANUARY 15, 2007

The company was a kilometre back from the river and trying to sort out a plan. HQ had decided that things were just too hot to go straight back over the river again to try and find our missing Marine. A better plan was needed, and in the meantime we had all driven up onto a high bluff with the low, flat valley spread out below us. In the distance the fort was still obscured by all of the ordnance being thrown at it. We were all outside of the Vikings, sitting on the ground and chatting about the morning's events. Our injured had been flown back to the surgeons at Camp Bastion, and in the end there had been four of them, all of them with gunshot wounds. Luckily none of their injuries were life threatening. Their arms, legs, and feet had been shot up, but their body armour had saved them from worse injuries. In particular, one of my friends caught a three-round burst in the chest that day, and lived to tell about it. The Nimrod surveillance plane had spotted the missing Marine across the river near the front of the fort where the wall had been blasted away by the big bombs. He wasn't moving and we all assumed he was dead. It was unlikely that anyone could have survived the concussions from all of those heavy bombs that had gone off so close to him. The big question was whether or not the enemy had spotted him. Short of cutting his head off on film, there is nothing more the Taliban would like than to parade the dead body of a Royal Marine for the whole world to see,

Since the moment we crossed the river there had been a non-stop expenditure of ammunition on the position, and once the body was discovered from the air the efforts were doubled. Every air asset we had was being used to keep the Taliban away from his body. Apache helicopters had been on a steady tag team from Bastion, leaving when they ran out of ammunition and stopping at Bastion only long enough to rearm and refuel. At any given moment there were two Apaches firing all around the body with rockets, Hellfire missiles, and 30 mm cannons. There were A-10 ground attack aircraft strafing all around the area, constantly swooping down to fire with their powerful 30 mm Avenger Gatling guns. This gun fires the same ammunition as the Scimitars, but instead of a few rounds a second, it has a cyclic rate of over sixty rounds per second. It was an awesome weapon, and when it fired it made a noise like no other. When the pilot pulled the trigger there were a couple of slow rounds as the gun spun up, but then it went into high gear and the sky was torn open with the roar that followed. It sounded like a cross between a foghorn and a zipper the size of a drag strip. It gave me goose bumps every time it fired, and until you hear that thing opening up overhead, you haven't lived.

The A-10s were also dropping five-hundred-pound bombs on enemy forces that were advancing towards the body, and every jet under the sun seemed to be present that day. The U.S. Air Force was sending all they had from Kandahar to help out their allies, and it was humbling to witness all of that effort and money being spent to protect a dead body. It made me proud to be part of such a dedicated organization. Everything was being coordinated by the Nimrod and I am sure the Brigadier was watching it all somewhere on a TV, trying to come up with a plan on how to get the Marine back to Zulu Company.

With the bombs exploding in the distance and the entire fort complex shrouded in dust and smoke, HQ came up with a plan. Two Vikings with only a couple of guys in the back of each were going to go back across the river. They would have Apaches directly overhead to give them fire support and to drive off the enemy while they made their way to the wall of the fort. Once they were there the guys would jump out, search for the body, and get it into the vehicles as fast as they could. It was going to be a very quick snatch-and-grab mission, and as the plan circulated throughout the company like wildfire we all wondered which Vikings were going to be picked to go. Everyone was ready and willing and the Sergeant Major knew this. If he asked for volunteers he would have had the whole company step forward, so he picked at random. Things happened very quickly after this, and once the Vikings and crews were identified, they grabbed more ammo, ditched any unnecessary kit, and went tearing off in a cloud of dust. There were some brave men that day who were willing to carry out some very brave acts, and the bar was just about to be raised again.

As the Vikings headed off for the river crossing, the Apaches were up above with an excellent view of what was happening on the ground. They could see the body and knew exactly where it was. The pilots came up with a plan of their own and quickly relayed it to HQ on the ground. HQ accepted the plan, and history was made. The Apaches came in and landed one hundred metres from where the company was milling about. As the Apaches came down to land, four volunteers were chosen and taken to the Apaches. One young lad was just walking past the CSM (company sergeant major) and was simply told he was needed to do something, as nonchalantly as if he were being told to move a few boxes. On the sides of the Apaches above the stubby wings there is a hard point that you can attach things to. These four brave men got up beside the cabs of the helos and sat down on the little wings, attaching themselves to the hard point. The new plan was simply for the helos to fly in with these men strapped to the outside (Apaches are not designed to take any passengers) and pretty much land on top of the body. There would be hardly any searching required as the pilots knew where the body was. Once they had the body they would attach it to the belly of the helo with a rope, then, once the lads were back on the wings, they would fly back out of there. It was a daring plan. The Apaches had never been intended for this role and were going to be very vulnerable to attack once they were on the ground. But speed and surprise would be used to maximum effect. And so, with the guys secured to the fuselages, the Apaches took off into the unknown.

The two Vikings that were heading off on the same mission were about to drive across the river when they were told to stop and provide some additional fire support for the new plan. The Apaches streaked in towards the fort, low and fast, heading straight for the section of the wall that the body was near. The two helos came in and landed with friendly high explosive bursting all around the area. Everything possible was being done to keep the baddies away from the helicopters, and if all went smoothly they would be out of danger in a few seconds. One of the pilots overshot his landing, perhaps losing sight of it in the thick swirling dust, and actually landed just inside the fort. The other helo landed out in the open and the four exposed men jumped down from the wings and fanned out to find the Marine. One of the pairs found him right away and lifted and dragged his limp frame towards the helo. The Taliban would have done anything and sacrificed hundreds of their fighters to disrupt this operation, and it must have been just a little uncomfortable to have been thrust into the hornets' nest again that day. But heroes rarely get to choose the time and place for their deeds. They had a nightmare trying to carry the huge Marine with all of his heavy kit across the pockmarked and cratered terrain, but they got him to the helo and attached him with a long rope. They clambered back up onto the stubby wings, secured themselves, and gave the pilot the thumbs up. The Apaches quickly took off from that small chaotic scene and banked away over the river towards the company. The whole thing had taken only a few minutes.

The whole company was standing up, on top of any vehicle they could find, straining to see what was happening across the river, and we could see the dust kicked up when the Apaches took off. We all hoped that he was still going to be alive, that some sort of a miracle was in the making. But as the helos came across the river and got closer to us we could see that was not the case. Dangling about twenty feet beneath the rear helicopter was a limp and very dead-looking person. Our spirits sank as the truth became clear. I don't know why, but the helos pretty much flew straight over top of everyone, and we all got a very good look at our friend and comrade. We were silent as we watched the Apache land one hundred metres to our rear. The medics and the CSM hustled out to the helos to unhook the body and see if against all odds a little life remained in him. They lay across his body to protect it from the sand and gravel as the Apache took off, and soon found that there was nothing that could be done. He was in rough shape and had apparently been shot several times, including one round to the head. Where he had been lying, if the gunshots hadn't killed him to start with, the bombs going off around him surely would have.

One of the lads ran over with a poncho to cover the body, and a few minutes later a big Chinook turned up to take him back to Bastion. It was all over. We sat and murmured among ourselves, and with the deed done and the last of the Vikings back at our position, we all piled into our vehicles and headed off to the gun line. There was nothing more we could do there, and as we turned our back on Jugroom Fort the jets continued to bomb and strafe the area. The Taliban were still very interested in what we had been doing with Apaches on the ground and were determined to try to find out. Targets were abundant that day . . . for both sides.

When we got back to the gun line we were all exhausted. The amount of adrenalin we had expended was immense and now it was the low after the high. But before we could have any sleep there was a lot of work to be done. The vehicles were a complete mess, with kit, garbage, and brass casings strewn from one end to the other. Weapons needed to be cleaned, ammunition redistributed, and vehicles fuelled and maintained. We all got straight to work on what needed to be done. The sooner we finished, the sooner we could crawl back into our holes in the desert and put an end to this long, long day. The oc called us all together to have a quick chat about the day's events. He expressed sorrow for the loss of our fallen man and vowed that it would not be in vain. But none of us was interested in what he had to say. We weren't happy with his leadership that day, and over time many stories came out from bootnecks of all rank about how the oc had conducted himself. It appears he had simply failed to lead. I can't verify or deny many of those stories, but what I can verify is that within forty-eight hours he had been relieved of his command and we had a new oc.

Finally, with a clean machine gun and a belly full of hot food, I fell into my hole and started to drift off. The sun was just going down and sleep would come quickly. I hadn't had a shower in weeks, I was slowly getting a beard, and stunk to high heaven. But one luxury was still available to me. Tonight I could have all the sleep I wanted, and I took full advantage. I was even too exhausted to dream that night, and didn't move a muscle for eleven hours.

CHAPTER 27

GARMSIR 3

The weeks wore on for Zulu Company in and around the Garmsir area. We broke into a routine, and although I can't say that things became dull, it was still a routine. Nearly every day or night our troop would be out on some type of a patrol. When we weren't on a patrol we would be manning one of the three checkpoints that were still exchanging shots with the enemy on a daily basis. There was very little time to catch up on much sleep. When we were back at the DC we were always roped into the sentry rotation, so if I ever got more than four hours of continuous sleep I considered myself lucky. The mortar line had moved right inside the walls of the compound now, and the three 81 mm barrels were ten metres away from my little piece of concrete floor. The only thing separating them from me was a mud brick wall. The noise was so intense it nearly made my body come off the ground when they fired. It would have been easier to try to sleep with someone yelling straight into my ear.

The ANP were trying to boost their image in the area to the north of the front-line road and we often headed off to their police station to liaise with them and generally express goodwill. We went on some foot patrols with them around the quieter areas and set up security perimeters for them while they conducted vehicle searches. Working anywhere near these cowboys was interesting, to say the least. The locals didn't trust them and neither did we. Most of them didn't wear uniforms so you couldn't really tell if they were police or not. They had all been issued uniforms at their academy, but most of them thought they were too hot and had sold them. I thought it was very foolish of them to go walking around with AKs over their shoulders and dressed exactly like the Taliban, but who knows what they were thinking? Maybe they were Taliban. There are numerous accounts of Taliban fighters infiltrating both the ANA and the ANP ranks.

When the ANP were off doing their own thing, the locals would wander up to the DC and complain about the police. They told us the police were corrupt and constantly stole from them. We were told that, right under our noses, the police were charging a toll to cross the bridge and pocketing the money. When they searched cars at roadblocks they were taking what they wanted and nothing could be done. They denied everything, of course, when we asked them about it, but we all knew it was going on and there was nothing we could do about it. We were not there to discipline the police and in fact were supposed to be working alongside them. It was all very frustrating to see our efforts to treat the locals well being destroyed by these so-called police. More than one local told us that this situation with the police would never have happened when the Taliban were in control. I wouldn't be surprised if more than one young man had joined the Taliban to get an AK and a little revenge on the police for the wrongs committed against his family.

One morning an old Afghan man came up to the DC to talk to the big boss. Well, I call him an old man, and he was for those parts, but in reality he was probably forty-five. People have hard lives there and the years show. That, and the Afghan life expectancy is just under forty-five, so technically he *was* an old man. He came up to the DC, tears in his eyes and clearly very distressed. He had a problem with the police, and as we tried to calm him down we got the story. He told us that the ANP manning the checkpoint at the end of the bridge a few hundred metres away from the DC had kidnapped his thirteen-year-old son, tied him up in the bunker beneath the little building, and used him as a sex slave for several days. Each day he had gone to the checkpoint to beg for his son back and each day they threatened him with arrest or worse if he didn't leave them alone. On the third day that he went there the police beat him up, and threw his poor son back at him, telling them both to piss off and never come back. This man had come to us for help. He recognized that we were there to try to bring stability to the region and get some confidence in the newest Afghan administration. So with that in mind he wanted us to do something about the police. What he really wanted was for us to go down there and exact some revenge on his behalf, to shoot them all as a lesson for the rest of the police in the area. It all sounded like a pretty good idea to us, but there was no way we could ever do that. All we could do was listen to his story with sympathy and tell him that we would pass the report on up the chain of command.

Old men in Afghan have all the power. They are the village elders, and whatever they say is law in their towns. This old man vowed to us that if something wasn't done very quickly, not only would he personally join the Taliban so he could kill the police, but he would recommend the same course of action to all the other males in the area. With that he left. All of the time and effort that we spent in an area to improve the lives of the locals could be wiped out in a day. This was the shit we had to deal with. This is the shit all of the boys over there are still dealing with.

Sometimes we would hear reports of impending attacks on the DC and we would send out patrols to lurk in the shadows and ambush the enemy. Sometimes our sentries would see people sneaking around in the night and we would be sent out to see what was going on. There was just no end to the little patrols we had to go on. We found some freshly dug mines on a road one day, so for twenty-four hours we sat in an OP, watching the IED to see if anyone came back to tinker with it. Our orders were to shoot anyone who went straight to it. Nobody came.

We would creep about in the dark setting up trip flares and claymore mines and then sit there all night. When the enemy came along at first light we would set off the charges and kill them with hundreds of ball bearings and flurries of machine gun fire. The patrols were endless, and they worked. Other parts of the province had serious problems with IEDs and mines in their areas. We had hardly any. I think the heavy patrolling we did at night dissuaded the enemy from crawling out and digging in their bombs in the dark. They simply never got the breathing space to plant their IEDs.

When we weren't on patrol, at a checkpoint, or on sentry, we would inevitably be part of the QRF, the quick reaction force. Every time a patrol went out there was an extra QRF in case they needed some help straight away. The checkpoints always had a section of QRF back at the DC as well, often sitting on or around their Wimiks so that they could get to the furthest checkpoints in a hurry. QRF was a good duty because it invariably included a bit of sleep. As long as your weapon was clean, your boots were on, and your webbing was within reach, you could do what you wanted. And for the most part that meant sleep.

We had all been living in pretty rough conditions for the last month or so and the hierarchy was starting to rotate troops back to Bastion for a few days to have a shower and a decent meal. So far all we had eaten was our twenty-four-hour ration packs, and it was getting a little old. Of course we wouldn't be the first troop to get rotated out, or the second. But we were third on the list, and when the day came for us to begin our move back to Bastion we were ecstatic. We had to make a vehicle move up to the gun line, where we would catch a lift on the next Chinook. With a new-found vigour the troop packed up their bergens and loaded everything up onto the Vikings. I was looking forward to a day or two of peace and couldn't stop thinking about salads and fresh fruit. I am a big meat eater and usually when I am starving I crave a large T-bone steak, but this time I guess I needed vitamins.

We went around the rest of the company and told them all how great it was going to be on Bastion and how much we would miss them. Naturally they told us to piss off, so we did. We roared out of there and up into the desert, smiling and joking all along the way. Things were looking good, and as we jumped out at the gun line on a sunny afternoon we were greeted by some disappointing news. It turned out that the schedule had changed and the troop wouldn't be heading back to Bastion that day. The next helo wasn't coming for another three days, so to pass the time we were told to dig a few holes and take over some of the sentry positions. The gun line had changed a bit in the last few weeks. It now had a high dirt mound surrounding the entire perimeter, and at the four corners and dispersed along the edges were some sandbagged enclosures used for the sentry positions. There were a lot of supply trucks parked in the compound, and it was from here that the DC in Garmsir was getting most of its food, fuel, and ammunition. It was a lot safer for the helicopters to land here out of the range of the baddies' guns, and convoys from Bastion could drive here straight through the desert without having to expose themselves to any IED threat.

We weren't completely broken, though, at the news that we weren't heading back for a hot shower. We were still going back, we had just been delayed for a few days, and at least out here we would be left alone to get some rest. The sentry routine wasn't all that demanding. We did two hours on shift and eight off for three straight days. There wasn't much to look at out there, and it was a challenge to occupy your mind as you stared out into the desert at night with a pair of NVGS, but it was the closest thing to rest we had had in a very long time. Quality sleep at the gun line was always an illusion. The 105 mm howitzers that were one hundred metres from us were firing often and were loud enough to knock the pebbles and dirt off the sides of my hole, sending it spilling onto me while I pretended to sleep. We got rained on while we were out there. In fact, it absolutely pissed down on us. Living in a hole is not the best place to be in a heavy downpour and we all scrambled like madmen to stretch our too-small shelters overtop of our too-big holes. It didn't work, and in the end we were scooping water out from beside us as we lay there thinking of Bastion.

The big day came, and as the hour for the helo approached we squared away our bergens and carried everything up to the LP. We were soaked and our kit was soaked, but our morale was soaring. The helo was delayed, as they always are, and we sat on our bergens, laughing and joking about our good fortune. Just when things seemed they couldn't get any better, they didn't. In fact, they got much worse. The boss wandered over to us with that "sorry but I'm about to ruin your day" look on him and came straight out with it. "Good news and bad news, boys," he said. "The good news is that the helo is still coming to pick us up. The bad news is that it won't be taking us to Bastion. It is taking us straight back to the DC. Intelligence believes there is the threat of a large-scale attack into Garmsir and all available troops are needed to counter the threat. I need a shower too, but orders are orders." Well, there was really nothing to say to that. Morale dipped a bit, and all we could do was accept the fact that we could look forward to a few more meals out of a foil bag. In the end, the attack never materialized and the troop was simply sucked back into the rotation. We never got our holiday back.

Eventually, in February, I got my own ticket to get back to Bastion. My R&R slot had finally rolled around, and for two weeks I was getting out of Afghanistan on my scheduled holiday. Everybody got two weeks off at some point and it was finally my turn. I had a firm date to fly out of Bastion and back to the U.K., but nobody could tell me when the helo would be showing up to take me as far as Bastion. It was just a waiting game, and as the days drew on and the hours went by I got more and more excited, to the point where I don't think my mates even wanted to be around me. I was bad for their morale, but they had all rubbed it in my face when it was their turn. I was showing no mercy and reminded them all of where I would be in a week and where they would be. I was going to be sitting on a beach in the Canary Islands with my bikini-clad girlfriend, having a Mojito, while they sat on sentry.

The next night my section was manning J-TAC hill, and as usual we rotated through keeping a watch out for the enemy and catching a bit of sleep. Everything was quiet during the night but just before first light as I sat behind my machine gun we began to pick up some heat sources moving about in the mist. There were a few figures about four hundred metres away that we could see bobbing up and down around some old blasted walls. There were only enemy down there, so as the sky slowly grew lighter we grabbed the FOO to bring in some artillery fire on them. We gave him a sight and talked him onto the targets and when he had eyes on them he called in some early-morning high explosive. As the rounds approached and we could hear the whistle of the shells soaring through the cool air I began to unload on them with my GPMG. They were dipping in and out of cover and too far away for me to lay down any real accurate fire. I just threw long twenty- and thirty-round bursts of slowly expanding clouds of tracer into their area. When the artillery started to land in among them they went into a frenzy and started running about into open areas, exposing themselves to my gun. I was letting rip and watching tracer kicking up all around one guy caught out in a field. He went down. Maybe I shot him. Maybe he dove in a ditch. I couldn't tell. It didn't matter. I was having a great time. Artillery came down and I carried on with my long bursts from the gun until I got a tap on the shoulder.

A vehicle had been sent to pick me up and they were waiting at the base of the hill to take me to the LP. My R&R helo was inbound and I only had a few minutes to get this ride. I couldn't believe my luck! Here I was having a grand old time, engaging targets with an awesome, flawlessly working belt-fed machine gun loaded with one-in-one tracer, with no danger to myself, and I was getting dragged away to go sit on a beach in paradise! I honestly couldn't decide if I was supposed to be thrilled or pissed off. Either way, the next thing to do was obvious. I grabbed our radio man, showed him where the enemy was with one last, long pull on the trigger, and moved over as he slid in behind the gun. I was on that truck, back to the DC, and heading for the helo in about three seconds flat. I was on a new mission now, and it involved getting the fuck out of Afghanistan!

A little over twenty-four hours after I'd been machine gunning people I was sitting in a pub in Lincoln, England, by myself, looking into a beer glass. I had managed to sneak out of theatre a few days before my R&R was actually scheduled to start, so I had some time to kill before Jennifer landed to meet me in London. I had a massive beard. My hair was long and scraggly, I was scrawny, and I felt weird. This was nearly the first drink I had had in months and the locals were all staring at me. They couldn't decide if I was a hippy or a psycho. I had come up to meet one of my mates who had come back early from the tour. He was the one from my room up at 45, the guy who had been shot in the arm, and he would be meeting me later after he got back from a funeral for another Marine.

I overheard a table near me talking about what was happening in Afghanistan. The two men were chatting about Marines and how much ass they were kicking over there. I really didn't want to get involved in what they were talking about, but I hadn't talked to anyone who wasn't in a uniform for nearly five months and I felt compelled to strike up a conversation. But even though I talked about Afghanistan like I knew what I was talking about, they didn't believe me. I told them I was a Royal Marine on R&R from Afghanistan, and they thought I was a liar. I could see them getting angry. They thought I was mocking their beloved Corps or something. Imagine a long-haired, bearded hippy having the balls to walk into their local pub and claim he was a bootneck. The conversation was over, so I sat back down at my own table and ordered another beer to stare into. *Fuck them*, I thought.

A few minutes later my friend walked into the pub to meet me. He had just come from the funeral and was still in his dress uniform, walking tall and proud with medals on his chest and an injured arm. I got up, shook his hand, and gave him a big pat on the back. I was happy to be with a bootneck again, and as we sat down to catch up on things I noticed the guys at the other table were the ones staring down into their beers.

CHAPTER 28

EASTERN CHECKPOINT

GARMSIR DC
FEBRUARY 24, 2007

R&R was finished, and I found myself jumping off the tail ramp of a Chinook just north of the DC again. I tried not to think about the beaches, cold drinks, and good times I had just been spoiled with. I was back at work and it was time to focus on the job. I tailed onto the back of the small foot patrol that had come out to secure the LZ and headed off towards the DC, struggling under the weight of a ridiculously heavy bergen again. As I neared the DC I couldn't believe the improvements that had been made while I was gone. A bunch of engineers had come down south to square away the defences and they had obviously been hard at work. There were high, thick dirt-filled walls enclosing the entire compound and some of the surrounding area. It seemed that business was booming and we were expanding. The sentry positions had been built up into small sandbagged strongpoints with thick protective roofs and steel plates to deflect bullets and shrapnel from the open doorways. Thick walls of barbed wire were set out around the perimeter and large obstructions had been placed on all of the roads that led to the compound. Once I got inside I saw that there were dirt-filled walls erected all over to compartmentalize any shrapnel that might zip around after a mortar attack. It was clear that the Brits had no intention of giving up our foothold in the area.

I wandered over and joined my troop, answering a million questions about everything that they had missed out on. I was sorry that my holiday had ended, but at the same time, I was glad to be back. It felt good to be surrounded by so many people that I could rely on. The entire company had been busy while I was gone, carrying on with their patrol schedules, checkpoint shootouts, and strike ops launched from the desert. Mortars and rockets were still being thrown at the DC most days, and a few guys had been sprayed with shrapnel and injured a few days before my return. I was glad to hear that no one else had been killed in my absence, but some had been shot while up on J-TAC hill and over at the Eastern Checkpoint.

In the morning we got to play with a new toy. It was a machine gun but instead of firing bullets it fired 40 mm grenades. They were similar to the bombs the guys fired from the UGLs on their rifles, but they were longer and had much more gunpowder in each casing to send them farther. It had a range of about one kilometre and was an awesome piece of kit. It was fed with a belt like a normal machine gun and could be fired on single shot or fully automatic. We were getting one gun placed up on each checkpoint and looking forward to firing bursts from that beast at those dirty bastards who kept shooting at us. We all learned how to fire it and clear any jams that we might encounter. We stripped it down for servicing and put it all back together with a fresh coating of oil. We couldn't wait to try it out.

One morning J-TAC was taking some fire from across the river. This was a firing point that the enemy had never used before, and someone called in some mortar fire to suppress the enemy. I don't know who was calling in the fire, but I do know that things went wrong. Perhaps we hit the wrong target, or maybe the enemy was firing at us from inside a small village to use locals as a shield, but the end result was two civilian casualties. About a half hour after the firing had all died down, a small battered pickup truck came crawling up to the gates of the DC. Two men got out, and once we had established that they weren't packing any explosives on them, we let them bring in a man and a woman who had been injured in the mortar fire. They pulled them out of the back of the truck and carried them into the DC wrapped up in some old blankets that were deeply stained with warm blood. Our medical officer went to have a look at them and when the blankets were pulled back it was clear that they were both dead. The man had a chest that was badly mashed up and the woman was missing a large piece of her head. It was heart-breaking to watch the interpreter try to explain to the two healthy men that there was nothing we could do for them. The men were in tears and begging us to help their loved ones, but it was hopeless. All we could do was send them on their way, hoping that they would get the message that if the Taliban had not been firing at us it never would have happened. They wrapped up the bodies and carried them back to the truck. They slowly drove off, heading for their village with their lifeless cargo, and we all went about our business.

The real excitement we were getting at this time came from the checkpoints and patrols down south. The Eastern Checkpoint was always a hot place, and you could count on getting shot at every single day that you were there. Contacts were very common. Usually two guys would be up on the roof to keep a watch, while the other six sat down below and slept, ate, or played cards. If some enemy fire started to come in and the guys up top went to work with the guns, all we would do down below is call up and see if they needed a hand. We were getting shot at so often that it usually wouldn't even break up a card game. Downstairs we sat behind a four-foot-high wall and calmly cooked our food and ate our meals with bullets often passing less than three feet over our heads. It is bizarre to think that you can get used to something like that, but I assure you it can be done.

Things were a bit more exciting when it was your turn to be up top, as you were the main targets. We were fully tooled up to deal with any trouble. We had our rifles, two GPMGS, the new GMG (grenade machine gun), ILAWs, Javelin missiles, and a radio that we could use at any time to call in mortar fire or have a QRF dispatched to our location. It was great to be left to your own devices with all that firepower, and the only thing that we had to ask permission for from HQ was to fire Javelins. Stocks in theatre were running low and the missiles cost well over $50,000 each. Nevertheless, we always had three missiles to hand. The mortar fire was always fast and effective and I was impressed with our bootneck mortar crew back at the DC. The enemy almost always fired at us from the same points, and all of these were prerecorded targets with their own X-ray number attached. If the enemy was spotted at one of these, we simply picked up the radio and said, "Fire mission, X-ray Two Six, ten rounds fire for effect," and that was that. A minute or so later, thirty high explosive bombs would land on target. It was great fun, and we could do that day or night. We used the mortar line to send up illum throughout the night as well. With a quick message sent on the radio, we could turn night into day wherever we wanted.

Up on top we had cover up to chest height and were surrounded by a decent wall of sandbags. We stood up there with binoculars pressed to our faces and constantly searched for anyone creeping around. Across the canal and a kilometre to the south was a massive Taliban compound where we often saw people moving about. Sometimes we would send them a burst with the GMG or a few mortar bombs in their direction. We spent a lot of time just observing their patterns and trying to see where their sentry positions were. Most days at some point as you stood there looking around, your peace and quiet would be interrupted by two or three loud snaps in the air around you as someone fired a burst at your head from his AK. This happened so often that we got very good at telling how close a bullet was to hitting you by how loud the snaps were. When the snap became a crack, it was close, and when the crack was loud enough to make your ears ring, you knew that you were probably only a few inches away from catching a bullet in the face. When the cracks were loud or the bullets struck the sandbags just below your chin, things got very serious very quickly. Your first reaction was to duck down. It would be unnatural not to. But you quickly remembered what your job was and slowly but surely stood back up to try and find the guy who was shooting at you. The idea was to find him and kill him, and that was hard to do if you were crouched down behind a wall. You also didn't want to be hidden away if this was actually going to develop into a serious attack. It is good to know about these things as soon as possible.

From the sound of the bullet you would usually have a good idea of the direction it came from, and sometimes we welcomed more shots because we hoped they would give away the enemy's position. Once we found where the enemy were or they gave away their position by moving, we would unload on them with everything we had. Usually we had one guy spotting with the binos while the other one engaged the target. It was the most effective way, especially when reaching out eight hundred metres with the GMG.

Sometimes the baddies would try and draw our attention onto one of their riflemen while some other ones crawled about to get into a position to let loose with their RPGs. We were starting to learn all of their tricks and weren't too bothered by engaging multiple targets shooting from different directions. If we needed more weapons firing we just had to call up another guy or two and really unleash the fury. The radio was always an excellent weapon and we put it to use time and time again. Few of these attacks were sustained or really pressed, though. They knew they would never win if they just tried to stand and slog it out with us, so usually after five or ten minutes things would grow quiet again.

One evening I was lucky enough to be just in the right place at the right time. I was observing the big compound with our thermal sights and was amazed to see an unbelievable target form. The Taliban knew that we could see them at night, and usually stayed out of view or moved about in small groups. But this time I watched a file of baddies come out of the front of the compound. From about 1,000 metres away I counted them as they came out, and when they were all out and standing in a group to the front of the compound I was bouncing around that little bastion with excitement. Eleven Taliban had just wandered straight out into my kill zone. The second guy up there was on the radio asking for permission to fire off a Javelin as I attached a missile to the launching unit. Because there was a shortage of missiles our HQ only wanted us to fire at worthy targets. One guy wasn't enough, but three or four would usually suffice. Eleven was a gold mine, and the answer came back straight away: "Clear to fire." As I got the missile shouldered and reacquired the target I was dismayed to find that the heat source had shrunk. My eleven targets had dwindled to probably five or six, but this was still a great opportunity to throw a large wrench into whatever these fuckers had planned for the evening. When all was prepped and the heat source was locked, I pulled the trigger and sent the missile off on its way. It came flying out of the launcher with its primary charge, and a fraction of a second later the main engine kicked in and sent it streaking into the night sky, accelerating at a ridiculous rate. It climbed into the sky a few hundred metres on its way to attack from the top, and as it reached its apex it searched for the heat source it had been sent to destroy. I watched the missile strike the group of men through the thermal sight, and one heat source became many as bits of person and warm earth and wall spread about the area. It was an accurate hit, and the whole thing from the time I pulled the trigger to the time the missile struck was about four seconds.

Overall though, the Taliban were shooting at us from that side of the canal much more than we appreciated. They figured they were pretty safe over there, and no matter what we threw at them from our side, they just kept on creeping about and taking potshots at us. We all knew that it was only going to be a matter of time before we had to head on over there and sort them out. Soon enough, the company began to prepare by sending out more and more patrols down south along the canal to root out Taliban sentries and see what was going on. We got into many little scraps down there in the dark, and spent a lot of time crawling about trying to keep an eye on things. Every time we got orders, we received a mission statement that was always repeated twice so that it could sink in. Time and again as we headed off down along that canal we had the same mission statement ringing in our ears: "Mission – To conduct a deep reconnaissance patrol south of the Eastern Checkpoint to gather intelligence for future offensive operations." There was no doubt in anybody's mind that sooner or later we would be trying to get over to that large Taliban compound that was giving us so much shit. The only questions were how and when.

CHAPTER 29

VODKA

EASTERN CANAL, GARMSIR DISTRICT
2115 HOURS
MARCH 7, 2007

"Civvies would pay thousands for this," I thought to myself as I started to move out over the canal. The bridge was still bouncing from the steps of the last guy who had gone across, and my movement was making it bounce worse. We were all loaded up with a ton of kit including the GPMGs Jay and I were carrying. At least the enemy fire was wild and not very accurate. It rarely was. The Taliban were poor shots. I bent down low and moved off as fast as I could, trying not to clang my machine gun off every part of the bridge railings for the whole fifty feet. I couldn't help but look at the water racing by beneath me and think about what would happen if this bridge snapped in half. I would be very dead on the bottom of a dirty Afghan canal, and the Corps would be down one very useful machine gun. I tried to spit out the chewing tobacco I had stuffed in while the bombs had started to pummel the target earlier, but only managed to get it and a bunch of black spit caught up in my beard. "Living the dream!" Jay had said to me before stepping onto the bridge. *Too right*, I thought. I wondered if my Spanish-speaking Brit buddy was still green from his chewing tobacco.

I got to the other side of the bridge in good order and quickly moved away to the far side of the canal bank. Visibility was still very poor with all of the smoke and dust, and the risk of getting split up was very real. But I quickly found the person I had been following, and Jay was hot on my heels, panting under his load. One by one the whole company was streaming over the bridge and we had to get moving to avoid any congestion. We were committed now, and there was no reason to give the enemy time to think. We leapfrogged through the engineers and a handful of bootnecks who were providing security at the eastern end of the bridge and moved east about thirty metres to wait for the whole troop to form up. The big bombs had stopped falling quite a while ago so visibility was improving quickly. Vodka was still being hit with artillery and mortars and was about four hundred metres east of us. Just to our south was the group of buildings called Sheppys, and this would be our first house call.

Our troop was the first to go into the attack and we had to move quickly. The whole company was pooling up behind us and itching to get to it. Jay and I were near the back of the troop, with the machine guns. They weren't exactly suitable for clearing buildings – too long and much too heavy to swing around quickly in a dark room. As we headed off south down a well-used track, we could see the two buildings of Sheppys looming up ahead on the left. Our guys were already stacking up outside the doors, getting ready to breach. In went the grenades – BOOM! – followed quickly by a few of the lads. They let off some rapid shots and as we neared the buildings we heard them yelling "Clear!" – letting us know there were no enemy in there or, if there had been, they were no longer a threat. We jogged up to the base of the buildings and I checked to make sure Jay was still with me. He was there and looked exactly the way I felt: sweaty and exhausted. It was a lot of work running around with that gun and all the ammo. I was just hoping we could start to engage targets right away so we could lighten the load. Five minutes of action with the gun means you head back fifty or sixty pounds lighter.

A couple of the lads in our troop had been gracious enough to carry some light aluminum ladders to be ready for just such a moment. They leaned them up against the buildings that had just been cleared and went down onto one knee facing south, rifles in the shoulder. This was our cue to make a move topside. Jay and I slung our guns and started to climb up onto the roof as the next two troops leapfrogged through, heading for the next objective. They had to go about one hundred more metres south and then face east to sweep through a large group of buildings called Strongbow on their way to the southern end of Vodka: the largest objective. Strongbow was about two hundred metres long and one hundred metres wide and had about twenty buildings in it. It was a large walled area with many small open spaces, walled corridors, and alleys. The troops were moving into their start position quickly and Jay and I had to get in position to provide some cover.

As I got up over the top of the ladder I lay down flat on my belly and crawled to the forward edge of the roof. The roof was sagging under the weight as Jay crawled up beside me. We were trying to stay low to reduce our profile, but the small-arms fire had tapered off a bit. The enemy that had been up close when we crossed the bridge were moving back further into their compounds so that they could use the buildings for cover. We quickly got our guns set up and started scanning for targets with the thermal and IR night vision kit. Thermal imagery is the way forward for finding the bad guys at night. Heat sources stick out like a sore thumb. You can even see bugs a hundred metres away in zero light. It's good stuff.

We were facing east, looking out over a large field towards the whole Vodka complex 350 metres away. One hundred metres to our right was the Strongbow complex that the boys were about to start clearing through. We were in a perfect position to cover everything to the north and across into Vodka, and if we had to we could fire south over top of Strongbow and the troop. We got on the radio and let them know that we were in position and everything was good to go. We unslung the bags of grenades we had brought with us and made sure they were nice and handy. If some Taliban shits decided to come anywhere near our building they would be met with a hail of high explosive and shrapnel.

Even as all of this was happening the artillery continued to fall in among the Vodka compound. The scene laid out in front of the two of us was impressive, and Jay and I had the best seats in the house. Without delay the troops started to sweep into Strongbow, and they were moving fast and hard. Many of them had brought ILAWs to fire into buildings as they advanced, and those 84 mm anti-armour rockets would wreak havoc when they came through the front door. Any building that didn't get an ILAW got a grenade or two. The troops were meeting little resistance as they moved among the buildings, which meant they could advance faster than expected. All of the enemy had clearly pulled back into Vodka when we had moved across the canal.

Back across the canal the security we had set up to protect our southern flank was starting to spot targets heading north to join the fight. A Javelin missile took off and grabbed my attention as it streaked south into the night. At fifteen hundred metres it slammed into a group of Taliban fighters hustling up the canal bank. More guys started to open up to the south with .50-calibre heavy machine guns and grenade machine guns. The baddies were trying their best to advance up to the scrap but were walking into a wall of heavy fire. Our southern flank was secure. Good positioning and superior weapons were doing the trick. Apache gunships were also operating overhead, as the artillery began to silence with our guys getting closer and closer to Vodka. One Apache a few kilometres southeast of us let rip with a Hellfire missile and a bunch of 30 mm cannon fire. We heard over the radio that truckloads of enemy reinforcements were being engaged and destroyed en route. Good news all around.

The two troops that were clearing Strongbow were about halfway through it when they started to get opened up on from the southeast. Jay and I had a perfect line of fire and could see the enemy's muzzle flashes about two hundred metres away. I got on the radio and let the troop commanders know where the fire was originating and requested permission to fire over their heads. They didn't like the idea of that and told me to maintain focus across to Vodka. The response seemed stupid to me because we were in a good position to do two things at once, but orders are orders, so I just had to sit there and watch my friends being shot at. There was so much chatter on the radio that there was no time to try to argue my point. The troop commanders already had more than enough things to deal with. After a moment the enemy stopped firing from there and moved off to some new, unseen firing position. It was a wasted opportunity to get some rounds down but there would be others.

A while back we had been issued with a bunch of pamphlets to spread around Taliban-held territory. The pamphlets were just single pieces of paper with a few words of Arabic and pictures of dead Taliban. I guess the idea was to scare the Taliban with pictures of all our superior equipment, and to convince them to abandon the cause. I had brought along a pocket full of these, and now seemed as good a time as any to spread them around, so I started chucking them off the side of the building. I was constantly scanning for the enemy while doing this, keeping an eye on the main objective. A lot of buildings were burning in among Vodka, and many other ones had collapsed.

But this certainly didn't mean the baddies were all killed. They had plenty of holes and tunnels in and about the compounds and we expected that they would defend Vodka viciously.

Our boys were nearing the far end of Strongbow and, as expected, they started to take a bunch of fire from Vodka as they got closer. It was hard for us to see all of our guys as they moved around the buildings and walls and just as hard to spot the Taliban. But it was easy to see all of the tracer and RPGs starting to fly around. The lads were pushing right up to the walls of Vodka and having one hell of a shootout. Incoming RPGs were met with outgoing ILAWS.

Jay and I spotted a few baddies starting to move down the outside of Vodka, towards our guys. We began to suppress the targets, and I was firing while Jay spotted. It is hard to fire over any distance accurately at night with a machine gun, so as I sprayed streams of tracer towards the target, Jay looked through the optics to tell me where to adjust. Up. Down. Left. Right. We couldn't be sure if we hit anything but we certainly stopped them from trying anything. We couldn't see any more movement there so began to fire on targets we could now see moving about in Vodka. The problem was that I was starting to lose the division that had existed between our boys and theirs. As the Marines began to push right into Vodka, they were getting too close to the enemy, and I couldn't be sure who was who.

I had to get on the radio and get someone to mark our most northerly position, and asked one of the guys to get out a firefly – a handheld strobe light that can only be seen with NVGs – and start waving it about. It took a moment for him to get into a position from which I could see the strobe, but once he did, the battle picture for us gunners was clear. We now had a specific point marking a clear division: we must not fire south of it, but everything north of it was fair game. And there was plenty of movement north of the strobe. As we blazed away into Vodka, the security team across the canal was still shooting up guys coming from the south. There was a shitload of Taliban in the area, and they had no intention of letting us stroll through Vodka.

But the plan was working. We had stirred up a hornet's nest and were drawing them out of their holes so that we could kill them. Things were coming to a head. We had pretty much achieved what we had set out to do, and up to this point we had not taken a single casualty. Not one guy had been hit – no land mines – no booby traps. Things were going well and it was nearly time to pull out and let our air assets go to work on the exposed enemy.

Jay and I, isolated up on our roof, were beginning to get some personal attention now from the enemy. The baddies over in Vodka could see the source of our tracer and were starting to fire back at us. Their fire was all over the place and only a very lucky shot from that range would hit us. We were in a great firing position and were able to send far more bullets than we were receiving. As our own little shootout unfolded, the jets overhead were getting itchy trigger fingers. They could see targets swarming all over Vodka and springing up out of the ground among the compounds. It was time for us to get the hell out of the line of fire.

I heard over the radio that the guys were going to disengage from the enemy and hustle back through our position and over the canal. Jay and I were to cover their withdrawal and then tag on behind the end of the company. A second later my heart skipped a beat when I heard quiet voices approaching our location from the south. Jay and I looked at each other. It seemed to us that some enemy had managed to sneak up on us without our security teams seeing them. My heart started pounding as I reached for a hand grenade and fingered the pin. If these guys were already in the building and decided to start shooting up through the roof, Jay and I would be in a world of hurt. I started to edge towards the side of the roof nearest the voices and suddenly realized they were speaking English. Happy days! What a relief. We hadn't expected anyone to get back to us that fast, but somehow these guys had made a two-hundred-metre sprint in about ten seconds. I put the grenade down, got my gun back in the shoulder and started firing towards the enemy again.

The Marines all got back from Vodka and out of Strongbow in record time, spurred on by showers of RPGs and plenty of bullets. The Taliban were already edging out of Vodka and into Strongbow. Time to go! Jay and I took turns crawling to the ladders and getting down off the roof. The company was quickly moving past us towards our bridge and we had trouble convincing the passing troops to take our ladders for us. We still had our big guns to carry, and I would have left the ladder behind if no one else had taken it. As we handed off the ladders the sky was torn apart by the sound of 20 mm Gatling guns and screeching jets. F-18s were getting in on the game. They were strafing the enemy that were spilling out of the southern end of Vodka and having themselves a turkey shoot.

We tagged onto the end of the company and headed back to the bridge. I couldn't believe how fast and smoothly the withdrawal was taking place. We were trying our best to get out of the killing ground. The jets were firing constantly now, and you could tell they were stacked up there, taking turns to strafe the enemy. As we neared the bridge we had to pause for a moment to let the troops ahead of us get over the canal. The artillery started to open up again on the targets. It sounded like it was going to be a repeat of the beating Vodka had taken earlier – only this time cannon fire from the air replaced the big bombs.

Time to move. I was up and across the bouncing bridge in no time and grateful to be much lighter than I had been heading the other way. The Taliban were firing wildly in our direction with everything they had, but that was all right. It kept them out in the open, presenting targets for the F-18s and artillery. On the other side of the canal, we headed northwest as fast as we could to get out of the

Taliban's field of fire. The security team would be left behind to cover the engineers as they disassembled the bridge. Our job now was just to get back into the DC without getting hit by a lucky bullet. As we advanced towards the town we were still taking RPG fire. The shots were all going way over our heads and exploding harmlessly in the fields to our left. I found it amazing that these guys were subjecting themselves to such punishment from above just to get off a few shots in our general direction.

A few minutes later we entered the town and were trotting at a quick pace for the DC. We got there in no time and everyone milled about the main gate as final head counts were conducted. It seemed that everyone was there and – amazingly – nobody had been hit. The bridge had been collapsed, and the engineers and rear security teams were piling back into the DC. We all started to relax a bit and listened to the show still going on a few kilometres away. The enemy were firing off RPGs at God knows what, and the artillery and jets were still pounding away. It was at least another hour before it started to quiet down. By then we were all out of our kit, had grabbed a bite to eat, and were thinking of getting some sleep. It had been a long day.

But it wasn't quite over yet. As we started to take our boots off and get ready to get our heads down, the Taliban sent some large 107 mm Chinese rockets in our direction. They were still up for a little revenge.

The rockets didn't hit the DC but a few managed to land within a hundred metres of us. I again found it amazing that the Taliban were still up for it. We started to hear small-arms fire in the distance as they launched an attack on the checkpoint that we had passed through earlier on our way in and out of no man's land. The boys manning the checkpoint repulsed the attack and called in some mortar fire for good measure. We had our boots back on and were cleaning weapons and gathering ammunition, getting ready to go back out and help our friends at the checkpoint if they needed any backup.

Luckily for us there was no crisis, and things finally started to quiet down for good. We were all hoping it would stay that way for at least a few hours. Sleep was quickly becoming a priority. I crawled into my stinking sleeping bag and settled down on the concrete in the dark smoky room with my thoughts. Shadows were flickering on the walls as some guys cooked bits of food or made some hot drinks. The familiar snores started to spring up here and there, the end result of a long, hard day. The whole company was very pleased with itself. We had gone into a Taliban stronghold, shot the fuck out of it, and got away without a single casualty. For once something had actually gone according to plan. I was tired as hell, and drifted off to sleep.

CHAPTER 30

THERE AND BACK

The attack on Vodka would prove to be the last big operation that I would be a part of through the tour. The routine from the DC continued on for another couple of weeks, much the same as before but with a marked reduction in the amount of enemy fire aimed at the Eastern Checkpoint. It was nearly the end of March and I had been in theatre for six months. I was getting tired of it all and longing to go home. And that didn't mean the U.K., it meant Canada. It meant *home*. One morning, with no warning, my wish was granted. It was one of the happiest days of my life.

The troop boss came in and started to lay out the plans for yet another patrol with the ANP. He designated the sections that were going out and those that would stay behind to help with the sentry rotations. But then he said it all applied to everyone except Tom and me. It seemed that the two of us had been drafted onto a heavy weapons course that was to start at the end of May, and if we were going to get all of the post-tour leave we were entitled to, we would have to go back to the U.K. right away. It was true that nearly a year earlier the two of us had put our names down for the course together, but I was still taken by surprise. The troop boss said that there was a helo inbound in a couple of hours with our names on it. I couldn't believe my luck, and as the rest of the troop shook their heads in disgust at our good fortune, Tom and I tried to conceal our excitement. We quickly emptied our kit of things that the troop would want: ammo, batteries, and NVGs. We happily handed over the last of our rations and any books, cards, tobacco, and fresh socks we had. We left behind everything that we could and stuffed the rest into our bergens in double quick time. We had no intention of missing this ride.

In a few days I was exactly where I wanted to be, back in B.C., and life was fantastic. The prawning and fishing were good, Jennifer was as lovely as ever, and my family was all around me. There was nothing for me to do but enjoy life.

This of course didn't last forever, and seven weeks later I was at the airport and on my way back to the U.K. to get on with the job. Camp up in Arbroath was packed with the whole unit back, and it was a good thing, because we had some very serious business to attend to. The Royal Marines have a tradition that they raise money for the families of bootnecks who have been killed on operations. We hold kit sales, and ask the families of the deceased to donate items from their loved ones' kit to be sold at auctions on camp. Nobody cares what gets donated, and usually we end up with a pair of boots, a few shirts, and some trinkets. The items aren't important because no matter what it is the guys will pay top dollar for it. Troop by troop and company by company the boys pool their money together and then head off to the auction. There is always a lot of beer involved and the families are usually present as the guests of honour to see how bootnecks mourn their losses. Items go up on the auction block and troops bid on them over and over, driving the prices up to ridiculous levels. I have seen single bootlaces get sold for over $1,000. A half-used pack of matches fetched $400 once, and a used respirator was suddenly worth a couple of grand to us, even though we all had one in our locker. Everybody drinks a shitload and talks to the family about how great their sons, brothers, and husbands were, and at the end of the night all of the money is given to the families. It is a fine tradition, and each company has a whole cabinet filled with items bought at these auctions. 45 Commando had more casualties from this deployment than any others in the recent past, so a number of items were purchased that night by every company.

My next stop was good old CTC. I took the train from Exeter, and that old familiar sick feeling crept back into my guts as the train passed the assault course and stopped in front of those gates. Many courses are held here for bootnecks going into a whole variety of specializations. Signallers, snipers, mortar men, and PTIs all return to CTC for further training. I checked in at the guardroom and then found Tom sitting in the accommodation. We were reunited again, and headed off down to Jollies for a cold one to catch up and gloat about how good our time at home had been. It sure was a different feeling to be walking around CTC with our heads held high and in no fear of a sudden thrashing. The world had definitely turned in our favour.

We were there for a month-long mortar course, and on Monday morning we got straight into it. The 81 mm mortar was to become our new weapon of choice, and to start with we had a lot of lectures on the mortar itself: weights, performance specs, and maintenance. Most of the course was hands-on, with the students constantly getting faster and faster at setting up the mortar and bringing it into action. The mortar had a three-man crew, and we cycled through each position over and over until we knew all of the jobs inside and out.

We had to take several written tests to ensure we were picking up all of the theory behind mortaring, but the emphasis was on accuracy and speed in changing the aim of the mortar from one target to another.

Most nights everyone in the course went out into town and hit the local pubs and bars. It was one giant piss-up, with even the training staff joining us most nights. Needless to say, we all really enjoyed the course, and towards the end were looking forward to putting our new skills into practice in Afghanistan. I knew from recent experience the value of a good mortar crew and couldn't wait to pound the Taliban with HE.

Near the end of June the course drew to a close and we all had to write down which units we wanted to go to. Hardly anybody on the course had been to Afghanistan yet so everybody put down 40 Commando as their first choice, since it was the next unit to go. Only three people would get to go to 40, and even though I had just gotten back from Afghanistan I still put it down as my first choice. I have trouble explaining what I was feeling when I did that. I badly wanted to be spending time at home but all the while I was dying to get back into theatre and carry on with the job. Even to this day I feel that way. Perhaps it is a soldier thing: an addiction to the action, camaraderie, and respect, yet simultaneously not wanting to leave your family. Anyway, I ended up passing the course with distinction and was awarded my top choice. On June 28, 2007, I headed off up the line to join the mortar troop at 40 Commando, Royal Marines.

40 Commando is based near a large town in Somerset called Taunton, about forty-five minutes by train from CTC. I really liked being in southwest England. There were plenty of green open spaces and it wasn't nearly as densely populated as many other parts of the U.K. However, before I barely had time to take a breath there, I was straight back into pre-deployment training, repeating the same lessons I'd taken the previous summer.

I spent much time at my new unit just getting to know the bootnecks I'd be working with and sampling cider from the local farms (Sheppys is king). The guys asked me a lot of questions about what it was like over there. Some of them had been to Afghanistan before, back in 2003, when they were chasing al-Qaida through the mountains of Tora Bora, but few had been into the Helmand province. I tried my best to pass on all of my up-to-date knowledge and plenty of tips. But soon enough we were out of time and the unit was focused on tying up loose ends and visiting with their families before we shipped out in October. I flew back to Canada again for three weeks of leave in August. When I saw Jennifer I could tell that something wasn't right. She wasn't her usual happy self, and after a bit of prodding she came out with it. She figured that we should stop seeing each other, that we had grown apart and that I didn't seem to have the commitment that she did. I knew that she was telling the truth and didn't feel right trying to convince her otherwise, so I simply said, "Okay." Another chapter in my life came to a quick end, and in my customary way I pushed through and tried to get used to being single again. But a blonde young woman named Sarah had other plans for me.

Sarah had heard all about me from some mutual friends and they'd shown her some pictures of me. When she heard I was single, she arranged it so that we would meet up at a local pub with some pals. She was beautiful, and we got along splendidly. She captured my heart instantly, and I was amazed at my good fortune to have met her. We spent all of our time together before I had to leave. Only three short weeks later, however, it was time to ship out. I told her that I was experienced in very-long-distance relationships, having just finished with one, and that it was very difficult. I suggested we put everything on hold until I finished my upcoming trip to Afghanistan, but she knew what she wanted and persisted. Hey, I am only a man, and my defences against the devices of a lovely young woman are only so strong.

So there it was. I had a new girl, and was just about to fly to Afghanistan for another six months at least. September flew by, and before I knew it, on October 11 I was on another Hercules that was touching down in Camp Bastion. This time everything was going to be very different. I was going out on the ground as a mortar man. I had managed to prove that I was very quick at adjusting targets and was the #1 in my crew. Instead of being at the pointy end of operations, this time I would mostly stay a few kilometres to the rear, sending bombs up into the air whenever the radio crackled to life.

We spent a few days on Bastion getting acclimatized and being briefed on the latest developments in the region. Things were very busy right from north to south with daily enemy contact. There were now a number of different FOBs (Forward Operating Bases) like the Garmsir DC set up throughout the province. It was most likely that we would be going to set up a mortar line in one of these FOBs, just like the one that had supported me so many times from Garmsir. Sure enough, after a few days we piled onto a Chinook with all of our mortar kit and headed out over the familiar landscape covered with compound walls and lonely, meandering tracks. I was back where I wanted to be, and one of the things that gave me comfort was knowing I had my Canadian flag stuffed into my pocket over my left breast. I had my lucky charm.

We were heading to a FOB called Inkerman that was situated up in the northern part of the Sangin Valley. It was on the eastern edge of the green zone and took an awful lot of incoming enemy fire. The green zone was what we called the belt of trees and irrigated fields that wound down through the centre of the Helmand province, following the river from north to south. FOB Inkerman was perched up above the edge of the green zone on a high point that was about one hundred feet above the valley floor and had a dominating view out towards the river to the west. A busy road ran from north to south at the base of the hill, and there was a small ANA base wedged in between the road and the hill. This was a fairly new FOB and was still under construction but its main outer perimeter walls had already been finished. Because of the FOB's exposed position on the hilltop, the enemy had many opportunities to crawl up to within two hundred metres using the system of drainage ditches and dykes that filled the green zone. Every day a few RPGs would be thrown at the FOB, and it was notorious for the mortar attacks that rained down upon it with regularity. There was nothing to the east of the FOB as it was right on the edge of the open desert, and it was in this endless open area to the rear of the FOB that the Chinook I was in settled down in an enormous cloud of choking dust. In the swirling, hot dust storm we struggled to get all of our mortar kit off the back of the helo, and with our bergens finally clear of the tail ramp we set up a defensive perimeter as the helo powered up and took off for Bastion. I was back on the ground in Afghanistan.

We were pointed over to a corner of the FOB and dropped our kit in a heap. This was a very dusty FOB, and in most places you literally sank up to the tops of your boots in a very fine, talcum-like powder. It was so light that if you closed your eyes you wouldn't even know you were ankle-deep in dust, and when the wind kicked up, it swirled around the FOB, coating everything, including your eyeballs and lungs. I immediately hated it, but this was where we were going to live for the foreseeable future. There was already a mortar line set up. One of our sections had arrived about a week before us and had set up shop in the opposite corner. We were all under the impression that our section was going to be the mobile section that would accompany any MOGs heading off on strike ops up and down the green zone.

We spent the next couple of days watching our brother mortar section in action and scrounging for bits of old wooden pallets and scraps of parachute to try to make our area a bit more livable. Each day the enemy would send a few mortar bombs over towards the FOB, and our boys would spring straight into action, pummelling the area from which the enemy bombs had originated. They had a great system worked out, and could often have bombs in the air less than thirty seconds after the enemy bombs had landed. This FOB was mortared so often that it eventually became known as "FOB Incoming."

The engineers were enclosing an area adjacent to the FOB with yet another tall, dirt-filled wall and needed some security out around them while they worked. Our section wasn't really up to much so we were tasked to go stand around for hours each day, protecting the engineers. One day as we stood about staring at neighbouring compounds for enemy movement, we came under heavy enemy mortar fire. We could all hear the bombs slicing through the air as they approached our position, and we ran towards a small cinderblock building that was in the middle of the area we were enclosing. The first bombs struck about thirty metres away as I ran across the open ground, hunched over to make a smaller target. A small piece of shrapnel glanced off the top of my helmet with the first burst and quickly reminded me of where I was. We piled into the structure and sat on the floor against the walls, listening to more and more explosions echoing around the FOB. Some of the bombs were landing in the compound but most were wide of the mark. There were about four of us from the section sitting in there, along with one of the engineers. Clearly he had not been under fire very much and was absolutely terrified by what was happening outside. He was huddled in a corner, telling us all how much he wanted to be at home. Not only was he wearing his own body armour like the rest of us but he had an extra set of armour that he was trying his best to hide his body underneath. The sight made the rest of us smile and our grinning comforted him a little. I was lucky enough to find some peanut butter from an American ration pack in a pile of garbage in the corner. Happy times!

For two weeks we sat in that FOB with no real task. So many things were exactly like they had been down in Garmsir, apart from the lack of action. The smell was an Afghan mix of the garbage burn pit, outhouses, dust, animals, and cooking fires. The local mosques were broadcasting prayers through loudspeakers at crazy hours, just as they had in Garmsir, and donkeys were braying all day and dogs barking all night. The mortars fell every day, and each time we put on our body armour and tried to carry on with whatever we were doing. One day an enemy mortar bomb hit the fender of a huge diesel tanker truck we had parked in the FOB. The bomb exploded and tore the whole fender and wheel well apart, peppering the diesel tank with a hundred holes. The tank was Swiss cheese, and the supply guys ran around for hours trying to plug holes and save what fuel they could in various containers. We were all very lucky that that tank had been full of diesel and not gasoline. Things could have been very different for us, considering the tanker was only about one hundred feet from where we sat playing cards.

Often times when a possible enemy was sighted, any jets in the area were called in to do a low and fast flyby to let the enemy know we had assets in the area. Unlike the situation in Garmsir, this was not simply a "free fire" zone. This was Card Alpha territory, and that meant you could only fire when fired upon, or when you were certain that you were about to be fired upon. There were many civilians still living and farming in the area. The most impressive show of our strength was when the huge B1 bombers would come down low. They are massive aircraft, and very good-looking. They have variable swept wings like an F-14 Tomcat. They would come screaming down the valley and pass just in front of the FOB, at about the same level we were standing. As they opened up the throttles and then pulled up and banked sharply away, the valley vibrated with the thunder of their four huge engines. Every time it happened I was impressed with the power.

Finally we were called into action at the very end of October. We were being recalled to Bastion to head out on a MOG. The section was happy to be thrown a bone and grinned the whole way back to Bastion. It took a little longer than usual because we were moved in large, heavily armoured trucks called Mastiffs, but it didn't matter. We were a mortar section, and it seemed that we would finally get to do some mortaring.

CHAPTER 31

MOG NORTH 1

NORTHWEST HELMAND PROVINCE
0200 HOURS
NOVEMBER 3, 2007

The night was already starting to get quite chilly as I sat down on the ground with my back to our Mastiff, staring up at the brilliant stars in the clear sky. I could see my breath as I exhaled and was happy that I was dry and had plenty of warm clothes on. It was my turn to be on radio watch, and for nearly an hour I had been sitting listening to complete silence coming from the headset. I thought about home, looked at the constellations, and fingered my new little St. Christopher medallion that Sarah had sent me.

We were leaguered up about thirty kilometres north of Camp Bastion out in the middle of the desert. The morning before we had left Bastion and headed straight north in a massive group of vehicles, leaving towering clouds of dust in our wake. We were MOG North, but our mission had still not been made clear to us. My mortar section was spread out between four of the large Mastiff armoured trucks. Three of us sat wedged in the back of each truck between our mortars and stacks of bombs. We were protected from the outside world by thick armour on all sides. The truck had six wheels, weighed around twenty-five tonnes, and had a crew of three. The driver and vehicle commander sat up front, while the third crew member manned the .50-calibre machine gun that was housed in a well-protected turret on the top. So far these vehicles had proven to be very resilient when it came to driving over large stacks of mines on the roads and so I felt very safe. They did get stuck a lot more than any tracked vehicle, but this was what we had to work with and there was a lot more room in the back of them than the Vikings that I was used to.

This MOG tasking was supposed to be a ten- to fourteen-day affair, and from what I could gather we were supposed to push north from Bastion about eighty kilometres to an area around a large settlement called Musa Qal'eh to generally locate and destroy Taliban forces. The strength of the MOG was tremendous. The main striking power was a group of twenty-four Warrior armoured fighting vehicles. These looked like light tanks, had a 30 mm cannon in a turret with a machine gun, and carried six riflemen in the back. Twenty-four of these full of troops constituted a formidable striking force. These were all army units that we were working with, as the bulk of 3 Commando Brigade had just been deployed when I was out with Zulu Company earlier in the year. 40 Commando was attached to an Army brigade for this tour, and time and time again over the next five months I would be reminded why I preferred to work with bootnecks.

In addition to the Warriors and the four Mastiffs filled with my mortar section there were eight other Mastiffs filled with an assortment of army riflemen and bootnecks. There were numerous logistics vehicles carrying a tremendous amount of food, water, ammunition, and spare vehicle parts for the MOG. There was a three-gun battery of 105 mm artillery with us, along with all of their vehicles to tow their guns, half a dozen Wimiks, command vehicles, rolling workshops, a large recovery vehicle (giant tow truck), and two large fuel tankers to feed the hungry diesel engines. Just getting all of these vehicles on the move at one time and heading in the same direction was an immense undertaking, let alone co-coordinating it all into a well-oiled fighting machine. As we had been moving north through the desert, the Warriors had been several miles ahead of us, fanned out to keep the route clear and to deal with threats as they arose. The soft vehicles, like the fuel trucks, artillery, and general cargo, all grouped together in the middle with a screen of Mastiffs and Wimiks to the sides and rear. It was very slow going for the most part. With all those vehicles spread out over such a large area, there almost always seemed to be at least one that was stuck.

In the evenings, all of the soft vehicles would bunch up together in the centre of a wall of steel that was at least two layers thick. The Warriors would form a protective screen a few kilometres out, in all directions. The Mastiffs and Wimiks would form a second screen, and in the centre we would set up our mortar line alongside the artillery. Our MFCS (mortar fire controllers) were the ones that spotted targets and adjusted our rounds onto them, and they would stay near the centre, ready to head to whichever side was being attacked. Our mortars had a range of nearly six kilometres, so overall the MOG was in a very strong position each night. Of course, with the old radio we always had plenty of fast air assets and Apaches just a few minutes away. We often had unmanned aerial vehicles way over our heads to keep an eye out for any heat sources that might have been approaching our position. The new flavour of the month for the Air Force was to fly their jets over the leaguer at night, very low and on full afterburner. It was always a wicked sight, and I envied the pilots as I watched the long blue exhaust from the engines rapidly disappear into the night sky, winking out completely when they let off on the throttle.

This is where I found myself on that evening, sitting in the leaguer next to the Mastiff with a radio headset on and my mortar about ten metres away. My crew was sleeping on the ground next to the mortar, and hour by hour the radio watch worked its way through the section. In the morning at about 0530 we would all get up and pack our kit away. At first light we would be sitting next to the mortar to repel any dawn attack, and after another hour or so we would quickly tear down the mortar, stow it away in the back of the Mastiff, and mount up for another long and dusty day, inching north across the barren landscape. Every few hours we might pass by a few compounds or a random herd of sheep, but for the most part it was very bleak. As we drove along there was always some motorcycle on the horizon, keeping tabs on where we were heading. These motorcycles were Taliban agents blatantly calling in our new positions, but unless we could prove it, we couldn't engage them. They never carried weapons and almost always managed to bury their cellphones before we could get to them. If we were under mortar attack or anything, the rules on dealing with these guys were relaxed, because they were likely adjusting the rounds, and that made them enemy combatants. On the fourth day of the MOG, this is the situation we were in.

We were all stopped for a vehicle that had gotten stuck in the sand and began to receive some enemy mortar fire. Our Mastiff gunner spotted what he thought was an enemy MFC and fired some warning shots to shoo him away. One of the large bullets broke up near the guy on the deck and a shard hit him in the calf. He went down hard and we ended up having to go over to him and capture him as a prisoner. We did a bit of first aid on him as he writhed on the ground, yelling all kinds of crazy shit with plenty of "Allah!"s thrown into the mix. We pumped him full of morphine to ease his pain and encourage him to calm down a bit. A Chinook was sent from Bastion to take him in for questioning and medical treatment, and half an hour later all was normal again. The mortar fire had ceased the moment this guy had been put on the ground. Shortly afterwards, our massive convoy roared to life again and snaked off into the desert.

Along the way there were a lot of wadis that had to be crossed, and some were very large. The biggest ones were several hundred metres across and basically old, wide riverbeds. There were steep banks leading down to the soft gravelly bottoms and equally steep exits up the other side. The largest of these wadis led northwest from the Helmand River, all the way up to Musa Qal'eh, a distance of about forty kilometres. This wadi was almost like a mini green zone and was heavily populated along either side. In the rainy season it filled with water and drew plenty of civilians to its banks. We wanted to get across this wadi to break out into the open areas to the north from where we would be able to dominate the entire northern sector of the province, right up to the start of the enormous Afghan mountain ranges. The crossing itself would make the convoy very vulnerable for a time because we would have hardly any room to manoeuvre and the enemy would have plenty of cover. We would be channelled into set routes and would likely be forced to stop in potential kill zones as we waited for other vehicles to get over and through obstacles. The day before we made our attempt, we stopped a few kilometres short of the crossing point and set up for the night. If the enemy had any brains at all, they would be able to see exactly what we were preparing to do, so to counter any bright ideas of theirs we had hidden an ace up our sleeve.

That evening, one of our sentries spotted a baddie burying a mine or an IED on the track that we were going to be driving along in the morning and took him out with a few long bursts from his GPMG. This incident meant the enemy definitely knew we were taking that route; if we got through with no major hassles we would have to consider ourselves lucky.

As dawn approached, a company of Royal Marines went on the move to come and help secure the crossing point. Half of the company came tearing straight up the wadi from the southeast in Vikings and secured a few pieces of vital high ground overlooking the crossing point, while the rest of them swooped down onto high points on the other side in the back of a pair of Chinooks. Although they met with some resistance, which we could hear from our location, it was nothing they couldn't handle, and as we prepared to move we were happy to know that we had extra security in place.

Just as we started to move off we had a delay. One of our supply trucks had driven into a large ditch and rolled over. There was simply no time to stop everything, so once Command had checked what the contents of the truck were, they made the decision to blow it up. So we had to blow up a perfectly good off-road supply truck filled with food and supplies, on account of somebody's poor driving. We did manage to offload some of the stores before we blew it, but we had only been going for a few days so all of the other vehicles were already full. Obviously, if HQ was willing to blow up vehicles rather than stop, there was a very important schedule that we were expected to maintain. The MOG headed off to the north to start our crossing and, as the last of the vehicles got clear of the disabled truck, the engineers detonated the charges they had set. There was a terrific explosion to our rear, and the telltale sign of a dusty mushroom cloud clawed its way into the sky. Later that day the Apaches would have another look at the vehicle, and if they felt it was necessary they would sink a few Hellfire missiles into it to make sure there was nothing of any use left.

The front of the convoy was soon pushing on into the flat wadi floor, following a route chosen by the Warriors the previous day. Everything up ahead of us was quiet and I couldn't see any action. There were two escape hatches in the truck's roof just above our seats, and I spent most of the time standing on my seat. I felt much better if

I knew what was happening in the outside world, and if worse came to worse I could at least bring my rifle to bear on any targets. Our mortar section was always near the front of the convoy so that we could be close to the action, and our MFC was riding in the back of one of the Warriors a few kilometres to our front. There was no point in having a perfectly good mortar line if you weren't going to be in a position to use it.

As our Mastiff crept down the bank at the start of the crossing, the lead vehicles were already making their way out the other side. All was quiet until we got about a third of the way across. The enemy began to fire at us from unseen positions beyond the hills with mortars and rockets. There was also the odd snap in the air as poorly aimed bullets zipped across the wadi. None of the fire was overly threatening and we had plenty of security on the flanks to deal with the threats, but for many of these army guys it was their first contact of any sort and they worked themselves up into a frenzy. The top gunners were spraying heavy bullets and 40 mm bombs in every direction, shooting at distant specks on the horizon. I could only assume that our top gunner could see things that I couldn't, so as he flapped about and got the rounds down I helped feed him fresh boxes of link. I could hear the Warriors up to the front somewhere, firing their 30 mm cannons, and some small-arms fire coming from one of the high points that our lads had secured that morning, but overall it wasn't much to be concerned about. As we made our way across the flat wadi bottom and climbed up the other side, everything started to get pretty quiet again. We simply had too much firepower concentrated in the area for the enemy to stand a chance.

Nearly every day at last light as we set up the leaguer we took a few incoming mortar rounds. The time 1730 became known as mortar o'clock, and we were always quick to have our own mortar line set up to try to get some fire returned. Sometimes our MFC would be able to spot the firing point and we would send back some suppressive fire, but most days the enemy would just shoot and scoot, never giving us a chance to get a fix on their position. At the same time, shooting and scooting meant they never stuck around long enough to adjust their fire and bring it to bear with any accuracy – it was always just a bit of harassing fire to let us know that they knew where we were. Every time we stopped and set up our mortar line we would dig holes to sleep in, and in the morning when we left we would fill them in again. Day after day we repeated the process, and our ten-day MOG slowly turned into a twenty-day and then a thirty-day affair. Each week we were told that we would be heading back to Bastion soon, but it never happened. Supplies for the MOG became an issue within a couple of weeks, so we began to be resupplied by air. Chinooks brought in what they could every few days, and about once a week we would get a large air drop by Hercules. In the middle of the night a Herc would come in low and slow, and we would all be staring up to try to see the black plane against the black sky. Usually we couldn't see it, but we would all hear the loud snaps up above as the parachutes attached to the supplies whipped open. They air-dropped food, fuel, and ammunition, and it was a little unnerving to have tonnes of supplies coming down out of the night sky and thumping into the desert a few hundred metres away. I have to hand it to the Royal Air Force for those drops. They were usually very accurate and only once did the parachutes malfunction, sending a large pallet of rations slamming into the desert floor.

Sometimes our mortar line set up quite far away from the main leaguer in order to get on level ground and we would put out claymores and trip flares around our position. The wadis always had small gullies leading down into them and we covered these likely approaches with machine guns and explosives. The chances of anyone sneaking up on us were slim because of our NVGs, and nothing exciting ever happened during the evenings, but we always took the precautions to minimize the risk. We worked hard to maintain a disciplined routine, and week by week we perfected it. It was on one of these groundhog days that we were shot at by the army lads for the first time. The leaguer was just getting settled into position at mortar o'clock when the enemy sent over their standard greetings. Our section quickly poured out of the Mastiffs and began to set up our mortars. All of a sudden there was an explosion right in the middle of the mortar line that we were establishing. It was too small to be an enemy mortar bomb and we all looked around to see where it had come from. After a bit of clarification on the radio we learned that a distant top gunner on a Mastiff had mistaken us for Taliban and had fired his grenade launcher at us. We are very lucky he only fired a single shot and not an automatic burst. How he managed to mistake us for Taliban in our British uniforms standing beside massive British armoured vehicles is beyond me, but we were all grateful that he was a bad shot. There was nothing that we could do about it, just get on with the job and get the mortars sighted.

That evening one of the army lads headed out for a piss in the middle of the night and managed to walk out from the leaguer and through our sentry pickets. I have no idea what he was thinking, but he managed to get lost in the desert and found himself in a very bad situation. If he wandered around too much and the sentries spotted him, there was a good chance that he would be shot. No civilians wandered around in the desert by themselves in the dark of night. Shouting out could attract the attention of any enemy in the area and even lead to getting his head chopped off for all to see on the Internet. He was in a pickle, no doubt about it, and likely scared shitless. He didn't have his rifle with him and hadn't brought his NVGs, infrared glow sticks, or any way to identify himself. In the end he chose to start calling out for help. The sentries headed out to find him and brought him back without incident, but it was a ridiculous situation.

What with all the crashed vehicles, being shot at by our own forces, poor discipline in the leaguer, and blokes wandering off into the night without their weapons, I was not very impressed with having to work with this bunch. It was a big difference from what I was used to, and for the first time I was glad that I wasn't heading out as a rifleman to look for scraps.

CHAPTER 32

MOG NORTH 2

After three weeks of driving through the desert we still didn't have a clear idea of exactly what we were trying to achieve. Somebody somewhere knew what was up, but for now we were just along for the ride. We kept pushing farther and farther north until we were the most northerly British troops in the province and in among the foothills of the mountain ranges that suddenly sprang up from the desert floor. In late November the Warriors all headed back to Bastion, and as a replacement the Household Cavalry showed up with their light armoured vehicles. They were the same Scimitars that the Light Dragoons had been using to support our operations at Jugroom Fort back in January.

As we had approached the foothills we passed through a number of built-up areas, always on our toes for an ambush. But nothing ever happened. We were not the only MOG operating in the northern half of the province and the Taliban were having a very tough time keeping tabs on everyone and guessing what we were up to. Even we didn't know what we were doing or where we were going, so the Taliban didn't have a chance of figuring that one out! The Taliban were always chatting away on their little hand-held radios that we could listen in on, but never carried out the attacks that they were announcing were about to happen. When we got into the foothills we tucked in behind a few high features and did our best to dig some holes in the rocky ground. Our MFCS got themselves up onto the hilltops, studied the terrain and identified likely enemy firing points. We were told that we were going to be staying here for a while and that we would be defending this position for as long as it took. We dug deeper and made storage pits for our ammunition next to our mortars.

The artillery was set up about twenty-five metres away, and in the middle of that first night without any warning they fired an illumination mission. They were firing on their maximum charge to reach the very tip of their range, and in that tight, rocky valley the noise was unbearable. We were so close to the guns that it felt like my body was being shaken apart. We had hearing protection that we called ear defenders, but mine just didn't do a damn thing, and all I could do was lie there with my hands pressed firmly over them, waiting for the fire mission to end. They fired a salvo five times between 2100 and 0100, and when they weren't firing the crews were yelling instructions back and forth. I really hoped that wasn't going to happen every night and looked forward to the time when we would get to fire and return the favour. If there were going to be any illum missions that had to be fired within six kilometres we would be the first choice. Our illum was much better. It was more accurate, burned brighter and longer, and was quicker to adjust.

The baddies were aware that we had set up shop in the valley and fired a lot of rockets at us while we were there. They fired from villages five and six kilometres away so sacrificed accuracy to ensure they could get away before they felt our response. Many of the 107 mm rockets slammed into the high, rocky feature to our rear with great crashes that echoed up and down our enclave. They were struggling to get the rockets to come down at a high enough angle that they would land among us, but if anything was ever going to be hit, it would have to be a very lucky shot. Each day the Scimitars and Mastiffs headed off to try to find and engage the firing points, and sometimes they got into some fair-sized firefights. They called in a bit of fast air now and then, but they were all armoured and could easily take on anything thrown at them out in the open. Their top gunners took a few minor casualties, and every couple of days a helo would show up to drop some supplies and take out the injured. One of these helo drops delivered some satellite phones for us to use, and for the first time in a month I surprised Sarah with a phone call. It was amazing to hear a Canadian accent, especially a female one as sweet as hers. She was shocked to get a call from me, and it was great to have someone as amazing as her to talk to out in the middle of the shitty Afghan desert. I felt like the luckiest guy in the world when I finished the call.

After two weeks of sitting in that tight valley we were off and moving again. It was around this time that we were made aware of our mission. The ANA, with American soldier support, were going to take Musa Qal'eh back from the Taliban. There were several MOGs satelliting around the large Taliban-controlled town, and at the moment of attack we would all close in to act as cut-offs. We were going to confuse the enemy with our presence, stop Taliban reinforcements from joining the fight, engage fleeing enemy, and generally isolate the battlefield. This town was the largest area still firmly in the hands of the Taliban, and it was going to be a major victory for the ANA, expelling large Taliban forces and boosting the ANA's image in the eyes of the public.

In the first week of December we moved off south about twenty kilometres and set up shop in a large compound at the base of a prominent hill. On our side there were a few compounds spread about, and on the other side was the large wadi that ran right up to the town.

It was the same wadi that we had crossed a month before, and we expected it would be used as a route by fleeing Taliban. As usual we got our mortars set up and dug in to stay for a while. We still had a few days to kill before the big attack and wanted to make sure that we were as ready as we could possibly be.

This compound became known as the Barnyard, and for very good reason. It had been occupied until we showed up, and the family had moved a few hundred metres away into a different compound. All of their animals were still wandering about, and it was good for a laugh. There were turkeys cruising around, pecking at our feet and gobbling away all through the day. Chickens and roosters jumped around on our kit, and cats were meowing in every corner. All over the place there were goats that managed to find their way up onto the roofs of the low buildings, a herd of sheep that was constantly in the way, and a donkey that loved to eat our rations when we weren't looking. The kid goats jumped about, tripping over our ammunition and kit, their floppy ears hanging down to their knees. We would pull up water from the well in an old bucket to give the animals a drink and fed them hand-fuls of hay. It was entertaining and completely harmless, except for the crazy dogs.

These dogs were no ordinary dogs. They were all massive, and tough as nails. They had no tails, their ears had been burned off by the owners, they all had limps and had been shot at numerous times. Pus poured from their faces and they snarled and lunged at anyone who came within ten feet. They had had hard lives and wouldn't take any shit from anyone. They made Cujo look like a pussy, and it wasn't long before someone got attacked by one of them. On the first afternoon we arrived, a dog attacked a Mastiff driver, so with good reason he shot it. A second dog ran away to the other compounds, and the third one just sat in a corner of the yard, growling and barking at all of us. He was the nastiest of the bunch, and in the middle of the first night he stood bristling at the edge of the #3 mortar's hole and barked at them for a full hour. They couldn't get out of the hole for fear they'd be attacked by this insane beast, and nobody wanted to start shooting in the compound in the middle of the night. When the dog wandered off a little bit they all made a break for it and came running over to my mortar, diving in the hole with this dog in hot pursuit. Clearly things were going to have to change.

At first light several of us crawled out of the hole, ready to do the deed. We lined out three abreast, and this crazy dog was right there in front of us, barking and snarling, lunging and daring us to make a move. We raised our rifles, cocked our weapons, and took aim. At that moment something inside that dog's head clicked. He realized we weren't messing around and that he was about to die. I guarantee that wasn't the first time he had ever seen a weapon cocked, but before any of us had time to fire, he stopped barking, slowly turned around, and loped off out of the compound. He headed off down the hill to where the rest of the settlement was and never came back. We were at the Barnyard for four days and we never saw him again.

When the battle for Musa Qal'eh started a few days later, it sounded like one hell of a fight. The explosions were distant but clearly audible, and at night the sky to the northwest of us was lit up repeatedly, flash after flash bouncing off the atmosphere. I wished we were closer to the action and had to content myself with climbing up the hill and watching the A-10s from a distance unleash the fury with their giant Avenger guns. We were just here to act as cut-offs and had to wait until something wandered through our kill zone. The battle lasted several days, and we did manage to engage and destroy some targets that came fleeing down the wadi, but for the most part it was uneventful just like the rest of the MOG had been. The only thing that kept me going some days was the knowledge that in a couple of weeks I would be off on R&R again, sitting on a beach once more with a beautiful woman by my side.

At night while the battle for Musa Qal'eh was on, there was often illum being sent up in the distance to the north, south, and west of us. People were getting into fights all over the whole area, and it was surprising that nobody had really tried to take us on yet. But the next day the baddies decided to attack our position from the compounds down below. They initiated the contact by sending a few RPGS up towards us and then they let rip with their AKs. We all dove into cover, reaching for our body armour as bullets snapped through the air all around us. It seems strange to say it, but it felt good to be back in a little bit of action. I had missed the adrenalin. I sprang out of my hole and went tearing across the compound to get into a good fire position. We had a GPMG up on the roof of a small building in the centre of the Barnyard, and the lads behind it were already starting to return fire down into the maze of dirt walls that the enemy was firing from. I got up to the edge of a wall and began to return fire, shooting at bits of movement bobbing about behind the walls. The Mastiffs were up on the high ground behind us and began to get their big guns into the game, tearing large chunks out of the compounds below with their .50-calibre Brownings. There was no way the enemy could keep up a protracted firefight without getting decimated, and as quickly as our little fight had started, it was all over.

That evening there was a lot of movement in the wadi on the other side of the hill and we sent up a shitload of illum to help our guys spot targets. We had a limited supply of illumination ammo with us. Every bit of space in the Mastiffs had been crammed with bombs, but nearly all of it was high explosive. We ran out of illum after a few hours, so the lads on the hill had to resort to calling in illum from the artillery battery that was established about six kilometres to the north of us. As we cleaned our mortars and cleared away the empty ammo containers, the first of the artillery illum went screaming overhead.

The artillery can fire their illum out to a distance of twelve kilometres or so, and to get it that long distance the part that burns and gives off the light has to catch a ride on a ten-pound piece of steel for most of the way. When the round gets near the area it is going to burst over, the ten-pound piece of steel is discarded and sent hurtling along its trajectory into the ground somewhere. The first time the artillery fired that night, we heard the steel slug coming out of the black sky straight towards our position. It was whistling and howling, and as we took cover it smashed into the ground about fifty feet in front of our #1 mortar. It landed with a loud WHOOMP! and kicked up a fountain of earth into the air. That bit of steel would seriously fuck you up if you happened to be in front of it, and we immediately got onto the net to get them to adjust their fire. They got the message and let us know that they had adjusted their fire away from us. Nevertheless, this was the army that we were dealing with, so we all got down into our holes in preparation for the next round, and sure enough they fucked it up. We heard the first round go whistling way overhead beyond the hill and then the steel carrier shell came hurtling down towards our position again. We all sat in our holes making ourselves as small as possible, listening to this thing screaming in towards us. I knew it was coming close as it got louder and louder, and then – SLAM! – it pounded into the ground about fifteen feet from the edge of my hole. I started yelling for the radio man to get back on the net and have those idiots check their fire, and when he did the artillery guys had the nerve to tell us that there was no way it had landed that close to us. They told us that it must have landed in another grid square, and that we were being paranoid. Even though they thought we had just been imagining it, they adjusted their fire again to appease us. How thoughtful.

As the ANA raised the Afghan national flag over the main buildings in Musa Qal'eh, everything began to quiet down. All along this had been the primary mission for the MOG, and with its successful conclusion it was time to be heading off. We packed up our mortars one morning and headed north again, into the familiar rolling desert and wadis where we had spent the last month. Our ten-day MOG had so far transformed into a forty-day epic. We were all in need of a shower and would have killed for some fresh food. But unlike the rest of the section, I had a pretty good idea of when I would be heading back to Bastion. My R&R was scheduled to start in the middle of December and I would be jumping on a Chinook a few days before then. We got out into the desert and spent the next few days doing exactly what we had done before. Set up, radio watch, wake up, pack up, and move again. As the days ticked by my excitement grew, and one morning the good news came. My massive beard and I were getting on a flight later that day, and with that news I handed out the last of my food and treats to the rest of the section and said my farewells. I wandered over to HQ with my bergen and waited for the helo.

A few days later I found myself back in the U.K. waiting at the train station in Taunton for Sarah to arrive. She had flown over to see me and I could barely contain my excitement. To be honest, we barely knew each other, and I was amazed at the giant risk this sweet girl was taking in flying halfway around the world to see me. When she arrived everything was perfect, aside from the airline losing her luggage. A few days later she was reunited with it and we jetted off to the Canary Islands to catch some sun, and spent a wonderful Christmas together on the beach and by the pool. I was back in heaven and had her to thank for it. I couldn't remember a time that I had been so happy. But all good things come to an end, and we parted ways in London, vowing to pick up where we left off after my tour was finished. Before I knew it I was back in Afghanistan and tearing north again, low and fast in the back of a helicopter, to meet up with my section.

CHAPTER 33

GIBRALTAR 1

FOB GIBRALTAR, SOUTHERN SANGIN VALLEY
DECEMBER 30, 2007

I landed in FOB Gibraltar at dusk on a cold and wet day. This was a new FOB; it had only been around for about a month and was located at the southern tip of a portion of the green zone known as the Sangin Valley. It was a built-up area, with the standard compounds and fields, interlaced with ditches and treelines. There were a lot of civilians around the area, and just as many Taliban. The Taliban flowed up and down the green zone regularly, terrorizing and stealing from the locals and stopping from time to time to pick fights with coalition forces. There were a huge number of tracks around the FOB that were hidden from view by walls, trees, and compounds, and this area was known to be full of IEDs and mines.

The FOB itself had been constructed in a month. The engineers had worked hard and accomplished a lot in that period. The three-metre-high dirt-filled walls were in place and enclosed an area that would accommodate a helicopter landing pad big enough for Chinooks.

Everyone had proper shelters, constructed with roofs that could take direct hits from mortar bombs. In the grots we had cot beds and lights. The mortar pits were well dug-in with areas for ammunition below the surface, and the CP (command post) for the mortar line HQ had its own protective shelter that looked out over the mortar line. It was a great set-up compared to what we had had back in the early Garmsir days, and the electricity and plugs all over the place were the icing on the cake. The section had been hard at work for the last two weeks improving our living area, constructing benches, tables, firepits, and areas in which to cook and clean. As it stood, we were scheduled to stay in this position for the next three and a half months, so we had plenty of time to work on making it comfortable. There was a company of bootneck riflemen based there, and when they pushed out patrols to dominate the area, it would be our job to support them whenever they needed it.

As I made my way off the helo and took in my new surroundings, a guy from the section came up to guide me to our area. Everyone was in fine spirits and glad to finally be settling into a proper mortar line. The section had done another week on that never-ending MOG before returning to Bastion for a quick shower and then moving to occupy this new position. They had taken over the mortar line from an army mortar section and had had to do a lot of cleanup and reorganization before it became workable, but everything seemed to be sorted out by the time I had arrived. There were radios to be manned twenty-four hours a day in the CP, and everyone had to stay near the mortars at all times. We had to be quick to react to any attacks on the FOB and equally quick to support the lads out on the ground. Whenever they went out on patrol, we would have mortar fire controllers (the MFCS) on the ground with them to ensure they got quick and accurate fire when it was needed. About four kilometres southwest of us there was another FOB with a mortar line. We were within range of each other so we could fire in support of each other's defence if necessary.

Whenever the patrols were out – and they went out almost daily – the MFC would lay the mortars onto targets as they moved about on the ground. He would identify likely enemy firing points as they patrolled and get us aiming at those points, so that if we had to fire the switches we would have to make would be small, thereby ensuring a rapid and, we hoped, lethal, response.

It was a very good setup overall. The only problem that I could foresee was boredom. It might be exciting from time to time when the shit hit the fan, but sitting tight in the FOB for over three months sounded like a prison term to me. It was both a good thing and a bad thing to be on the mortar line. We often got out of shit jobs that had to be done around the camp because we could never be far from the mortar, but at the same time it was often very boring to just sit there doing nothing. As they say, 99 per cent of soldiering is sitting around, and the other 1 per cent is full-on action. The mortar line was no exception to the rule.

Within a few days of the riflemen heading out on patrol they began to get hit by IEDs. The first casualty got hit on New Year's Eve by some sort of bomb and was stitched with shrapnel in his leg, arm, and face. He was in stable condition when they brought him in but obviously firmly in the hurt locker. He headed straight back to Bastion on a helo a half hour later and made a full recovery. That night at midnight we were all up and ready to fire off a bunch of illum to bring in the New Year, but at the last minute we had to check fire. There was an American foot patrol in the area that we would have lit up accidently.

The first few days of 2008 were spent improving the living quarters for the section. We laid down thick rubber matting in the accommodation for flooring and adopted a cat that we named Augie. The charges that we placed on the base of the rounds to propel them out of the barrel were called augmenting cartridges, so the cat fit right in with this name. We helped the engineers upgrade and waterproof the roof on the CP, beefed up the sandbag defences in the nearest sangar, and put doors on our accommodation. There was never any escaping sangar duty, and for the bulk of the next few months our section had to have at least one man up there on sentry. The only exception was when we were busy firing our mortars. In that case we would get some riflemen to come and take over for us so we could get on with our real job.

Things picked up for the boys on the ground as the days slipped by. The enemy really didn't like the cold (they were wearing flip-flops after all), and on any day when the weather was clear and warm they were sure to make an appearance. One day in mid January a troop-sized patrol came under fire from a compound a few kilometres from Gib (FOB Gibraltar) and had to call in some mortar fire to suppress the target. We hit it with a bunch of high explosive and threw some white phosphorous into their faces to cover our lads' advance across an open field. When our guys broke into the compound they found a massive cache of parts to make a shitload of pressure plate–activated IEDs. This was a full-on IED factory and we had been lucky to find it. Everything was photographed and a few bits and pieces were brought back for our engineers to study before they blew the lot sky-high.

After a few weeks, nearly every patrol that went out got into some sort of a contact on the ground, and most of January was very busy. Some were minor shoot and scoots, and others turned into all-afternoon affairs with Apaches ending the fights with showers of rockets and Hellfire missiles. Most of the time, though, everything could be handled by the firepower our mortar line packed. We got into a groove and became a very slick section. We could often get our mortars on target and ready to fire long before they were ready to actually pull the trigger on us. We always followed the patrol around on the ground with our barrels, and our mortar fire controllers were very good at pre-empting targets – aiming us towards likely targets that then became real targets just seconds later.

Around this time we received another new toy to play with. It was a shiny set of brand-new Austrian-made 60 mm mortars. Decades before, the British military had done away with the 60, and now they decided it was time to reacquire a medium-sized mortar. Our 81s were fantastic pieces of kit but also just a bit too big to be trucking around in the back of Vikings. The weapons themselves weren't the problem, it was the ammunition. It was simply too heavy and too big to allow us to carry enough bombs. The 60 mm bombs were about half the size and a third of the weight. Every couple of weeks one or two of our mortar crews would load up the backs of two Vikings with a ton of 60 mm ammo and the mortars, and go tearing off around the desert following the riflemen. We would set up in the desert a few kilometres away from whichever compounds were the lads' targets and provide them with an instant cover of HE. It was a great piece of kit and worked flawlessly for us. It was very accurate and had a high rate of fire, but the best part was the fuses. The new 60 mm bombs came with proximity fuses that we could set to burst two metres above the ground, which ensured a wider spray of deadly shrapnel, helped us to hit targets behind walls, and let us spray shrapnel down on top of people who were hiding in holes. It was a brilliant set-up and we wished we had the same fuses for the trusty old 81.

Part of the program to get the locals onside was to employ them whenever we could. Obviously there were serious security issues involved with letting them into Gib, but sometimes we made exceptions, and the well diggers were among the exceptions. We had hired two local well drillers to come into the FOB with their primitive drilling rig and dig us a well. They had to stay in the FOB for the duration of the project so that they only had the one chance to sneak in anything that might be bad for us, and we gave them food and water while they worked. It was only supposed to take them a few days to drill the well, and after ten days we were all wondering what was taking them so long. They were getting paid a fortune for it, and had probably agreed to come and drill knowing full well that their drilling set-up wasn't up to the task. It kept breaking down and falling apart, and one day, one of the two drillers got permission to go to a local town to buy some parts. The other guy stayed behind to work on the rig and became concerned when his friend was late returning. After a few days with his friend not being able to get in touch with him on his cellphone we all began to fear the worst. We heard on intercepted enemy transmissions that they had caught a spy who worked for the British in the town. We had to assume that that was him and that he was likely already dead. The friend who was still in the FOB hung around for a few more days before abandoning his equipment and heading off into the unknown to meet his fate.

Most nights we got up several times to send up a few illum rounds over random points on the ground. We did this a lot, to get the enemy used to it, so that they would think nothing of it and wouldn't even bother getting up to check out what was going on. This way, when we were actually launching attacks at night and needed to put up some illum for the boys, it wouldn't startle the enemy. The company rarely patrolled at night. There were just too many IEDs around for us to be stomping about in the dark. But if everyone had patrolled hard at night I think it would have seriously impeded the enemy's ability to creep around and set up their deadly traps. In Garmsir our fighting patrols had been done almost exclusively in the dark and we had had almost no IEDs or mines to deal with. But who knows which came first, the chicken or the egg?

Towards the end of January the weather began to get very cold, and we started wearing long johns, and heavy sweaters underneath our jackets. It began to snow quite regularly, and we often woke up to find a crisp layer of the white stuff covering our mortars and ammo covers. On one particular day we had giant flakes floating down around us, and everything was so quiet that you could hear them landing gently on the ground. It reminded me of being back at home, out on my dad's property. It was the little things like this that made me miss home and impatient to get out of that damn FOB. At such times it felt just like a prison. We had high walls around us with barbed wire on the top, crappy food, and very little entertainment and a homemade gym to pass the time. The only difference between us and prisoners was that they had hot showers and got to live indoors. If we wanted a shower we had to heat up a pot of water on a smoky fire and pour it into a rubber bag with a spout that we hung up and stood under for a moment.

The mortars needed constant love and attention, being stuck out in the elements for weeks on end. We cleaned and oiled them up almost daily, and every time we had a big fire mission the barrels were scrubbed to no end. A routine had established itself once again, and this time there was no escaping it for several more months. I always volunteered for every patrol that I could get on to get outside of those walls for a bit, and several times I found myself out on the ground as an extra rifleman. We got in some small firefights while I was out on patrol. We would return fire to try and pin the enemy down while the MFC worked out the position. After a few adjusting rounds to get them onto the target there would be a massive mortar stomp of thirty rounds, and usually by the time the smoke cleared it was all over. Sometimes there would be a second small adjustment and then another big stomp and then that would be it. Our MFCs were very good at their jobs and rarely failed to get the bombs exactly where they wanted them.

The IED threat was certainly no illusion in our area. A patrol that had been coming back after a hard fight had made it nearly to Gib when a young Marine triggered a bomb and was seriously hurt. Everybody in the FOB had known that the patrol was almost in, and we all heard the blast as clear as day. It was only a few hundred metres from the FOB. There was no doubt in any of our minds what had just happened and I had felt sick thinking about it. We had all hoped that everyone was fine, but the chances of a happy ending were slim. A few minutes later the patrol came hustling back through the gates, carrying one lad on a stretcher. The medics swarmed around him and got him up to the med centre as fast as possible. One of his legs was gone, and the other was in bits. Everyone in the FOB was quiet as the Chinook came in to fetch another broken Marine, each of us thinking about how much that young man's life had changed in a fraction of a second.

CHAPTER 34

GIBRALTAR 2

From time to time the baddies would attack our FOB and we were forced to defend it. As usual, the attacks would be unannounced and the action would start with a few RPGs sent our way and then a whole bunch of small-arms fire. The boys up in the sangars would start to return fire with the GPMGs that they had at their disposal, and everyone else would sprint to take up positions and bring bigger and bigger weapon systems to bear. Our MFCs would go tearing up onto the walls to try and get a good fix on the enemy shooters while the rest of the lads responded with grenade machine guns, sniper rifles, and Javelin missiles. The mortar section would run and jump into our mortar pits, manning our weapons and waiting for a fire mission to come through on the radio. Many times the attack would already be over by the time we got a fire mission, and the OC was very reluctant to just start smashing up every building in the area with our mortar fire, even if it was clear that that was where the enemy fire was coming from. He was trying to befriend the locals, and blowing someone's house to bits was not the best way to achieve that. We had to assume that the locals were letting the Taliban use their homes for cover against their will, and for the most part that was probably true.

But sometimes as the RPGS slammed into the front wall of the FOB the OC would give our MFC the nod and we would spring into action. Whether we had permission to fire or not, we would already be laid onto the target with a bomb in the #2's hand. All we needed was that nod – and once we had it the enemy fell into a world of hurt. My mortar in the middle would fire one round for the MFC to adjust from. All of the barrels were perfectly parallel, so we only ever needed to adjust with one. When I moved my barrel, the other ones moved the same amount, so we were always aimed at the same point on the ground. Once the MFC had seen my first round land, he would make a correction: add, drop, left, right, or whatever. Normally, with the second round we would be on target and receive an order to "Fire for effect." With that command, each of the three mortars would drop ten bombs down the barrel as fast as they could, and the end result would be thirty bombs in the air all at the same time, all aimed at the same spot. The enemy on the receiving end was in a very bad position once the bombs started to hit the deck, and within a few seconds three hundred pounds of high explosive and deadly shrapnel would have turned his world upside down.

We could repeat that drill over and over again, all day long. Or at least until we ran out of ammunition, which was unlikely in the FOB. We had absolutely shitloads of it, and when things got really heated up we would have a chain of extra bodies from around the FOB feeding us ammo from our big shipping containers. We had plenty in our mortar pits to begin with but always had a few thousand more bombs nearby. It was great when we had a massive fire mission on the go. We would be chasing targets all over the battlefield with ten-round salvos, and the ammo helpers would be screaming about how much their ears were hurting them. The mortars were very, very loud and could easily blow your eardrums if you weren't quick enough to get some protection on over your ears. We had all been issued with new battery-powered ear defenders that cut out loud noises but let in quieter ones, so even in a ridiculously noisy environment like a mortar pit you could talk to each other without having to yell. After a big bout of action there would be empty ammunition containers piled high around the mortar pit, and the barrel would be sizzling away, far too hot to touch till it had cooled for at least half an hour. Those were the good times as a mortar man.

The weeks, and eventually the months, slipped by, ever so slowly, as we sat behind our walls and in our pits. Sometimes time dragged and I could barely handle thinking about home and Sarah for so many hours each day; other times, when the air above the FOB was thick with bullets, entire afternoons disappeared in the blink of an eye. When things were at their most dangerous, with RPGs falling within the walls of the FOB, that was when we had to stay exposed to the danger to return fire. Everyone else got to seek shelter and crouch down behind walls, but we stood there and took it in our mortar pits, ready to respond to a fire mission. We were the ones that could put an end to an attack, and we had to be at our post.

We certainly weren't the only ones getting hit in the area. FOB Keenan to our south was hit regularly too; the Americans were always getting into scraps just to our north; and to the west the Danes constantly called on us for fire support. We had a lot of customers in the area and strove to fill every order as fast as we could. The Americans liked to use their air power above all, and we would often climb up onto the walls to watch their air assets go to work. We watched F-15s strafing ground targets and dropping bombs from low level in close support, and the infamous A-10s were often about, tearing apart the sky with the telltale growl of their massive Gatling guns. I never got tired of watching the show, and on one particular night we got a special treat. The Americans had identified some targets about five kilometres north of our FOB, and with an AC130 Spectre gunship began to lay into a village. This was an awesome piece of kit and could really tear apart ground targets. It was a huge four-engine transport aircraft with a whole bank of heavy weapons jutting out one side of it. It had Gatling guns, 40 mm cannons, and a massive 105 mm howitzer, and all could be pointed at the same target at once. We stood and watched this thing blazing away that night, flying in a big lazy circle around the target, with tracer and tongues of flame reaching down towards the ground. It was an amazing sight and would have scared the shit out of me if it had been directed at me.

The sights the next morning, however, were not nearly as impressive.

FOB Gibraltar was the nearest coalition position to the village that got hit, so they brought their problems over to us. A small tractor came up to the gates pulling a trailer that was filled with dead people. There must have been a dozen of them, with women and children among the pile. Unfortunately, there was nothing that we could do, and it was impossible to explain to them that it wasn't our fault. I am not sure how it all got sorted out, but when civvies were killed there was usually a little cash thrown at their family members. The tragedy is that the Taliban often used human shields to protect legitimate targets. But, on the other hand, it was hard to believe that all civilians were completely innocent. Every time we talked to them they all told us there were no Taliban in the area, and they had no information on where the IEDs and mines were. Yet none of them ever stepped on mines or triggered IEDs. That can't be all luck.

The Danish army was operating just across the river from us and constantly stirring up a hornet's nest. They were very gung-ho and liked to kick ass whenever they could. They cruised around with main battle tanks and shot the shit out of compounds that offered up any resistance, using 120 mm cannon fire from point-blank range. They even had giant shotgun shells they could shoot from their tanks to cut down enemy fighters. We had a liaison officer attached to them, and more often than not we ended up firing across the river to help them out. They used us sporadically at first, but once they discovered that we were a battle-winning asset that could be in action in only a minute or two they leaned heavily on us. We didn't mind of course. Getting the rounds down range was what our entire existence was about, and we loved it. The biggest fire missions we received while at Gib were in support of the Danes. They weren't shy, and as long as we had ammo they were happy to throw it all over the battlefield. It was hard work to fire round after round, constantly switching targets and making sure your bombs were going to go where they were supposed to be. The best mortar team was the fastest, and my group of three mortars competed endlessly to be ready to fire before the other two. Nothing was more fulfilling than when you heard over the radio, "Target round, end of fire mission, good shooting." A target round was, of course, one that landed right on top of the target and eliminated it.

March rolled around and the weather became warm again, and then, a week later, it was hot. We were obviously glad to be rid of the rain and snow, but this change in weather signalled something much more important. It meant the end of our tour was near, and our morale began to soar as the first of the Paras began to show up. The Parachute Regiment was taking over for us, and day by day they began to trickle into the FOB to come to grips with their new mission. We didn't care much for having a FOB full of army boys, but considering what it signified we found a way to handle it. Until of course they decided to start shooting at us . . .

One of the bootnecks on camp had been showing a few of the Paras how to use a 66 mm rocket launcher. It was one of those ones that you often see in movies. When you pull it apart it gets a bit longer, and then you throw it over your shoulder and fire. He gave them a quick little familiarization lesson, then put the weapon down and started chatting to someone. On operations we never have any drill rounds or practice weapons. Never. This is so that there are never any mistakes. Everything is live and everybody knows it. Plus, if we did have practice weapons, they would be painted up as such, and you still *never* point even practice weapons at anyone. But this dickhead seemed to have forgotten all of those things. One Para picked up the 66, opened it, cocked it, aimed it at our mortar CP that was full of people, and from about twenty metres away he *pulled the trigger.*

Beside our CP was a large tent that had about six people living in it. The rocket tore straight through the tent at chest height and slammed into the thick, dirt-filled wall of the CP. The walls on the CP were about a metre's thickness of compacted dirt, and the rocket smashed a cubic metre of the wall into bits. I was sitting with four guys from my section on the other side of the CP by the open door, and with the explosion an instant wall of dust and debris came flying out of the CP through the open doorway. Seconds before I had watched four guys from the section wander in there, and I fully expected to see guys coming out of the CP missing bits of their bodies. As we jumped up, thinking it had been a lucky shot by an enemy mortar or something, the other four came out of the CP, covered in dust, choking and sputtering. Three of them came out on their feet and the last one came out on all fours. As we checked them out we were happy to find that they were all okay. Their ears weren't working very well but they were all in one piece.

We left them as the medic came running down from the top of the FOB, and as we all headed for our mortars to return the favour we looked across to see a Para holding an empty 66 tube with a small group around him in a panic. A guy in the section figured it out and started screaming, "It was the Paras! It was the Paras!" over and over again as he hopped about pointing at the culprit. He wanted every bootneck at the FOB to know damn well who had screwed up. We walked around to the side of the CP that he had hit and found that an entire section of the wall had collapsed. The tent the rocket had gone through was in shreds, and thankfully nobody had been in there, because all of the kit and cot beds were filled with hundreds of holes from the shrapnel. One of the Paras was in serious pain with ear injuries. He had been unlucky enough to be caught up in the back blast. A standoff ensued, with all of the Paras forming up on one side of the FOB and the bootnecks on the other. Things were threatening to get nasty as we pointed out to the sergeant majors who the culprits were, and if they hadn't intervened to settle things down I think we would have lynched that prick. Nobody had been hurt but that was just down to luck. Our last run-in working alongside the army had ended in near disaster again, and as the Para was flown back to Bastion to be charged with negligence, the engineers got to work repairing our CP.

In the first week of April we finally took our mortars out of action and pulled all of our kit out of the mortar pits. The Paras jumped straight in there and set up their own mortars while we lugged everything across to the LZ. They had moved into our accommodation the day before, and as the Chinook thundered into the FOB to pick us up, my second tour in Afghanistan came to an end. We still had a bunch of loose ends to tie up at Bastion before we flew back to the U.K., but other than cleaning weapons and packing away stores, we were finished. The section made its way to Kandahar to await our flight, and as I sipped on a coffee and had a Boston Cream donut from Tim Hortons I was relieved that I had come out of thirteen months in Helmand province without a scratch. Many of my friends and colleagues weren't so lucky, and once back in the U.K. I would be reminded of this time and again as we went off to attend bootneck funerals.

The scene when we touched down in the U.K. was moving. There were people running up to the boys as they walked out of the airport, grinning from ear to ear. Wives and girlfriends threw their arms around their necks and babies were pressed up against their chests. Wonderful reunions were taking place all around me with hugs, kisses, and tears of joy everywhere. With everyone occupied and caught up in seeing their loved ones, I wandered off by myself and got on the bus provided by the Corps. Though I was happy for everybody else, there was nobody there to greet me and I felt awfully alone.

But I pushed all of that aside and thought of better things. I had eight weeks of leave ahead of me and planned to spend every second of it with my sweetheart and family. Sarah was waiting for me in B.C., and I got home to her just as fast as I possibly could. I kept myself busy, and with Sarah by my side May and June flew by. But no matter what happened I could never get all that comfortable because I always had a flight looming on the horizon. It is a far bigger price to pay than many people will ever realize: constantly flying away from those you love is tough. I had to remind myself a lot that I had volunteered for it.

PART 3
THE LONG WAY HOME

CHAPTER 35

MOVING ON

Six weeks after leave I gave my twelve months' notice to the Corps. I had done everything I had set out to do. I had earned my green lid and had my fair share of action stories without incurring any injuries. With Sarah waiting for me and B.C. beckoning it was an easy decision to make.

The troop had a lot of chill time on camp for the next couple of months. We had a ton of equipment and vehicles to sort out and maintain, and it was a good chance for everyone to get back into some sort of normal routine. We trained and kept up our mortar skills between the odd field exercise, but we also spent a lot of time sitting around with cold beers. In late October the troop was given a new task that would take us up to a camp near London for about a month. Back when the Brits acquired their ICBMs (intercontinental ballistic missiles) from the United States they made an obligation to guard these nuclear assets with nothing but the best, so the Royal Marines have been tasked in this role ever since. They provide security at the big base in Scotland where their missile submarines park up, but the U.K.'s nuclear deterrent has more to it than the missiles themselves. At this camp you will find deep bunkers and underground command centres that all have to do with the Brits keeping control of and launching their nukes. To provide the muscle that keeps these things safe you will find a bunch of bootnecks. Apparently the guys that were doing the job before us were called away to go and hunt pirates or something, so they needed to fill the gap. Somehow, out of all the bootnecks in the country, they picked my troop.

It certainly wasn't a hard job to do, but as you can imagine there was a lot of procedure involved. The day we showed up we just had to shadow the crew that was still working. There were patrols around the camp to conduct, gate duties to be carried out, and posts to be manned throughout the most important buildings. We were always armed with at least a pistol and spent plenty of time sitting in bulletproof rooms watching security camera monitors, pressing buttons to open doors, and checking IDs. It was tedious work, but in some ways it was a nice change, especially when we knew that it was only going to last for a month or so. Some guys had done that job for years and I didn't know how they endured the boredom.

One of the biggest pains of it all was the ridiculous number of salutes you had to throw up as you moved around camp. This place was jam-packed with command centres and buildings full of people with huge paycheques who moved soldiers and ships around the globe like chess pieces. There were officers everywhere, and not only British ones. NATO had their North Atlantic Maritime Operations HQ there, and around that building you would find brass from nearly every NATO country. A Canadian flag flew proudly out front of that one.

We constantly drilled on what to do if we came under attack, and practised securing the camp. As with all other operations we had a QRF ready to respond to any threats at a moment's notice. We had to lock down the most important buildings and practise escorting VIPS with vital information to rendezvous with various other agencies. Nothing was left to chance there, and the procedures that were in place were numerous, to say the least. When you were underground, you couldn't go twenty feet without having to produce ID, swipe cards, and fill in forms half a dozen times. It was a high-security nerve centre of Britain's capacity to wage war, and it was damn near impregnable. At the push of a button you could have a metre of solid steel sealing off any number of passages. The most important points could take hits from nukes and continue to function.

Our troop was relieved in early December 2008 by some other guys from 40 Commando, and we headed back to Somerset to continue with our training program. We had some live-fire shoots scheduled between then and Christmas and were up on Salisbury Plain, not too far from Stonehenge, for a big shoot with the whole unit. We had to practise firing from the back of our BVS in preparation for a large exercise we had scheduled in the New Year, and spent hour after hour standing up on these things in the cold December rain that always came down sideways. BVS are an old version of the Vikings that we had used so often in Afghanistan, and we had our own mortar variant. The rear cab wasn't designed for carrying troops – it was just a flatbed with a huge turntable on it. We set up the mortar right on the back of it and fired from up there, a few feet off the ground. It was a great way to fire and allowed us to switch targets much faster than we could when it was deployed in the ground role. One of the main tasks within NATO for the Royal Marines had been to secure the Northern flank in Europe in the event that the Cold War turned hot. If the Russians were to have come sweeping through Finland and Norway we would have headed up there to cut them off at the pass, and our mortars would have been useless in the snow without the BV variants. On solid ground our mortar base plates can easily sink knee-deep after a good round of firing, and if we had ever had to set up on top of the snow in Norway we would have lost the mortar after the first shot.

Christmas rolled around and as usual I found myself on the old London-to-Vancouver flight. This was the first time in three years that I would be home with my family at Christmas and I was very excited. I loved seeing everyone during the holidays and had missed it all very much. I couldn't think of anything better than seeing my niece and nephew on Christmas morning, and for the second year in a row I would get to wake up next to Sarah on the big day. The West Coast had a lot of snow in the winter of 2008/2009, and I was well pleased at having a white Christmas for once. We had wonderful mornings with our families and great meals in the evenings. Sarah took me snowmobiling and I couldn't believe how great it was just to be back in B.C. and to be able to have a beer in good company and go tearing off on snowmobiles right from someone's front yard. It was all amazing and helped to reassure me that I had made the right decision in giving my notice. My favourite thing to do was to go walking slowly along my dad's property in the winter when there was snow on the ground and large snowflakes lazily drifting down among the trees. At those times I really felt at peace. That Christmas it happened, and as Sarah and I walked down there it was so calm we could actually hear the giant, heavy snowflakes landing on the ground. The sound of the crisp river gurgling and bubbling as it passed the frozen banks added to the tranquility, and I knew exactly where to find happiness.

For better or for worse, I still had responsibilities back in the U.K., and with another tearful goodbye from Sarah I was gone again. 40 Commando was getting prepared for a huge exercise that would start in late February, and many of us were going to be gone for four months. While 40 Commando was in the U.K. doing its thing, the rest of 3 Commando Brigade was overseas again, and taking casualties. My old partner Tom had been drafted down to 42 Commando in Plymouth and was now operating in a mortar team working near Kandahar. On his first tour he was the one who had been shot in the head within a few days of arriving, and on this second tour he was in a vehicle that drove over a mine less than two weeks after he arrived. He was broken up badly enough to spend a month in hospital in Kandahar, but he refused to be flown back to the U.K. with tour-ending injuries. He stayed there, and probably much sooner than he should have been, he was back with his mortar crew raining shrapnel down on the enemy. He was a very lucky man, and I sure hope the "three strikes you're out" rule doesn't apply to him. As I write this, Tom is in Iraq, having volunteered to go there as a rifleman.

In January an MFC who knew many people in the troop was killed in Afghanistan, and he was going to have a large funeral with full military honours. We were the only mortar troop in the country and we pressed to be the ones to make up the official Royal Marine funeral party. The funeral was going to take place just outside of Manchester and we all headed up one week ahead of time to the Royal Marines Reserve detachment in Manchester to rehearse our role and prep for the big day. His closest friends volunteered to be the pall bearers and the rest of us were tasked with lining the route that the hearse would follow on its way to the large cathedral where the funeral was set to take place. We went through our routine again and again, working to ensure we didn't make ourselves look like fools when the time came, and after a few days we were ready. The troop was in full dress uniform, and those of us in the street-lining party had our rifles, so that we could present arms to the family of the fallen.

We headed for the cathedral early and all lined out in our set positions. We were standing there as still as statues as everyone showed up to pay their respects. Nearly a thousand people came to the funeral. There were many bootnecks there, many of them limping with recent injuries of their own. Retired veterans from all the services came in droves, and I was amazed at the support the community as a whole gave to the grief-stricken but proud family. As the hearse and cars carrying the family came down our route we all came to attention and saluted the family with our rifles. We slowly dipped our heads as the cars crept past us, and as the last of the pall bearers disappeared into the church carrying their friend, we made our way inside to watch the service and try to get a little warmth into our hands. It was freezing that day, and standing perfectly still hanging onto an ice-cold rifle had been anything but pleasant.

The guys who had lined the street were doubling as the firing party too, so we snuck out of the service a moment before everyone else and marched smartly down the long lane that ran through the well-manicured cemetery to the crematorium. We got set up in ranks outside the front entrance and shortly behind us came the funeral party, slowly carrying the coffin draped with a massive Union Jack. The coffin went into the building, and the priest said a few words before it was rolled into the incinerator. As the doors closed behind the coffin, we took aim out over top of the crowd and fired our rifles. The crowd jumped at the noise, and three times the cemetery echoed with this world's final goodbye to another Royal Marine.

The wake was a traditional bootneck affair that started out with everyone on their best behaviour. As the afternoon turned into evening and the beer kegs were drunk down, things got a little livelier. It was a time for many of us to catch up with friends that we hadn't seen in ages and to trade stories about our latest deployments. As I was walking along outside the main building I heard someone call out "Canada!" I turned to look for whoever had called me but couldn't see anyone that I recognized. I wandered over a little bit closer and then realized why I couldn't recognize the speaker. His face was wrapped in bandages, but I discovered that he was a friend that I had served alongside in Afghanistan the first time. He had been the driver of the Wimik that was hit by the suicide bomber in Kandahar so long ago, and it was from his weapon that I had washed the blood and gore. He had just been in Afghanistan a second time and had been hit by another IED. He had very nearly been killed but was one tough Welshman and lived on. His face was in bad shape, and although it was hidden beneath bandages I could see that some of it was missing. He was missing fingers too, and had a cane to help support him on his one good leg.

At first I was appalled at my inability to recognize one of my own friends. He was just too smashed up, and I felt awful that such a great guy was going through this ordeal. He has a wonderfully supportive wife and great kids, but life must be tough for him. We chatted for a while before he headed off to use his amazing sense of humour to lighten up some other part of the wake. This guy had been to Afghanistan three times, and twice he had been blown up. I went there twice and never got a scratch. I know that it is simply a matter of chance, but sometimes I can't help but feel guilty.

CHAPTER 36

TAURUS 1

In late February, my mortar section found itself on a ship heading south past France and Portugal. The big exercise was finally underway and we were attached to a company group embarked on RFA Mounts Bay. It was a very modern amphibious assault ship that was only a few years old. It had been designed specifically for the needs of the Royal Marines, and was one of four Bay Class ships in the Royal Navy. All of the corridors and stairwells were extra-wide to allow Marines to move about quickly and easily with their full kit and bergens on. There was a large helicopter landing pad on the back deck, and the stern was one giant door that opened up to allow landing craft entry right into the ship. The ship was hollow, and a large portion of it would be flooded inside whenever the big door opened to enable the landing craft to pull up close to the internal ramps so that bootnecks could get on and off easily. Half of that deck was for parking vehicles which could drive straight onto the landing craft. The landing craft could stay in the ship when the door was shut and sit on the dry deck once all of the water had been pumped out. It was a brilliant design and worked very well for us.

The U.K.'s armed forces place a heavy emphasis on amphibious operations because they are an island and have always had to transport their soldiers by sea. An amphibious force can influence events on shore without ever having to actually get troops onto a beach. The mere threat of an invasion has a powerful effect. A striking force can mill around just over the horizon waiting for events to develop on shore, and by first light the next day, attacks can be launched with surprise and deadly effect. The first few months of the exercise were intended to get us practised in doing exactly that. We were going to sail from country to country, launching amphibious assaults all over the globe, honing the skills of not only the bootnecks but also the navy. This was my first time ever being on a warship for any length of time, and it took a little getting used to. As much as I disliked the fairly cramped quarters on board Mounts Bay, I was certainly looking forward to doing what bootnecks do best. The Royal Marine's motto is "Per Mare, Per Terram," or "By Sea, By Land." I had done plenty of the "By Land" portion over the last few years and it was now time to get back in touch with the "By Sea" bit.

The company group, which we were a part of, was a strong force with many different components. The core was a full company of riflemen, and attached to it was our mortar section, anti-tank detachments, assault engineers, signallers, vehicle drivers, landing craft operators, an intelligence detachment, a recce section, and our own bootneck chefs. We had all of our kit with us and plenty of ammunition. If some sort of crisis had kicked off while we happened to be sailing past, there would have been a serious ass-kicking in the cards for somebody.

Throughout the first week we adjusted to life on board and spent our spare time doing phys up on the flight deck or in the gym. We played a lot of cards and tried to come to terms with a world that rocked to and fro all day, every day. One night after we had all drifted off to sleep in our swaying room, this random rifleman, who was stuck in with all of the mortar men, decided it was a good time to start sleepwalking. Rather than simply walking about mumbling random crap, he jumped out of bed and started tearing lads' curtains aside, screaming at them to get up because we were sinking. He was banging and kicking on the lockers to wake us all up, yelling, "Abandon ship! Abandon ship! We're sinking!" Being in a dark cabin that was swaying heavily from side to side in rough seas with some guy screaming in the dark to abandon ship was not a comforting experience. Thankfully, before we all started scrambling for our life jackets, the lad stopped yelling and calmly got back into his bed to drift back to sleep.

A few days later we were standing up on the deck as the ship slipped between the Pillars of Hercules, two promontories at the eastern end of the Strait of Gibraltar that mark the narrow entrance to the Mediterranean Sea. Our first stop on the trip was in Gibraltar, the city at the base of the rock that the Royal Marines had captured hundreds of years before, and we were all looking forward to it. This wasn't a training stop, it was a social call, and after a week on ship we were all getting a bit thirsty. The riflemen were going to be on parade and the rest of us were going to be set free for a few days. I had never been to Gibraltar before, and I found it a strange place. It was just like a mini England, with the same sorts of buildings, pubs, currency, menus, and shops. The differences were that it wasn't raining, and there were warm-weather plants and monkeys all over the place. I thoroughly enjoyed it there, and one night a few of us had headed across the border into Spain too.

The lads did their parade, in front of a friendly crowd. Then, early one morning, we were all forced into the infamous rock run. This is a run the Marines do whenever they are in Gibraltar, and you just run from the ship all the way up the winding track to the top of the giant

Rock of Gibraltar. We did it very early in the morning before first light, and most of the guys had been out on the town the previous evening. Half of the company was still drunk, and I passed more than a few who were heaving up their guts along the way.

With the fun and games of Gib out of the way, it was time to move into the training phase of the exercise. We set sail east, stopping in the warm, blue waters of Cyprus for a quick amphibious exercise, then headed to Turkey for the next round of training in a large area near Izmir. This was a joint exercise; we would be working alongside Dutch Marines, Belgian troops, and Turkish forces. Our mortar section was tasked to launch with the Dutch Marines from their own ship, so a day before the assault was to begin we jumped on a helo and headed to HNLMS *Rotterdam*. Their ship was very similar to our own Bay Class vessels and we were treated very well onboard. They put on a late meal for us and gave us a large accommodation that was about twice the size of what we actually needed. The ship had been designed to take the same LCs as ours, so in the morning we headed on down to the vehicle deck and got on another LC for another run to the beach. This exercise was pretty much exactly like the last one, only it lasted five days and was much more interesting with more moving parts. Each day we would yomp off to some other spot to set up a mortar line in support of another company attack, and each night we were surprised at how cold it was in Turkey. We had moved a few hundred miles north of where we had been in Cyprus and each morning our kit was covered in frost. We had a great show put on for us one morning as we watched the Turks storm ashore from their giant LCs and go sprinting about in the sand with their AK-47s and RPG launchers over their shoulders. I was impressed with the size and abundance of their landing craft, and considering who and what their military was geared up against, it made sense. Historically, they hated the Greeks and the Greeks hated them, and they have fought numerous wars in the past. The area separating the two of them has hundreds of strategically important islands, so it was imperative that the Turks have a decent amphibious capability if they wanted to stand a chance against the Greeks. We caught a few rides in a Turkish Air Force Puma helicopter as well, and the pilots and aircrew were all wearing leather jackets like Maverick from Top Gun. It was a little bit dodgy flying with them, but they got us pretty close to where we needed to be, and we never crashed.

We had to work hard on that exercise and covered a lot of ground on our feet, so we were all very pleased when we learned that the next stop was for a few days off in Crete. We were on ship for a couple of days before we hit Heraklion, and there I bumped into an old friend. Good old Steve, from way back in the early days of training, was on the ship with the signals detachment. He was still up to his old tricks, trying to do everything he could to cut corners and stir up a shit storm everywhere he went, but he was also still a great guy with a good head on his shoulders. He knew his job and that is what counts in the Corps. We spent a lot of time catching up over the next few months, on the ships and in various ports. The community of the Corps is quite small in some ways, so it seems that no matter where you go in the world, you will always bump into at least one bootneck that you know.

I had been to Crete a few years before with Jennifer and I loved that island. The weather was great, the ocean was blue, and the food was fantastic. I and two other guys grabbed a map and a car and headed off to explore. We travelled from town to town, setting up shop for a night at each place. The three of us went to Suda Bay and checked out the battlefields where the Germans had landed their elite paratroopers in World War II and narrowly defeated the British. The area was thick with military cemeteries, both Commonwealth and German.

With hangovers and battered bank accounts, we got onto the larger amphibious ship, HMS *Bulwark*, and headed off for the Suez Canal. We had to wait around the entrance for all of the other Navy ships to arrive and for our slot to open up, and then, once we got the green light, we entered the canal. For most of the twelve-hour journey we were expected to stay inside so that nobody could shoot at us from the shore, but we obviously stood out on the deck as much as we could. There was a lot to look at, and as far as you could see to the front and the rear there were warships steaming through in a long line. We were all going through together, and every couple of hundred metres along the entire route there were Egyptian soldiers posted to provide security. The canal itself was much narrower than I had expected, and the monuments and buildings along the way were bizarre. There was one huge monument that was just a massive AK-47 muzzle and bayonet standing straight up in the air, and directly beneath it was a giant floral sign that said "Welcome to Egypt." As dusk began to fall, the canal slowly began to get wider and wider until we were out of it. We entered the Red Sea surrounded by enormous jellyfish and schools of flying fish, and headed south for our next trip ashore.

CHAPTER 37

TAURUS 2

The temperature had soared the moment we slipped into the Suez Canal, and it only got hotter as we moved farther south through the Red Sea. We spent a lot of time up on the flight deck doing phys to try to acclimatize, but we didn't have much time before we went ashore in the KSA (Kingdom of Saudi Arabia). This was going to be another joint training package, this time with us working alongside Saudi Marines, and the day before it was all going to kick off we pulled into a port midway down the Saudi Coast and loaded a bunch of Saudi Marines and their vehicles onto our ship. The Saudis were given their own grots on the ship and we only really saw them in the galley, trying to make sense of our food and drink, in particular sorting out what might or might not have pork in it. We now headed back out into the open sea and carried on south until we were off the training area somewhere to the north of Jeddah.

We went through all of the same routines that we had done the last few times and headed for shore on one of the largest LCS. This time we were taking the BVS ashore with us, which was good news. Driving around the scorching Saudi desert is a lot better than walking around in it. The only bad thing about it is that the vehicles had been designed for use in Norway. They didn't have air conditioning and the hot engine is in the middle of the cab with a thin fibreglass cover, between the driver and whoever was riding shotgun. The heater only had one setting, full blast, and it was on all the time. Considering the air temperature alone was well over forty degrees Celsius by 0700, we had some serious discomfort ahead of us.

Meanwhile, we were bobbing around halfway to shore, waiting for who knows what, so the coxswains dropped the anchor and lowered the front ramp for us to go for a swim and cool off. Most of the section stripped down immediately and dove in, hoping for a little respite from the evil sun. But the water was as warm as a bath, so that even in it we were sweating. When we got back on the ship we learned that the temperature of the sea surface, which extends down about a metre, was a full thirty degrees too.

With our swim finished we re-embarked, only to splash ashore into yet another sand-filled Muslim country. It was nearly last light by the time everything was sorted and we were all successfully ashore, so we set up camp right there by the beach. I went for a late-night swim to try to cool down but it didn't work. We were all just sleeping on the ground under some mosquito nets we had and it was ridiculously hot throughout the night. I lay on top of my roll mat completely nude, sweat pouring off my whole body until around midnight. From four until six in the morning the temperature was comfortable but we still didn't require any cover to stay warm. Then, at about seven, the evil sun would reappear, and the whole thing started again. I would sweat continuously day and night, apart from my two hours of peace between four and six in the morning. We had hardly any time to properly acclimatize and were very fortunate that we didn't have much labour to do in the sun. There was a lot of ammo to prep, and when we did that task many of the guys nearly passed out, but that was about the worst of it.

The first morning that we woke up on shore we loaded up the BVS with mortar bombs and tore off into the desert to the grid where we were supposed to set up our first mortar line. The riflemen were going to be storming ashore each day in successive waves, and would then be extracted back to the ships each evening. They were going to repeat this drill three times, and on the fourth day they would do it with Saudi Marines attached, before an audience of members of the Saudi royal family. Our mortar section wasn't going to be nearly as lucky as those who would be retiring to an air-conditioned ship each night. We were stuck out there for the extent of the exercise. As in all deserts, when you drive around in them in heavy tracked vehicles at high speed, you kick up a shitload of dust, something that we could have done with- out. We were so sweaty that the dust just stuck to us in thick, clogging layers, and there was no point in opening the windows while we drove because instead of a blast of fresh air we would get a blast of dust blowing in. It was hell driving around in those BVs. I am certain the temperature got well over fifty degrees in there. Maybe even sixty. Every ten minutes or so our little convoy would have to stop so that everyone could pile out of the vehicles and have a breather. Even standing in the forty-degree Saudi desert was cool compared to the inside of those things.

When we finally arrived at our designated patch of scrubby desert, we got into position, opened up the backs of the vehicles, and set up the mortars for firing. We prepped our ammo, adjusted the sights, and got our radio masts up to start chatting with the MFCS who would be coming ashore with the rifle troops. We were set up and ready to go with only one last thing to do, which was, of course, to wait. So we set up a few shelters to keep the sun off our heads and then waited for most of the day. A Saudi mortar team turned up in the afternoon and we watched with amusement as they set up their two mortars just off to the side of our own mortar line. They were working as if they had never even touched a mortar before and we wondered how they were planning on hitting targets without any sights. They didn't prep the ground under the base plate and were in no position to properly bed the mortar in once they started firing.

Our MFCS got ashore in the end and called in a few adjusting fire missions to properly record the targets for all of the subsequent attacks. We wanted to be absolutely certain that our bombs were going to go where we wanted them to go and took no chances. The last thing we needed was a stray bomb to hit a member of the royal family. The Saudi mortar team had different ideas, though. When they fired their first bomb with nobody supporting the mortar at all, the whole assembly flew back six feet and fell over. This wasn't exactly precision mortaring. They set it up again and with a little advice from our guys managed to fire again without it falling over. They still weren't really aiming it, and as they passed the bomb from man to man down a long chain they were all yelling, "Allah Akbar! Allah Akbar!" ("God is great"). When the man whose turn it was to fire finally dropped the bomb down the barrel and sent it on its way, they all cheered and praised Allah again. It seemed to me that if they had any hope of actually hitting a target they would definitely need their God to personally guide the bomb.

We slept beside our vehicles again, and in the morning the first of the attacks went in along the beach. We couldn't see any of the action as we were about five kilometres inland, but we fired a lot of bombs into the surf to give a bit of visual effect. It was hard work mortaring in the hot sun and we were going through a lot of water to try to keep hydrated. Daily, I was managing to drink about eight litres of water and pissing maybe twice. We stayed set up in that same location and repeated the same serial the next day as the OC ran different troops and Saudi contingents through the drill. The section packed up that afternoon and headed off to a different mortar line to get prepared for the final big attack scheduled for the next day. It was a big show for the dignitaries and they had set up a large tent off to the flank of where the troops were going to come ashore. The tent floor was covered with red carpet, and big plush chairs were brought in, along with servants to serve cold drinks and snacks.

The next morning the last attack went in without any problems and we fired off a lot of bombs. We held up a good steady rate of fire throughout and didn't stop until all of our ammo was gone. We were dying to get back into the air conditioning on the ship and didn't waste any time in consuming all the ammunition. We were packed up and heading back for the beach a short while later, and arrived early enough at the pickup point to ensure we had hours to wait in the blazing sun. Most of us spent the afternoon moving back and forth between any patch of shade we could find around the vehicles and the hot sea. Slowly but surely, the troops waiting on the beach were ferried back to ships a few miles offshore, and when our turn finally came we waded into the LCS with our vehicles in tow. Before we could relax on ship, we had to clean a lot of kit. The vehicles were absolutely filthy and doused in salt water, as was most of our mortar kit. We were finished mortaring for a couple of months, so everything had to be sorted out before we stored and locked it all away. The entire exercise was shifting gears for us, moving from an amphibious orientation to river and jungle ops.

Before our next stop in Bangladesh we had to sail through the pirate-infested waters of the Gulf of Aden, and needed to keep a sharp lookout for any threats. One day we came right up alongside a vessel that was clearly packed with pirates. We couldn't see any weapons onboard and had no mandate to search the boat, but what was a fifty-foot boat doing out in the middle of the shipping lanes with three smaller boats with huge outboard engines in tow? The intelligence section got a few photos of the pirates and added them to the collection. There is a famous photo of a few large parcels of ransom cash being parachuted down onto the deck of a massive Saudi oil tanker in late 2008. The pirates that we had just passed by had a parachute stretched out over their deck as a sun shade, and when you compare the two pictures you can see that the parachutes are identical. We all got a chuckle out of that.

Then I got some bad news from home. It all started with a phone call to Sarah. I was missing her tremendously and had counted down the days until I would get to hear her sweet voice again. She didn't pick up for a few days, but when she finally did answer she was in tears. She had met another man, though she swore she still wanted to be with me over the next few weeks. I tried to call in every favour I had ever earned in the Corps to arrange a panic flight home to sort this all out. I desperately wanted to be with her and I wanted the future we had envisioned together. She was having some very hard times at home. The previous summer when I was home her mother had passed away and it had devastated her. She needed someone to be there with her and as things unravelled it became clear that there was nothing that I could do. In the end she binned me for a fisherman named Bob, and that was that.

Luckily for me, there were a lot of stops left throughout the trip, and plenty to keep me occupied. We stopped in a large city on the east coast of India for a few days to show off our ships and to try to sell some to the Indian Navy before we headed up to Bangladesh for our next big exercise. This was going to be an interesting one, with lots of moving parts, in the Ganges River delta. The exercise was going to involve the Bangladeshi Marines, Coast Guard, and Navy, and their intelligence agency. The scenario was that an HVT (high value target) was coming down from a large city through the river system and out into the open sea. We were tasked with setting up a series of OPS throughout the delta to report his movements. After he had passed through and out into the open sea, the Coast Guard would nab him, job done. The bulk of the company would go racing up and down the river in their high-speed gun boats and LCs, locating and launching attacks against various enemy positions in conjunction with the Bangladeshis.

The weather was very warm and very muggy and within a few minutes of being out on the LC we were soaked in sweat. The water was a combination of stinky, shallow sea water and even worse-smelling brown water flowing out of the mouth of the Ganges. We were heading into one of the most diseased and water-logged areas on the planet, where every bit was covered in mud and mostly below sea level, and we knew we had a lot of work ahead of us. When we finally hit the beach, we had to wade in thigh-deep water for about a hundred metres, and with every step we sunk into knee-deep heavy mud. If you stopped you would become stuck, so the trick was to press on. If you went down with your heavy bergen on, there was no way you would be getting up again without someone else's help, and it happened to a few of the guys. I stopped to try and pull someone up and that was the end of me. I was on my hands and knees in deep mud wearing a heavy bergen. One of the deckhands on the LC who wasn't wearing any kit waded out to help us and I managed to go the distance with no other mishaps, but others were not so lucky. Some of them ended up dragging their bergens through the mud for the last fifty metres, struggling to stay on their feet. It was an inglorious landing and proved again why time spent on a recce is rarely wasted.

As it began to get dark we all sat on the beach around a giant map model tucked in beneath some trees to receive a set of orders. The plan was laid out, and areas where we were to set up the OPs were identified on the map. Comms schedules were established, and our section was broken down into different Zodiacs with different OPs to occupy. Our section was teamed up with a section from Recce Troop, and together we figured we had one of the best tasks. We were supposed to get established in our OPs before first light and occupy them for the next seventy-two hours, reporting on suspicious activities and trying to identify the HVT when he passed by us. As the last bit of light faded away we made our way to our boats with our bergens, rifles, and plenty of spare radio batteries. There were four of us in each boat with the coxswain, and with all of the fuel bladders and our kit it was a tight squeeze, but one by one the six boats headed out and formed up into a file. All we could make out of the boat in front of us was a tiny sliver of dull light escaping from a mini glow stick. As we drove up into the mouth of that river the lighting changed dramatically. I couldn't stop watching the water to the sides of the boat and the wake to our rear. The whole area around us was alive and brilliantly lit up with phosphorescence. I found myself wishing that we had phosphorescence like that back home in B.C.

A team had been deployed out to the area a few weeks before we arrived to conduct recces and organize the training package. The report from them was that the area we were going into was excellent for setting up OPs and that it would be a piece of cake to achieve our training objectives. That night we learned that this was anything but true. Hour after hour we searched for suitable places, but we couldn't find anything. There were civilians everywhere, up and down the entire length of the river, and even at three in the morning they were milling about to see what the British were up to. Other areas simply offered no cover or were tidal plains that would be several metres under water twice a day. We couldn't find anywhere suitable to hide the boats, and anywhere that we did find that was remotely suitable was quickly dismissed when we tried to get in touch with HQ and couldn't. You simply don't set up an OP with no radio coverage. No comms equals no bombs.

The boats in our group had dispersed to try and find their own locations as laid out in orders, but eight hours later we were all grouped together again, twenty kilometres up the river with no OPs established and first light rapidly approaching. We had been in and out of the Zodiac into knee-deep mud for nearly twelve hours and were just a little bit pissed off with the shitty area we had been tasked to cover. The recces that had been done had either been ignored or were inaccurate. One OP near the mouth of the river was established that night, and in the morning they had to pull out because they were being swarmed by curious civilians. It was a ridiculous scenario, and we had no choice but to head back down the river to one of our floating bases and find a new task. Halfway back to the sea with the sky growing light, we finally got through on the radio and were told to just stop where we were and wait for the man who was supposed to be in charge of the OPS to come up the river on a local boat with a new plan. We found a partially constructed bridge and tied up to that in the middle of the river, and in a few minutes we had all fallen fast asleep to the sound of the gurgling river and the crowds of children lining the riverbanks.

CHAPTER 38

TAURUS 3

The new idea for our Bangladeshi river ops was much more work-able and proved to be a great success. We rented a few local dhows and their crews, and, with an interpreter, hopped on board to ply up and down the river, dropping anchor here and there. The river was absolutely filled with these wooden boats. These boats averaged thirty feet in length and had a big hold in the centre that was used to carry cargo. On our boat the four of us were the cargo. These boats weren't exactly clean or comfortable, and the crews were a little bit creepy, but as far as ops in the Ganges delta go, they are the way forward. We promised to give them a few drums of diesel at the end of the exercise, and the three-man crews were only too happy to accommodate us. We cross-decked from the Zodiacs into these dhows and went puttering up the river to disappear into the network of tributaries and fleets of other dhows plying the delta.

For the next few days we moved about in the river system, hiding down below as much as possible during the days and coming up onto the deck in the evenings. We had several dhows keeping an eye out for the HVT, each in its own designated zone, and other than cleaning our weapons and taking shifts on watch there wasn't a whole lot to do. When it got dark the boat swarmed with enormous cockroaches that the crew didn't even seem to notice. The crew often offered us food that they cooked in pots and pans that had been covered in cockroaches only moments before. Most nights there were spectacular lightning storms and torrential downpours, but for the most part they were welcome. It was very warm during the days and we were filthy, so the heavy rains refreshed us and helped to wash away some of the stink. We showed off our night vision capabilities to the crew and it absolutely blew their minds. The NVGS sent them into a frenzy and they couldn't believe that man had invented such things. Once they saw the infrared glow sticks they were convinced it was all magic. These glowsticks look like any others but when you crack them they don't give off any light that you can normally see. However, through the NVGS, they glow very brightly.

One night the locals worked with nature to put on an exciting show. On shore near where we were anchored there was some sort of a town meeting that was getting heated. The interpreter said there was a debate going on between local politicians, but it sounded more to us like they were lynching someone. All of a sudden a huge wind came up out of nowhere, with a very violent lightning storm hot on its heels. The locals all started going crazy on the shore, screaming at the top of their lungs through megaphones to each other and scurrying about. Women were gathering up their kids as fast as they possibly could as the wind got stronger and stronger, until the largest of the dhows began to drift straight towards us. Their anchors could no longer hold them in place and their crews were running about trying to drop extra anchors and screaming down at us to prepare for an impact. A few minutes later the large boat struck us and stopped.

A second massive boat hit that boat, and in the end we were all tied up together. The other lads and I sat up on the deck of our dhow with the much bigger ship alongside, and for the next three or four hours the crews from both of the other ships squatted up above us on the edges of their boats, just staring down at us curiously with Arabic music blaring out of an old radio. The lightning was crashing down all around us, splitting the sky with great forks of lightning and accompanied by thunderous crashes. The local mob was still lynching someone at the top of their lungs and the cockroaches were swarming around our feet. It was an evening that I will never forget.

By the end of our Ganges cruise we had spotted the HVT and the Coast Guard had pulled the trigger, apprehending him as he tried to get away on the open seas. The exercise had been a bit of a fiasco all along, but the local forces that we had worked with had learned a great deal and were already looking forward to working with us again. We said our goodbyes to the crew of our dhow and filled up their drums of diesel from our floating supply depots. Soon we were back on our ship, cleaning our weapons and getting settled down for a long sail to Malaysia. I spent most of that time just trying to figure out what in the hell had happened with Sarah, but I just couldn't find any answers.

The company had a lot of jungle lectures and lessons as we headed for Malaysia, and when we arrived late one night we all felt pretty well prepared. The Malaysian Army met us at the port and drove us to one of their large camps right in the southern tip of their beautiful country. Our convoy had a full police escort, and traffic had been completely blocked off on the freeway and roads in preparation for our coming through. In the morning we had a huge welcoming ceremony, with prayers offered to Allah on our behalf by their chaplain and much singing by their regiment. Malaysian jungle warfare instructors would be taking us through a number of different lessons at their school before we headed out into the jungle to practise patrolling and operating out there. The Corps had sent over a number of lads a few months early to learn the tricks of the trade prior to our arrival, and when we went into the trees they assumed the role of the instructors, with Malaysian gurus keeping an overwatch. But first the Malaysians had a lot to show us at their camp, and troop by troop over the next few days we rotated through various stances.

A very important one was the jungle survival school, where we learned how to make all sorts of different traps for catching animals and about some of the different shelters that can be quickly and easily constructed in the jungle. There are an infinite number of different plants over there, and although many of them are dangerous, many of them are very useful for food and shelter. Just like scenes out of Hollywood movies, there are vines all over the place that you can hack open and drink clean water from. They even taught us which plants you can eat to help with circulation, which happens to be the same plant the locals use as a Viagra substitute. We were shown many different animals and bugs to stay away from and how best to avoid some of them. They showed us how to kill large pythons and monkeys and where to look for quail eggs. And at the end of the training they had a large feast prepared for us, all of the dishes made from local plants and animals and cooked in the fashions they had taught us. The monkey was a bit chewy, but with a little salt and pepper I think it would have tasted fantastic.

Once they were convinced that we could survive for a while on our own if we got lost, we headed out to start practising all of the other important aspects of operating in the jungle. It was a demanding environment in every way. It was hot and very humid, and you were soaked from head to toe for nearly twenty-four hours a day. Everything around you was alive, even the forest floor, and the overwhelmingly stagnant air was thick in your nostrils. It was suffocating, and you constantly felt as if you couldn't take a proper deep breath. The insects are very large and everywhere. Sticks and leaves come to life and walk away from you, while ants the size of your thumb go through your kit when you're not looking. The one bonus of being in the jungle is you tend to get a lot of sleep. When it gets dark around six o'clock, all movement has to stop. It gets very, very dark in the jungle at night, and there is no way you could cover any ground through the trees in the blackness. It would be ridiculously slow and you would just make too much noise. So, for about twelve hours each night, we got to lie in our hammocks, soaked in sweat, listening to the animals all around.

Navigation in the jungle is much different from anywhere else. It is usually very hilly, with numerous streams, and your visibility is extremely limited. Maps are notoriously inaccurate, and trying to count your footsteps while quietly walking on a bearing is not easy. The conditions of overwhelming heat and thirst, vines and prickly bushes to entangle yourself in, dangerous snakes in the trees overhead, a radio buzzing in your ear, an objective to achieve and the constant careful watching for any sign of the enemy make it a very demanding place to do your job. The saying is that if you can soldier in the jungle, you can soldier anywhere, and I agree 100 per cent. The humidity and jungle stink eats everything, including your clothes and body. If you get a cut or any type of injury, infection can set in immediately, and even the smallest cut may never heal. Imagine cutting your finger and then holding it under water for a week: chances are it still wouldn't be very far along the path to healing when you take it out of the water.

Slowly but surely we began to roll into the more tactical phases of the exercise. We couldn't just rush straight into it because we had to become accustomed to the heat and weather. Day by day we increased the amount of activity we did, until eventually we were navigating and patrolling all day long, setting up our hammocks and shelters only at last light. This whole training session was in preparation for the real exercise in Brunei, but all the while the company was still making plenty of attacks on enemy villages over the days. Patrols would go out to recce the enemy positions, and when everything possible had been observed and noted, the attacks would go in. None of this was live firing, except for when the company rolled through the set live-fire lanes in the trees. Live-fire exercises in the trees are very dangerous because you can lose sight of your friends so easily, and many precautions had to be taken. But even with the restrictions it was all good practice, stalking along jungle paths and pumping rounds into targets hiding among the trees. With our skills finally coming together and the company becoming comfortable with the routines of jungle operations, we wrapped it up with a large final series of patrols and attacks. By the time it was over, the lads were in serious need of a good shower. We all stunk to high heaven, to the point where even the smell of yourself was disgusting. It is the most musty, moist, choking stink you can imagine, and if we came within one hundred feet of a clean civilian he would have run the other way. Back at the Malaysian camp it was all hands to the pumps to get the weapons cleaned and everything packed away for going back to the ship. We had all been away from home for over three months by this time, and we worked quickly, thinking it would somehow speed things along.

We left Malaysia with invites to come back and train with them again whenever we wanted, and after a few days off in Singapore the whole company group was back on ship again, heading even farther east to take up positions off the Brunei coast. This exercise was the culmination of the entire trip, and every skill we had practised in the last few months would be brought into play. The unit had deployed two more companies to Brunei a month before we arrived to get trained up at a different jungle school, and all three companies were going to be taking part in the final exercise. One company was going to play enemy, while the other two would be the hunters. There were going to be large-scale amphibious assaults made in LCs and helicopter assaults launched from HMS *Ocean*. Gunboats and LCS would be tearing up and down the river system while lads patrolled through the jungle, catching rides in the boats when they needed them. The enemy had boats of their own, and a series of camps up and down the river, starting near the ocean and extending about fifty kilometres inland. It was a massive unit-level exercise, but the most important thing for our section was that once this was over we would be finished all of the field work on the trip and just waiting for flights home.

Again our section was tasked as a mortar section that could easily be turned into a rifle section, and once more we found ourselves strapping mortar pieces to our bergens. We were heading off into the exercise by helo, and had sailed from Malaysia on HMS *Ocean* in preparation. On the morning we flew, we all gathered in the hangar to form up into our separate helo lifts, and when it was our turn, we stood on one of the massive elevators used to lift aircraft up to the flight deck. With blue skies above, we were lifted up with all of our kit, and foot by foot we came even with the helos waiting for us. The air was filled with the sharp stink of aviation fuel, and helicopters were all over the flight deck, some with rotors turning and some with them swept back into the storage position. Crewmen were running around all over the place, and one of them ran up to us to guide us to the right helo. He grabbed the first man in our stick and led us off to the rearmost helo, waiting for us with its side doors open and the rotors turning hard. One by one we tossed our bergens in for the crewmen to stow away, slipped on our lifejackets, and crawled up and into seats. With everybody on board we took off right away, gaining a few metres of altitude before slipping sideways out over the open water.

We gained height quickly as we made for the shore, passing over the beach and levelling out over the endless jungle canopy. The contrast between the blue sea and the green jungle, separated by a thin ribbon of white sand, was acute, and soon the two-minute signal was being passed around the helo. It didn't take long for these powerful machines to cover twenty or thirty kilometres, and in no time we were settling down in a small gravel pit in the middle of the jungle to unload. There weren't many clearings large enough to take these big helos, so once we had piled out we had to wait a few minutes for a smaller Lynx helicopter to come and move us farther forward, to an open area near which we were supposed to set up our new mortar line. It was helo leapfrog, and I was loving the change from carrying our mortar kit everywhere.

We got set up on the edge of a large grassy opening in the jungle and immediately sent out patrols to clear the area and ensure we weren't surprised by the enemy. These patrols were kept up by the section twenty-four hours a day, and for two days we maintained that position. We had trouble keeping in touch with our MFCs, but from what we could gather they were moving towards enemy positions and getting into small contacts along the way. They were moving slowly and having trouble getting so many people through the thick foliage, but progress was being made, and on the second morning we supported a large attack that went in on a village. By 0900 everyone was on the move again, including us. We had our bergens as heavy as possible once again and patrolled off to the riverbank a few kilometres away. We had a boat pickup scheduled and were supposed to be moving quickly upriver to link up with the rest of our company for advances farther inland.

We found the river easy enough and set up a tight defensive perimeter as we waited for our pickup. Large red caterpillars the length of a pen fell out of the trees onto us as we lay there watching monkeys fight it out in the treetops across the river. It was a crazy place we were in, and everywhere we looked our eyes met something bizarre. There were enormous lizards all around the riverbanks – I saw one that was over a metre long and must have weighed at least fifty pounds. He was eating a large fish, and at first I thought he was a small crocodile, but I would meet those later.

The Zodiacs we were waiting for turned up and ferried us up the river to some LCs which we boarded. Half of the company were in the gunboats to rapidly get into attack positions with heavy fire support, and the other half were in the LCs with us to act as mobile reserves that could be placed where they were needed. As the attacks developed, our mortar section was supposed to get ashore and establish a mortar line to support the operations, but this was easier said than done in the jungle. There were very few suitable places along the river, and we simply didn't have time to constantly push in from the river through the dense jungle to find a good spot while a quick attack was being mounted. Eventually we managed to set up a few lines here and there, but soon enough they did away with the mortar coverage and turned us into an over-strength rifle section.

Day by day we pushed farther and farther upstream, clearing through enemy positions as they presented themselves, and each night we pressed into the jungle far enough to have space to set up our hammocks and shelters in section areas. It was quite creepy to be moving around the riverbanks in the dark. We had seen a number of crocodiles over the last few days, sunbathing on the muddy banks, and some of them were at least ten feet long. They were absolutely fearless creatures, and when we pulled up right beside them in the boats they never even batted an eye. In their ancient minds they were at the top of the food chain and had absolutely no reason to fear anything in that river. This gave us pause for thought as we scrambled up and down the slippery banks in the dark.

On what we hoped was the last day of the exercise, our section was launched into one final attack from the banks of the river. A few of the patrols that had gone downstream ahead of us had been ambushed and fired on from enemy positions up on top of a hilly bank looking down on the muddy river. Our section was already on our assault boats and nearest the action, so we were quickly given a task.

As the guys checked over weapons and did a final bit of kit tinkering, we grouped the boats together and had a hasty chat about what we were up against. Details were sketchy, but speed was the name of the game. There were more boats heading downstream that needed the route cleared, and with virtually no information about the enemy strengths we roared off down the river to pick another fight.

As we got closer to the target we could hear intense machine gun fire mixed with a chorus of rifles. We rounded the final bend and saw a pair of our gunboats in a fire position, hammering the enemy and waiting for us to arrive to mop up the mess. The boats and guns were British, but the guns were all being manned by U.S. Marines who were involved in some sort of exchange program with us. They had those guns working to capacity, and the hulls of their boats were filling with empty brass casings and bits of link. As it all came into view we could see the area the enemy was firing from and figures darting about in the tall grass. We were tearing in towards the shore and had no time to come up with any plan from where we were. There was only one place on the riverbank that was suitable for us to get out from in a hurry, and one by one the three boats pounded their bows into the soft muddy beach about fifty metres up from the nearest enemy. Some guys jumped out over the bows and landed in the mud, while others just went over the sides of the boat into waist-deep water. Getting out of the boats quickly was essential, and as we splashed out of the river we clutched clumps of grass and scrambled up a short, steep bank. The boats threw it into reverse and the powerful jet drives pulled them off the mud and sent them hurtling back upstream, out of harm's way. At the top of the bank we rolled into a small dip in the ground and began to formulate a quick plan while hidden in the tall grass.

Our sergeant assessed the situation while we all took up defensive positions. At the top of another steep bank off to our side the ground levelled out and there was a large clearing in the trees that looked out over the river. This is where the enemy was concentrated, and in the clearing there was a large house along with a number of grass-covered dirt piles. Speed was still the priority. Our sergeant told us the plan and we were off. The section broke down into two separate fire teams and spread out down the bank, preparing to assault up onto the position. When we were all ready, we went over the top and began.

The sections drills were slick as we moved to the attack. My fire team was on the left closest to the riverbank and the other team was off to our right. One fire team would stay put on the ground and provide covering fire while the other team ran forward twenty feet to the next bit of cover. When they stopped and began to fire we moved, and in this way we advanced towards the enemy. There were four or five bad guys that we had to contend with and we took them completely by surprise when we came up on their flank, advancing and firing into them. They withdrew as we pushed on, and when we hit the house a few of our guys peeled off the main attack to clear it out. The enemy were beginning to play dead now, falling prey to our blank training ammo. The section continued to move forward, leapfrogging each other as we pushed right through the position. We had gone up to the far edge of the clearing in only a minute or so, and I was pouring with sweat again in the humid jungle heat. The guys were screaming at each other, pointing out positions and letting everybody know if they were moving, firing, or changing magazines. Communication, speed, and aggressiveness were all in good supply. As the section cleared the last of the positions in the treeline another enemy firing point revealed itself off to our flank. The guys that had swept through the house were ready to get back into it and went tearing off down to our right side to mop up the final threat.

It was all over as quickly as it had started. We had some fake casualties to deal with and as we administered first aid to them we dragged them back down towards the river. We had immediately radioed our boats to come for our pickup, and as we slid down the bank they rammed into the shore just below us. We were in the boats and tearing off downstream again, the familiar stream of camouflage face cream and sweat making our eyes sting. My rifle was hot and it had worked flawlessly. My final attack in the Corps had been one of my smoothest ever, and the experience of the section showed. I felt privileged to be a part of such a professional group.

The stink and the filth had built up on us, and as the last of the enemy positions were taken further downstream by other assault sections, we were all overjoyed to hear that we were heading back to a large Brunei army camp to sort our kit out for two days before heading back onto the ship for the return journey. The hard part was finished. We rendezvoused with some trucks a few miles from the beach and headed to the camp to have a shower and a decent meal.

It was a wonderful change to be sleeping inside a solid building again on a bed with a mattress, and the icing on the cake was the immaculate Olympic-sized swimming pool just a few minutes' walk from our accommodation. Each morning we worked quickly to finish cleaning and packing away mortar kit and personal weapons, and in the afternoons we went for wonderfully long swims in the pool. We were counting down the hours until our ride back to HMS *Ocean* arrived, and on the final morning in Brunei we piled into LCS for the last time and headed back out to the ship. Exercise Taurus was over.

CHAPTER 39

ONE-WAY TICKET

I really didn't have much time left to spend in the Corps. It was mid June and in less than two months I would be on my way home to Canada. Between now and then I simply had to wind up my life in the U.K., tie off loose ends and prep for a whole new life. I was going to have to get a job and would be faced with bills again like a normal person. The thought of it all was daunting, and I was really having trouble thinking of jobs that I could do at home, jobs that would keep me from getting bored. I just couldn't quite picture myself in an office after all that I had been through in the last five years.

I passed the time I had on camp packing up all of the crap I had acquired while in England, throwing out a ton of kit and sifting through what I wanted to keep. There was plenty of paperwork to do when you wanted to leave the Corps. I knew that I was going to miss serving in the uniform of a Royal Marine. It was a lifestyle that simply couldn't be re-created as a civilian. I really wanted something exciting to do for work on the outside, and at the same time I wanted to spend much more time at home. I somehow doubted it would be possible to have both.

The weeks slipped past, and before I knew it I was at the local pub with all of the boys from the troop celebrating my big send-off. The troop presented me with a large statue of a Royal Marine carrying a mortar barrel. It was their opportunity to get me pissed and they did just that. Plenty of port and pints of beer got right on top of me and by the end of the night I was wandering the streets of Taunton by myself, drunk and depressed. In a way it was fitting, because I now felt adrift.

As I wandered I found myself reflecting back on my time as a boot-neck. I remembered the highs and the lows, both of which brought a grin back to my face. I thought about the times I was lying in half-frozen puddles all night, wishing I could feel my hands, and when Taliban bullets had cracked the air around my head. I remembered the intensity of sitting in orders before a violent attack, and the bursting pride that filled my chest when I had earned my green beret. I smiled to myself. I had accomplished my own mission. Without a doubt I knew the answer to that question I had asked myself so many times throughout the last few years. "How in the hell did I end up here?" It was simple. I had volunteered for it, and was damn proud of it. After successfully passing through Commando training and doing my job overseas, I knew that there was no obstacle too big in my future. Anything I wanted to accomplish, I could. And I can assure you, that is quite a feeling.

It all ended with me standing in front of the Commanding Officer of 40 Commando with my discharge papers in hand and a final salute. He thanked me for my service, offered to take me back at any time, and dismissed me. I was out of the Royal Marines. I was a civilian, and at least for the time being, there was no turning back. My flight was booked, and as desperately as I wanted to get back home, I knew that I was going to just as desperately miss my place in the Corps.

On August 1, 2009, I boarded a direct flight from London to Vancouver at Heathrow and left the United Kingdom and the Royal Marine Corps. My time was finished and this adventure was over. This was a one-way flight.

GLOSSARY

.50	.50-calibre belt-fed heavy machine gun widely used by coalition forces.
105 mm	Standard British medium artillery.
107 mm	Chinese rockets fired at coalition forces by the Taliban.
2IC	Second in Command.
51 mm	51 mm light mortar.
60 mm	60 mm light mortar.
66 mm	66 mm shoulder-fired anti-tank rocket.
81 mm	81 mm medium mortar.
A-10	U.S. Close Ground Support aircraft mounting a 30 mm Avenger Gatling gun.
AC130 Spectre	Heavy ground-support gunship based on the Hercules airframe.
AE	Assault engineer.
AK/AK-47	Standard enemy rifle, also widely used by friendly Afghan forces.
ANA	Afghan National Army.
ANP	Afghan National Police.
AO	Area of operations.

Apache	U.S./British attack helicopter.
Avenger	30 mm Gatling gun mounted only on the A-10.
B1	American heavy bomber.
Battery	Four artillery pieces grouped together.
BCR	Battle casualty replacement.
Bergen	A large backpack.
Bootneck	A Royal Marine.
BRF	Brigade Reconnaissance Force.
BST	Battle swim test.
BV	An old version of the Viking and designed for use in Norway.
C4	A type of plastic explosive.
C-Scots	Canadian Scottish Regiment.
Casevac	Casualty evacuation.
Chinook	Large twin-rotor supply helicopter widely used by coalition forces.
Claymore	An area defence weapon initiated by an electrical trigger that sprays an area with hundreds of ball bearings.
Contact	When friendly forces are engaging the enemy.
CP	Command Post.
CTC/CTCRM	Commando Training Centre Royal Marines.
CV	Cardiovascular.
DC	District centre.
Det cord	Detonating cord, used to initiate larger charges.
DL	Drill Leader.
ETA	Estimated time of arrival.
Ex	Exercise.
F-14	U.S. Naval air superiority fighter.
F-15	U.S. air superiority and ground strike fighter.
F-16	U.S. air superiority and ground strike fighter.

F-18	U.S. and Canadian air superiority and ground strike fighter.
FIBUA	Fighting in Built-Up Areas (Urban Warfare).
FOB	Forward Operating Base.
FOO	Forward Observation Officer.
Gib	Short for FOB Gibraltar.
GMG	Grenade machine gun – 40 mm automatic, belt-fed grenade launcher.
GPMG	General-purpose machine gun – 7.62 mm automatic, belt-fed machine gun widely used by coalition forces.
Grots	Accommodation, sleeping quarters.
H&K	Heckler & Koch, a German arms manufacturer.
H-Hour	Scheduled time for an attack to start.
HE	High explosive.
Hellfire	Missile fired from the Apache attack helicopter.
Hercules	Large four-engine transport aircraft widely used by coalition forces.
HQ	Headquarters.
HVT	High value target.
ICBM	Intercontinental ballistic missile.
IED	Improvised explosive device used by the enemy in a number of different compositions, such as roadside bombs, trip wires, homemade mines.
ILAW	Interim light anti-armour weapon – 84 mm single-use, disposable anti-tank weapon, usually used to fire at enemy emplacements.
Illum	Short for "illuminating rounds" fired from artillery and mortars.
Infrared (IR)	A type of light that is invisible to the naked eye, but easily seen when using NVGS.
IRC	Inshore raiding craft.

Javelin	Heat-seeking anti-armour missile that can also lock on the heat from a human body
J-TAC	Joint tactical air controller – this is the guy on the ground with a radio on his back who calls in air strikes.
KSA	Kingdom of Saudi Arabia.
LCA	Landing craft assault – medium-sized for moving troops or vehicles from ship to shore.
LCU	Landing craft utility – large-sized for moving troops or vehicles from ship to shore.
Lynx	British light helicopter used for transporting VIPs and reconnaissance.
LP	Helicopter landing point.
LZ	Helicopter landing zone.
Mastiff	A heavily armoured truck with a turret on top for mounting weapons.
MFC	Mortar fire controller.
Minimi	Light belt-fed air-cooled 5.56 mm machine gun.
MOD	Ministry of Defence.
MOG	Mobile Operations Group.
NATO	North Atlantic Treaty Organization.
NBC	Nuclear, biological, and chemical.
ND	Negligent discharge of a firearm.
Nimrod	Large British surveillance aircraft.
Nod	A Royal Marine recruit.
NVG	Night vision goggles.
OC	Officer in Command (company commander).
OP	Observation post.
ORC	Offshore raiding craft.
Paras	Short for Parachute Regiment or members of the Regiment.
Phys	Physical training.

PT	Physical training.
PTI	Physical Training Instructor.
QRF	Quick reaction force. A group of men on standby to respond to threats or provide reinforcements.
R&R	Rest and relaxation. We refer to our two weeks of holidays when overseas as R&R.
RMA	Royal Marines Association.
RO	Radio operator.
ROE	Rules of Engagement. These define what we can shoot at and when we can shoot at it.
RPG	Rocket-propelled grenade – widely used by Taliban forces and friendly Afghan forces.
RV	Rendezvous.
SA-80	Standard British military rifle – 5.56 mm.
SAS	Special Air Service – British Special Forces.
Scimitar	British armoured reconnaissance vehicle; mounts a 30 mm cannon.
Scran	Means food, or to eat.
Section	A team of eight soldiers. Three sections are in a troop, plus headquarters.
Slug	Sleeping bag.
STG	Shit Tasking Group.
Stripey	Sergeant.
UGL	Underslung grenade launcher, attached to the underside of the SA-80; fires 40 mm bombs.
Viking	Tracked, articulated, amphibious armoured vehicle for transporting troops.
Warrior	British armoured fighting vehicle capable of carrying six soldiers in the rear; mounts a 30 mm cannon.
Webbing	Load-carrying vest covered in pouches for ammunition, grenades, water, etc.

Wets/hot wets   A hot drink, coffee or tea.

Wimik   A Land Rover variant, stripped down and with a hand-operated turret in the back for mounting weapon systems.

Yomp   A long march with full field kit.